f Wight 1970

The View From The Crowd

A Photo Album of
The Afton Experience

by

Alan Stroud and Tom Stroud

Now and Then Books © 2021

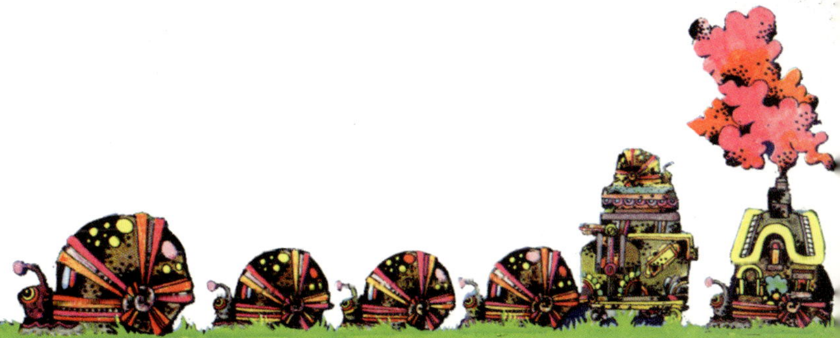

Isle of Wight 1970

The View From The Crowd

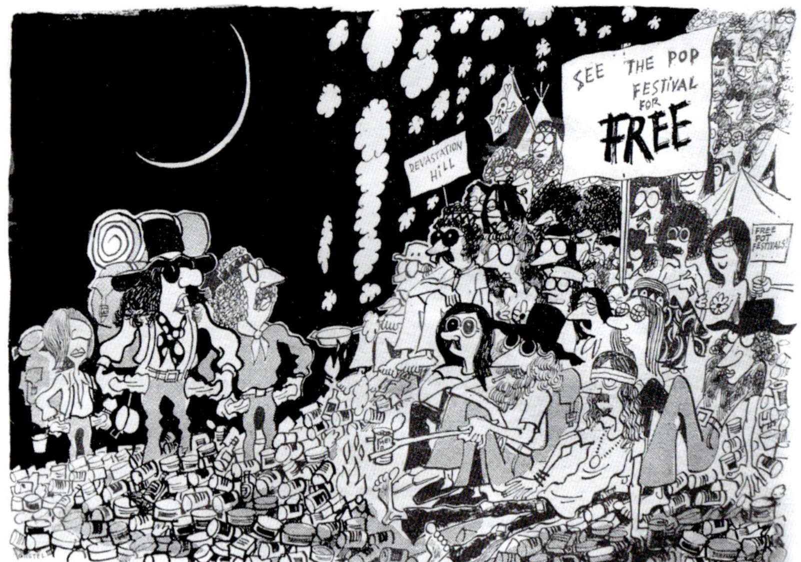

"Mind if we join you? – We're the organisers."

Daily Sketch, August 29, 1970

ISBN 978-1-8381740-1-9.
Typeset and layout by Alan Stroud.
Printed by Short Run Press, Sowton Industrial Estate. Exeter. EX2 7LW

nowandthenbooksiw@googlemail.com

The Afton Experience - Five Days In A Field

In August 1970 hundreds of thousands of people flocked to the Isle of Wight to attend what was then, and still is today, the largest crowd gathered at a music festival in this country. It was a remarkable moment and a peak point in popular culture; the hippie movement, the love generation and international rock superstars, all gathered together for a long weekend in the sun, outside a small town in the West Wight.

For festival organisers Ray, Ronnie and Bill Foulk it was the high point of a rapid trajectory established just two years before, outside Godshill, with the Jefferson Airplane and a year later they had brought Bob Dylan to Wootton. By 1970 Fiery Creations had established themselves as the biggest festival promoters in the UK, capable of booking acts like Jimi Hendrix, The Who and The Doors. For their audience it was a bargain. For the sum of just £3, equivalent to the price of a double album, they could spend three days watching some of the biggest international artists on any festival bill anywhere - "the world's top talent for two bob a head," as *Disc and Music Echo* described it.

Although it's a metaphor that doesn't hold up to close examination on some levels, for many it definitely was 'the British Woodstock'. The audience came from far and wide, across the UK and from around the globe. Press officer Peter Harrigan told tv news crews, "We've had people writing from Asia, Kathmandu, heavy ticket sales in Australia and charter flights from America. I should think one in six, one in seven people at the festival will be from overseas."

It was an international gathering of the tribes, and for most people their Isle of Wight experience began at the sea end of Ryde Pier. With live music beginning on Wednesday August 26th and running until Sunday 30th, Ryde town was alive with festivalgoers for several days around the bank holiday weekend. Young people alighted from the passenger ferry and made their way to Ryde Esplanade to get on a bus for Freshwater.

Their destination was a field at Afton, a controversial site, and not the first choice of organisers Fiery Creations. The arena could easily be viewed from the nearby hills of Afton Down, which as Michael Watts of the *Melody Maker* noted, "resembled a huge natural grandstand, and a high proportion of the human influx is making use of its position overlooking the stage by pitching their tents and establishing squatters' rights."

Hundreds of thousands of people arrived without having already purchased a ticket. On discovering that they could watch from the downs where the view was in many ways better and was free, many spent their £3 ticket money elsewhere, which would cost the organisers dearly. "It was an impossibility to wall that down off and we were trying for weeks beforehand," Ray Foulk explained. "As fast as we could build a wall, people were taking it down at night."

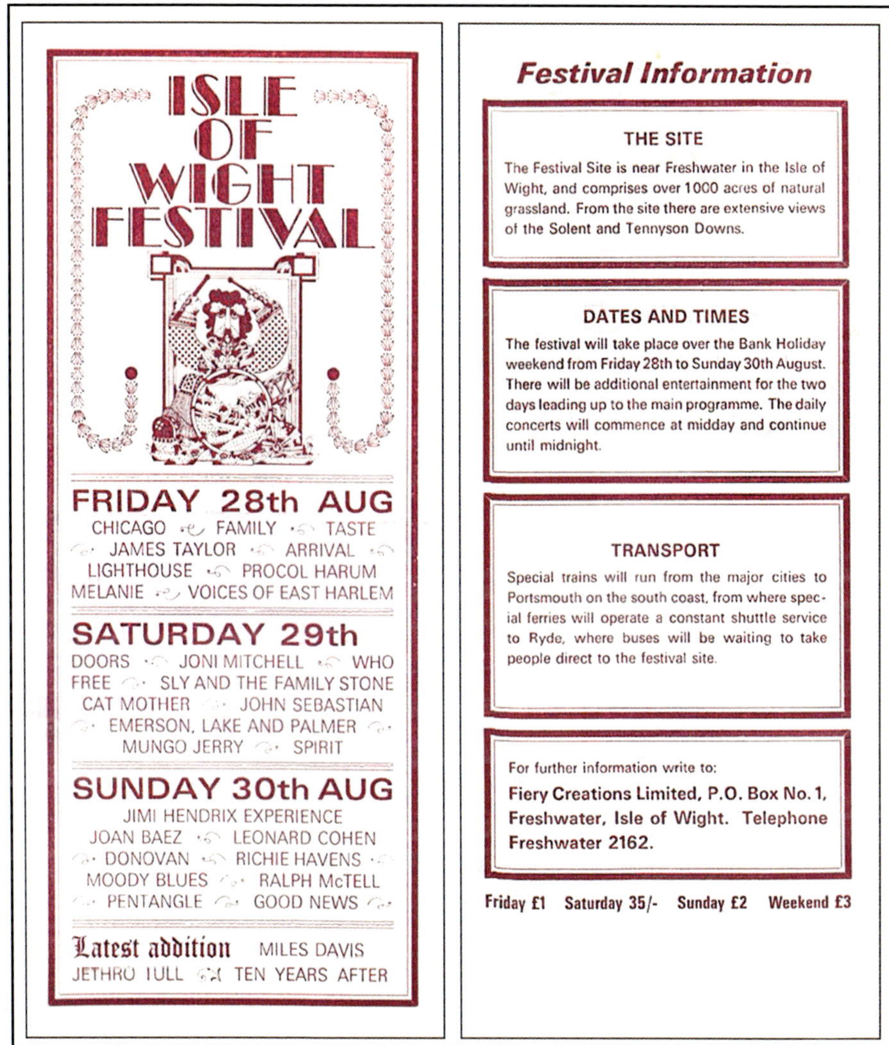

ISLE OF WIGHT FESTIVAL

FRIDAY 28th AUG
CHICAGO · FAMILY · TASTE · JAMES TAYLOR · ARRIVAL · LIGHTHOUSE · PROCOL HARUM · MELANIE · VOICES OF EAST HARLEM

SATURDAY 29th
DOORS · JONI MITCHELL · WHO · FREE · SLY AND THE FAMILY STONE · CAT MOTHER · JOHN SEBASTIAN · EMERSON, LAKE AND PALMER · MUNGO JERRY · SPIRIT

SUNDAY 30th AUG
JIMI HENDRIX EXPERIENCE · JOAN BAEZ · LEONARD COHEN · DONOVAN · RICHIE HAVENS · MOODY BLUES · RALPH McTELL · PENTANGLE · GOOD NEWS

Latest addition MILES DAVIS · JETHRO TULL · TEN YEARS AFTER

Festival Information

THE SITE

The Festival Site is near Freshwater in the Isle of Wight, and comprises over 1000 acres of natural grassland. From the site there are extensive views of the Solent and Tennyson Downs.

DATES AND TIMES

The festival will take place over the Bank Holiday weekend from Friday 28th to Sunday 30th August. There will be additional entertainment for the two days leading up to the main programme. The daily concerts will commence at midday and continue until midnight.

TRANSPORT

Special trains will run from the major cities to Portsmouth on the south coast, from where special ferries will operate a constant shuttle service to Ryde, where buses will be waiting to take people direct to the festival site.

For further information write to:
Fiery Creations Limited, P.O. Box No. 1, Freshwater, Isle of Wight. Telephone Freshwater 2162.

Friday £1 Saturday 35/- Sunday £2 Weekend £3

The first flyer for the festival. With the site still uncertain Fiery Creations play it safe and describe the location as "near Freshwater."

The Fiery Creations team had been building the site since August 1st. On one side it was bordered by Afton Down and on the other by the Middle Road. At each side of the arena was a campsite, 'Newport Camping' on the western side, and 'Freshwater Camping' on the east (see the map on page 7 for much more detail on the layout of the site). Some early arrivals pitched their tents alongside the public footpath along the far edge of the arena (see pages 16 and 17). This commune of campfires, abandoned car parts and metal sheeting was referred to as Desolation Row, taking its name from a Bob Dylan song. The Downs would become known as Devastation Hill, although the two locations would often be confused with each other.

The rectangular festival site itself was ringed by an eight foot high double wall made of two miles of corrugated iron fencing, seen prominently on pages 21 and 23. "The double wall system was potentially a great idea because it served a few things at once," Ray Foulk explains. "One is the additional security it provides – you have two walls to get over rather than one. Secondly, you can have your security within the double wall zone so nobody sees them unless they are in the business of trespassing, and thirdly, you have a roadway all the way around the site to service shops, toilets and backstage and keep vehicles separated from the people." There's no doubt that for a sector of the crowd, the metal perimeter walls would prove unpopular. Although the vast majority of attendees were happy with the line-up and prices, anarchists intent on a "free festival" were determined to breach the fences, with some ugly scenes occurring over the weekend, described as "battles" in the press. The attempted incursions were quickly dealt with by security but cast a sour note when included in Murray Lerner's 1995 film, *Message To Love*.

The organisers recognised that the fences looked austere. They gave fans free tickets and buckets of paint in the hope that they might brighten them up. "Rikki Farr stupidly gave them the tickets before they'd done the paint job – they just sploshed it around and wrote slogans and made a terrible mess," Ray Foulk remembers. Graffiti like "Tear Down The Fence," "HM Prison," and "POW" can be seen on many of the fences.

The photograph on page 21 offers a view of the backstage area in context; it can be seen in more detail on page 60. The green van adjacent to the stage housed the recording equipment of the Pye mobile, hired by Fiery Creations to record the entire five days on eight-track tape. The marquees were used as dressing rooms for the artists, and it's likely that one of those tents is where Ray and Ronnie can be seen in *Message To Love* counting out money to pay Friday's headline act, Chicago.

For those who had arrived without a tent, Canvas City (pages 44 to 51) was the answer. At 300 feet long, 75 feet wide and 50 feet high, the unmissable inflatable marquee was the largest structure on the festival site. Festivalgoers could sleep in this huge dormitory tent for just 2 shillings a night, rising to 10 shillings a night on the main days. Canvas City and the area around it provided a focal point for the underground fraternity and some of the festival agitants. Something of an alternative "festival within a festival" it featured live music from bands like Hawkwind and the Pink Fairies, whose drummer Twink can be seen shaking a tambourine on page 46 and bottom left of page 99.

The security for Canvas City was provided by a group of Hells Angels, an organisation which hadn't yet been intrinsically linked with violence at festivals, an association that would be set in stone by Altamont in California a few months later. Nonetheless, the tribe of Angels was imposing and their swastika flags fluttering in the breeze make uneasy viewing now, especially alongside the adjacent 'Jesus Revolution' tent seen on page 97.

Many of the concessions were run by Fiery Creations, including the bar and food stalls (pages 31, 35 and 27), which operated using pre-printed tariffs to ensure fair pricing. Both *Melody Maker* and a subsequent IW Council report agreed that the standards of the catering were fair. Vendors like those on page 71 almost certainly weren't licensed by the organisers and employed a much less democratic pricing structure.

The Foulks took the matter of feeding their attendees very seriously, setting up a division called 'Exhibition Catering', with army-style kitchens housed in the huge marquee seen behind the stage on page 21, and on the left on page 42. The food shops would be serviced from within the inner wall system. The photos on pages 38 and 39 show the food and drink stalls along the wall of the 'Freshwater' campsite, with the back of the stage seen over the top of the wall. The same shops can be seen on pages 18 and 20, behind and just to the right of Canvas City.

For most festivalgoers the bands at Canvas City would be the closest they got to a performing act. Although the sound from the main stage could be heard clearly around the site using a state of the art sound system, in the days before video screens, performers were largely a dot in the distance. Photos like those on pages 66 and 67 are good examples of the view, with a largely seated crowd listening to the performers, rather than watching them intently.

Although tickets were required from Friday, the live music began on Wednesday with a further two free days of lesser acts and smaller crowds, as seen on pages 40 and 41, where the spectator arena is noticeably less busy and, unaccountably, someone has managed to park their car near the stage. As well as being open to festivalgoers without tickets, the turnstiles also welcomed curious Islanders who had come to see what the festival was all about. In many of the crowd photographs, particularly on the non-ticketed Afton Down, are people who really shouldn't be there. Older, conservatively dressed and definitely from another generation, they look amusingly out of place. Writing in *The Times,* David Wilsworth observed that "the throng of young people... had themselves become a minor tourist attraction."

The act Arrival can be seen on page 61, playing second on the bill, mid-afternoon on the Friday. In front of them is the VIP area at the very front of the crowd, shown up close on page 56. As the photograph on page 113 clearly shows, the VIP enclosure was far from full and would be reduced in size as the weekend proceeded.

During the weekend, Fleet Street's finest were rewarded with scenes of actual nudity as festivalgoers took a dip in the sea at Compton (see pages 80-84). Scenes of the 'love generation' splashing without inhibition in the waves to cool off, raised the notoriety of the festival in the next day's papers.

At its peak the crowd swelled to several hundred thousand. Local newspaper *The County Press* noted that "estimates of the attendance varied from 150,000 to 400,000". On the Sunday festival MC Rikki Farr told the crowd that up to 600,000 people had come to the festival, a figure organiser Ray Foulk describes as "absurd."

The faces of the festivalgoers tell their own story. Mostly male, and mostly in their late teens or early twenties, the crowd was well behaved and not troublesome as some locals had feared.

By the Sunday it was clear to the organisers that the event was not a financial success although all was not lost perhaps. They had yet to receive ticket money from agencies and they hoped to sell the film footage of the weekend. Perhaps with the film in mind and certainly providing a moment of theatre for the crowd, they declared the event free on the Sunday afternoon. With the turnstiles abandoned, non-paying attendees and inquisitive onlookers could once again enter the site. Any idea that the fences were torn down by a baying crowd who then rushed into the main arena is fanciful and a fake memory fostered by the editing used in *Message To Love*.

"There's a lot of mythology about those fences," Ray Foulk says. "After the festival was declared free, on the Sunday evening, a short stretch of the northern boundary was torn down. The walls were ripped down from the inside – not the outside – by people either thinking they were making a statement but mostly from those wanting to use the corrugated iron to make huts. The sheets were scattered all over the site at the end."

The music had run late and well into the night throughout the weekend. The "man with the guitar", Jimi Hendrix, took to the stage in the early hours of Monday morning and a few hours later as the sun rose, Richie Havens played the final song of the festival.

Perhaps a little bleary-eyed after a weekend of long days and late nights, the crowd dispersed quickly and peacefully on the Monday afternoon. The next day, as seen in the film, was cold and wet as the organisers began the clean-up operation. They had two weeks to return the site to its former state.

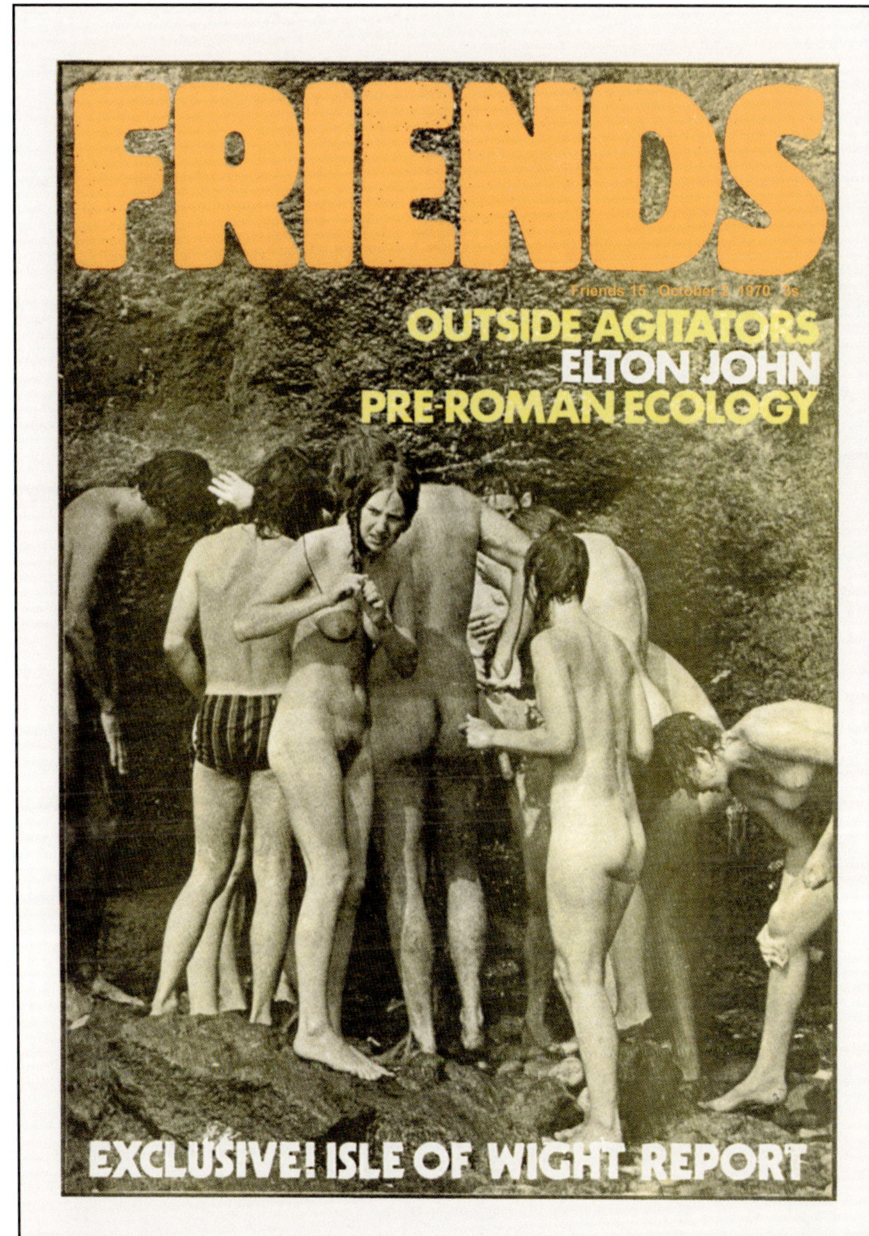

In its October issue 'Friends', a popular underground magazine reported at length on the festival. Its front cover featured festivalgoers taking a shower on Compton beach. Compare this with the photo on page 83.

The photographs in the final pages are taken in early September and have an eerie, almost post-apocalyptic quality, with the spectacle of the festival now contrasted with the bleakness of the empty arena strewn with the litter of the love generation and the discarded fence panels used as makeshift shelters (page 126). The panorama across pages 124 and 125 shows the perimeter fence is still standing several days after the festival has finished. Workers are beginning to dismantle the wall and load panels onto a flatback truck.

Page 133 documents perhaps the last musical performance at Afton, another man with a guitar, playing to an empty Desolation Row on September 10th. Pages 127 and 135 make a neat juxtaposition; one final look at the empty stage, followed by the view from the stage, looking out into the empty arena.

On a cultural level the UK had not seen anything like the festival, and arguably the Isle of Wight would spend decades living it down, or attempting to live up to it, depending on which side of the proverbial fence one sat. Until the resurrection of a different sort of Isle of Wight Festival in 2002, the 1970 event cast a long shadow. The idea had powerful opponents too and anyone seeking to put on another festival would be constrained legally, with an act of Parliament devised specifically for the Isle of Wight.

Twenty five years after the cameras rolled at Afton, a finished film emerged, edited by director Murray Lerner who now owned the footage after an expensive legal tussle with Fiery Creations. *Message To Love* featured wonderfully shot musical performances, intercut with scenes of tension and anger. To use Ray Foulk's phrase, it was "an essay in conflict". It's worth stressing that although all of the disturbances, protests and arguments did occur, almost all of them took place backstage, in the middle of the night, or outside of the weekend in which the festival took place. Were it not for MC Rikki Farr ranting at rogue elements of the audience from the stage, most of the crowd would have been none the wiser.

"Ever since 1970 I have made a point of asking festivalgoers what their experience was," Ray Foulk says. "Almost all of them say they enjoyed the festival and didn't see any trouble. It's been exaggerated. We know what trouble there was but it was a flea bite on an elephant."

Absent from the film at any point is the view from the crowd out in the arena, or the thoughts of the audience. The fans we see talking were interviewed while the stage was still being built, at which point these early arrivals had yet to witness a single act.

The photos in this book offer a more authentic view of the festival, from within the crowd, from the hill and from inside the campsite. This is the festival as most would have seen it – with the stage a dot in the distance, surrounded by a sea of like-minded people. For many attendees the most profound feeling of the weekend was "being surrounded by hundreds of thousands of people who looked like me."

In 2020 the authors of this book published *Rocking The Isle Of Wight*, intended to complement Ray Foulk's definitive personal accounts of the festivals, in this case by telling the story from a purely local and intentionally detailed perspective. The book is now out of print and is already a collector's item. Some of the photos used within it appear here but in large format for the first time. After the publication of our book a further cache of photos were discovered and they appear here for the first time anywhere.

In these pages you'll see the festival from the ground. It's the fan's eye view, through the lenses of keen local photographers who knew they were documenting a moment of social history. The organisers were inventing the British rock festival but it would be their swansong and the Isle of Wight 1970 was the last of the truly big festivals in this country.

It was the end of one line but it was also the beginning of the modern era. Today's festival crowds look much like the Afton audience. The hair might be longer then and the clothes cut slightly differently, but in their T-shirts, denim and leather, the young people of 1970 still look familiar more than fifty years on. In the late sixties youth culture flowered and something arrived that can still be felt today. Because of *Message To Love* the Isle of Wight is often misremembered as an unhappy or violent event. These photos prove otherwise; the crowd is friendly and respectful to each other.

You can never go back - but in these pages you can get close. The faces, the fashions, the fences and even the queue for the yoghurt stall – it's all here, in glorious colour.

Tom Stroud, 2021.

The Afton Experience - The Site

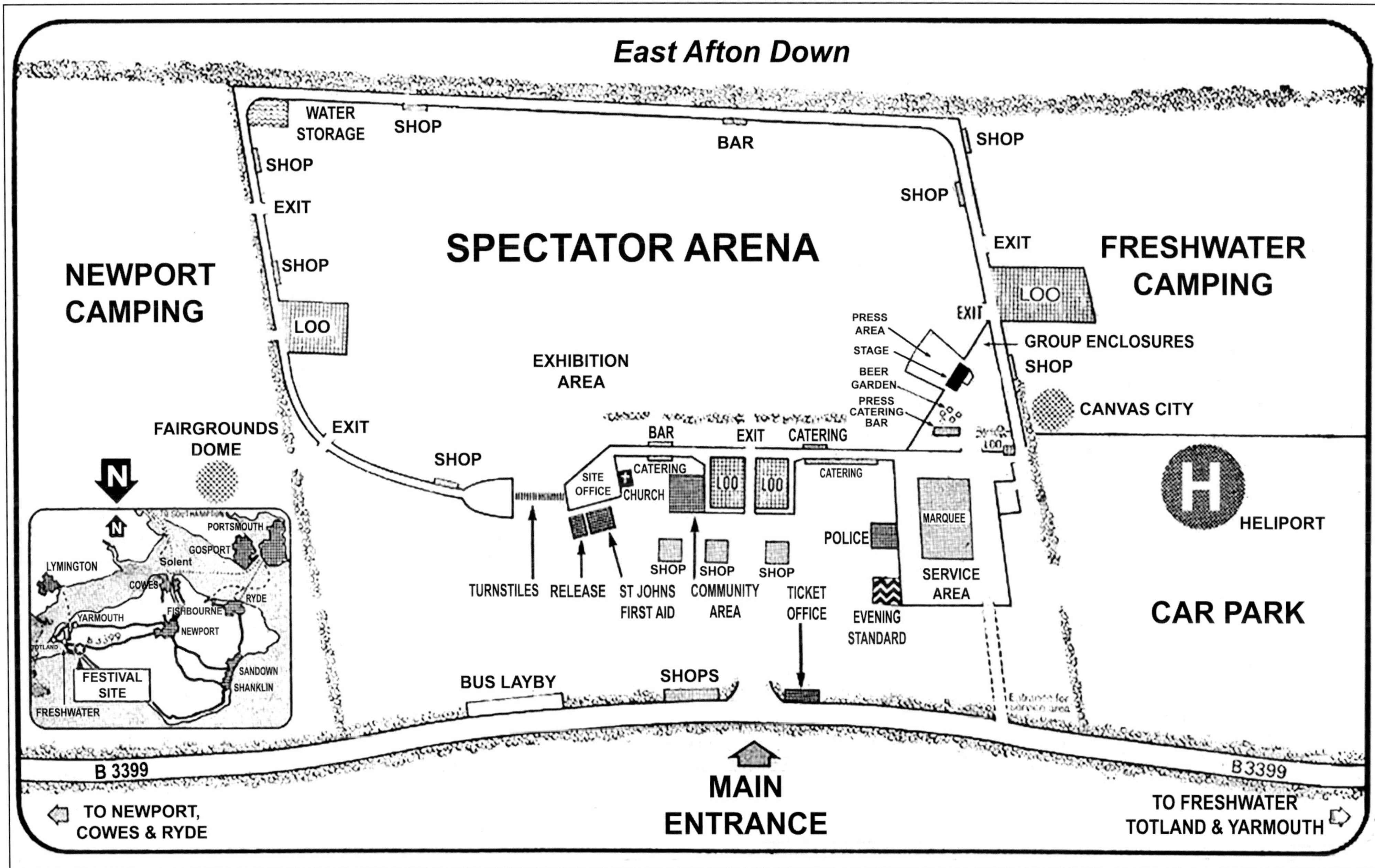

Capturing Afton – The Men With The Cameras

Some of the festivalgoers who came to Afton in 1970 didn't just bring money and a sleeping bag - they brought their cameras. What follows is the work of five of them, four named and one unknown, who had the foresight all those years ago to take high quality colour photographs of the 1970 festival. Their photographs of events at Afton and the thousands who came to watch some of the biggest musical acts of the time are not only a fascinating body of work but with the passage of time they have become a social document. This collection of their work provides a welcome alternative to the professional photographs of the festival which, due to the demands and whims of Fleet Street editors, tended to concentrate on the performers rather than the crowd.

Amateur photography had undergone a sea change by the time of the 1970 festival. During the sixties, camera technology had advanced in leaps and bounds and by the end of the decade high quality 35mm cameras with interchangeable lenses were flooding in from the Far East, Russia and East Germany with names like Nikon, Practika and Zenith becoming commonplace. Prior to their arrival many of the photographs taken by the general public would have been taken on Kodak box cameras or on the mainstream 'compact cameras' of the day, the Kodak Instamatics and Ilford Ilfomatics, using the new drop-in cartridges. Over 50 million of them were produced from 1963 to 1970 and while they were undeniably cheap and simple to use, none of them were known for the quality of their lenses.

The new arrivals, especially those from Japan, took photography to a new level; they came with high quality lenses and what's more, they were affordable. They quickly took over the 'serious' amateur market and swept the compact camera aside.

The other leap forward that amateurs were to benefit from in the sixties was a dramatic drop in the price of colour film. Colour photography up until then had been seen very much as a luxury and a rare treat for most people, reserved for weddings, high days and holidays. In a sign of the times, all Ilford colour film prices were drastically cut in 1968, in a "Two for the price of One" campaign. The cost of Ilford 'Colorslide' was halved to 8/9d (44p) for a twin pack of 36 exposure rolls, and with processing costs 36 slides cost less than 7d (3p) each. In another sign of the times Ilford stopped making their 'Ilfomatic' compact cameras. Almost overnight, colour photos taken using SLR cameras became the norm, quickly displacing black and white as the general public's film of choice.

Ironically, this wasn't the case for the Fleet Street professionals at Afton. Newspapers were still printed in black and white and there was little demand for colour work. The *Sunday Times* had published the first colour supplement in 1962, other newspapers quickly following suit, but the use of colour in them was still minimal and it took another twenty years or so for colour to creep into daily news.

For that reason it is almost certain that amateurs took far more colour photographs at Afton than the professionals - and much of it, as we shall see, was of outstanding quality. Also, it's fair to say that Fleet Sreet had only a passing interest in the festivalgoers unless, of course, they were naked or 'freaking out.' Newspaper editors did not pay their photographers to capture art - they wanted action shots of performers. Hardened Fleet Street photographer Bob Aylott, in his book *Isle of Wight Festival 1970 - Six days That Rocked The World* made no bones at all about his motives in photographing the Festival, "We're all waiting for a disaster to happen ... I'm knackered and want to go home but what stops me is the thought of being on the spot when a disaster happens, something that is in the blood of every press photographer....If Jimi Hendrix drops dead from an overdose I've got to be there to capture it."

Free of such cold-blooded considerations our amateurs arguably captured the real essence of the festival in a collection of images that will chime and resonate with anyone who attended, far more than the over-familiar shots of performers.

First among the amateurs whose photographs appear here is my own late father-in-law, Harry Matthews. Unknown to me at the time, while I was attending the festival Harry, accompanied by wife and two teenage daughters, visited the site on the Sunday afternoon equipped with his Praktica camera and 200mm telephoto lens. He also paid a return visit to the site a week later to take some rare photographs of the clear-up operations.

Eric Moth, of Cowes, took shots on the hillside but also made his way to the beach at Compton where hundreds of naked festivalgoers were frolicking in the surf. His photographs are now part of the Cowes Heritage and Community Group archive and we thank Barry Groves for allowing their use here.

The third photographer is unknown, his or her treasure trove of colour slides having only come to light recently in a box that had lain forgotten in a cupboard for 40 years. The photographer was certainly painstaking - not only are there scenes on-site but there are also unique colourful shots of festivalgoers on Ryde Esplanade, en route to Afton. Once again, all the work is of very high technical quality.

Then there is the work of Ken Box. While all the photographers in this book are to be congratulated on the quality of their work, Ken's collection of photographs stands alone. Some readers will know of him from their schooldays at Carisbrooke Grammar School in the 1960s and 70s, where he was a popular art teacher. What they probably didn't know at the time, self included, is that out of school he was a keen and highly skilled photographer who took thousands of photographs across the Island. Aged 43 at the time of the festival, Ken spent several days photographing the site and the festivalgoers using high quality lenses, and cameras loaded with fine grain Kodak Ektachrome colour film.

Capturing Afton - The Men With The Cameras

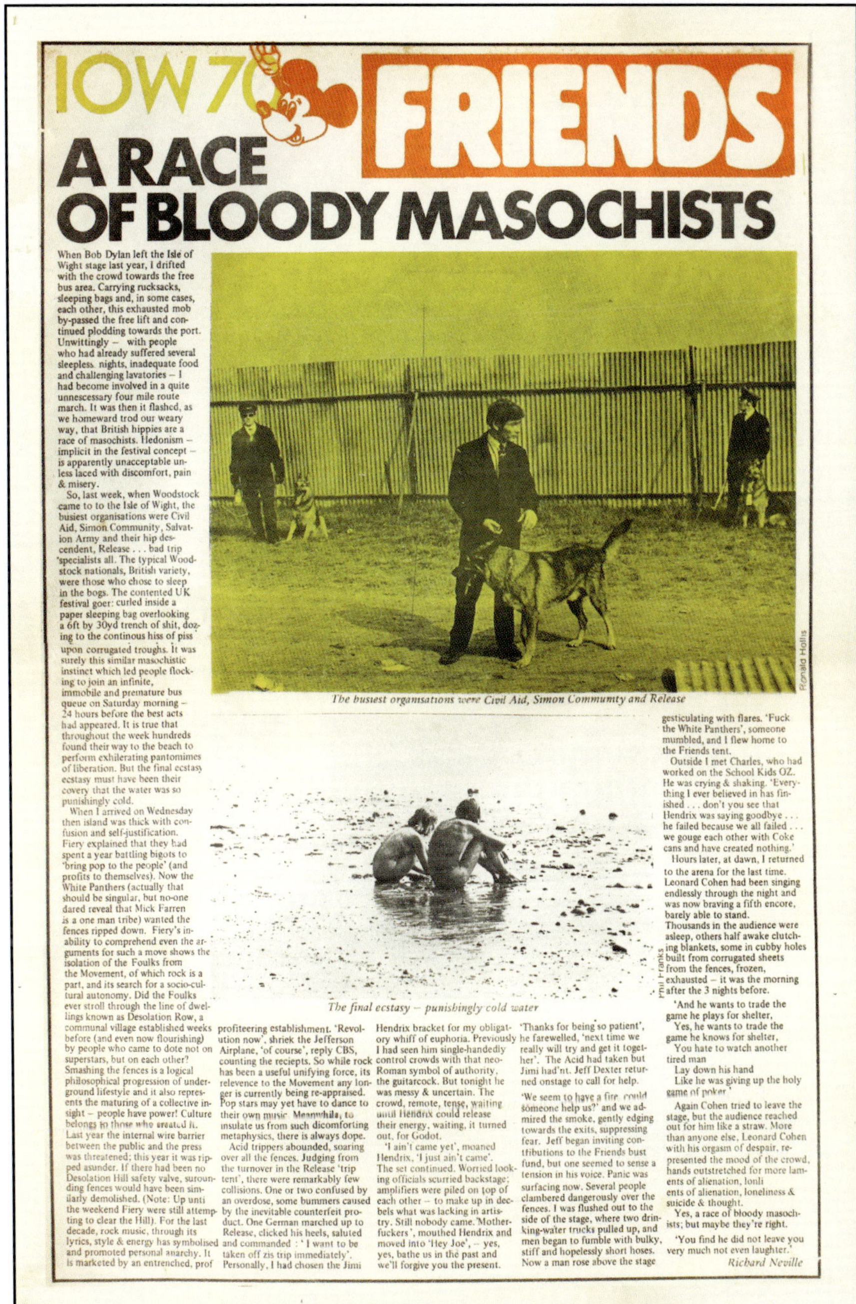

IOW 70 FRIENDS

A RACE OF BLOODY MASOCHISTS

When Bob Dylan left the Isle of Wight stage last year, I drifted with the crowd towards the free bus area. Carrying rucksacks, sleeping bags and, in some cases, each other, this exhausted mob by-passed the free lift and continued plodding towards the port. Unwittingly – with people who had already suffered several sleepless nights, inadequate food and challenging lavatories – I had become involved in a quite unnescessary four mile route march. It was then it flashed, as we homeward trod our weary way, that British hippies are a race of masochists. Hedonism – implicit in the festival concept – is apparently unacceptable unless laced with discomfort, pain & misery.

So, last week, when Woodstock came to to the Isle of Wight, the busiest organisations were Civil Aid, Simon Community, Salvation Army and their hip descendent, Release . . . bad trip specialists all. The typical Woodstock nationals, British variety, were those who chose to sleep in the bogs. The contented UK festival goer: curled inside a paper sleeping bag overlooking a 6ft by 30yd trench of shit, dozing to the continous hiss of piss upon corrugated troughs. It was surely this similar masochistic instinct which led people flocking to join an infinite, immobile and premature bus queue on Saturday morning – 24 hours before the best acts had appeared. It is true that throughout the week hundreds found their way to the beach to perform exhilerating pantomimes of liberation. But the final ecstasy ecstasy must have been their covery that the water was so punishingly cold.

When I arrived on Wednesday then island was thick with confusion and self-justification. Fiery explained that they had spent a year battling bigots to 'bring pop to the people' (and profits to themselves). Now the White Panthers (actually that should be singular, but no-one dared reveal that Mick Farren is a one man tribe) wanted the fences ripped down. Fiery's inability to comprehend even the arguments for such a move shows the isolation of the Foulks from the Movement, of which rock is a part, and its search for a socio-cultural autonomy. Did the Foulks ever stroll through the line of dwellings known as Desolation Row, a communal village established weeks before (and even now flourishing) by people who came to dote not on superstars, but on each other? Smashing the fences is a logical philosophical progression of underground lifestyle and it also represents the maturing of a collective insight – people have power! Culture belongs to those who created it. Last year the internal wire barrier between the public and the press was threatened; this year it was ripped asunder. If there had been no Desolation Hill safety valve, surounding fences would have been similarly demolished. (Note: Up unti the weekend Fiery were still attempting to clear the Hill). For the last decade, rock music, through its lyrics, style & energy has symbolised and promoted personal anarchy. It is marketed by an entrenched, prof profiteering establishment. 'Revolution now', shriek the Jefferson Airplane, 'of course', reply CBS, counting the reciepts. So while rock has been a useful unifying force, its relevence to the Movement any longer is currently being re-appraised. Pop stars may yet have to dance to their own music. Meanwhile, to insulate us from such dicomforting metaphysics, there is always dope.

Acid trippers abounded, soaring over all the fences. Judging from the turnover in the Release 'trip tent', there were remarkably few collisions. One or two confused by an overdose, some bummers caused by the inevitable counterfeit product. One German marched up to Release, clicked his heels, saluted and commanded : 'I want to be taken off zis trip immediately'. Personally, I had chosen the Jimi Hendrix bracket for my obligatory whiff of euphoria. Previously I had seen him single-handedly control crowds with that neo-Roman symbol of authority, the guitarcock. But tonight he was messy & uncertain. The crowd, remote, tense, waiting until Hendrix could release their energy, waiting, it turned out, for Godot.

'I ain't came yet', moaned Hendrix, 'I just ain't came'. The set continued. Worried looking officials scurried backstage; amplifiers were piled on top of each other – to make up in decbels what was lacking in artistry. Still nobody came. 'Motherfuckers', mouthed Hendrix and moved into 'Hey Joe', – yes, yes, bathe us in the past and we'll forgive you the present. 'Thanks for being so patient', he farewelled, 'next time we really will try and get it together'. The Acid had taken but Jimi had'nt. Jeff Dexter returned onstage to call for help.

'We seem to have a fire, could someone help us?' and we admired the smoke, gently edging towards the exits, suppressing fear. Jeff began inviting contfibutions to the Friends bust fund, but one seemed to sense a tension in his voice. Panic was surfacing now. Several people clambered dangerously over the fences. I was flushed out to the side of the stage, where two drinking-water trucks pulled up, and men began to fumble with bulky, stiff and hopelessly short hoses. Now a man rose above the stage gesticulating with flares. 'Fuck the White Panthers', someone mumbled, and I flew home to the Friends tent.

Outside I met Charles, who had worked on the School Kids OZ. He was crying & shaking. 'Everything I ever believed in has finished . . . don't you see that Hendrix was saying goodbye . . . he failed because we all failed . . . we gouge each other with Coke cans and have created nothing.'

Hours later, at dawn, I returned to the arena for the last time. Leonard Cohen had been singing endlessly through the night and was now braving a fifth encore, barely able to stand. Thousands in the audience were asleep, others half awake clutching blankets, some in cubby holes built from corrugated sheets from the fences, frozen, exhausted – it was the morning after the 3 nights before.

'And he wants to trade the game he plays for shelter,
Yes, he wants to trade the game he knows for shelter,
You hate to watch another tired man
Lay down his hand
Like he was giving up the holy game of poker.'

Again Cohen tried to leave the stage, but the audience reached out for him like a straw. More than anyone else, Leonard Cohen with his orgasm of despair, represented the mood of the crowd, hands outstretched for more laments of alienation, lonli ents of alienation, loneliness & suicide & thought.

Yes, a race of bloody masochists; but maybe they're right.

'You find he did not leave you very much not even laughter.'

Richard Neville

The busiest organisations were Civil Aid, Simon Communty and Release — Ronald Hollis

The final ecstasy – punishingly cold water — Phil Franks

Inner front cover of Friends Magazine, October 1970 issue.

For the most part his photographs are aesthetic gems and technically near flawless. Ken produced a remarkable body of work amounting to over 200 photographs taken all around the site during and after the event. It is photographic reportage at its best, carefully and thoughtfully compiled by a man who knew what he wanted, and clearly had an artist's eye not only for subject matter but also for composition. Ken roamed every corner of the site to assemble a stunning collection of photographs which range from crowd shots to intimate portraits of festivalgoers. It is a superb piece of work.

Following Ken's death in 2014, his sons Richard and Pete became custodians of his large collection of photographs, including those taken at Afton, and they have been kind enough to permit a selection of them to be included here. We are indebted to them for this very kind gesture and thank them both for their help and their trust in us. Special thanks must also go to Pete Box who provided us with his top quality scans of Kens's slides.

The last few photographs in the book were taken by me, Alan Stroud. Aged 19 at the time, I was already a keen photographer with a primitive darkroom at home, so it remains a matter of everlasting embarrassment to me that I did not take my Russian 'Zenith' camera to Afton armed with rolls of colour film. I redeemed myself a little by going back to a desolate Afton a week later to take some shots of the deserted site but even then I only shot in black and white for some forgotten reason.

Finally, to sum up, our 'amateurs' were anything but amateur. Between them they have captured a magnificent alternative view of the festival. Frozen in time by their lenses are the youth of 1970 in all their finery and glory, taking part in what was and still is the largest tribal gathering ever seen in this country. Our contributors had no particular end game in mind when they took their photographs - they had no ambition beyond capturing for themselves memories of an exciting world event taking place on their doorstep. They were not to know they had witnessed and recorded for posterity what was to prove a cultural crossroads - not only for 1970's festivalgoers but also for promoters Ronnie and Ray Foulk.

The men with the cameras would be pleased and proud to see their work live on, giving us a new perspective on the 1970 festival – The view from the crowd.

Alan Stroud, 2021.

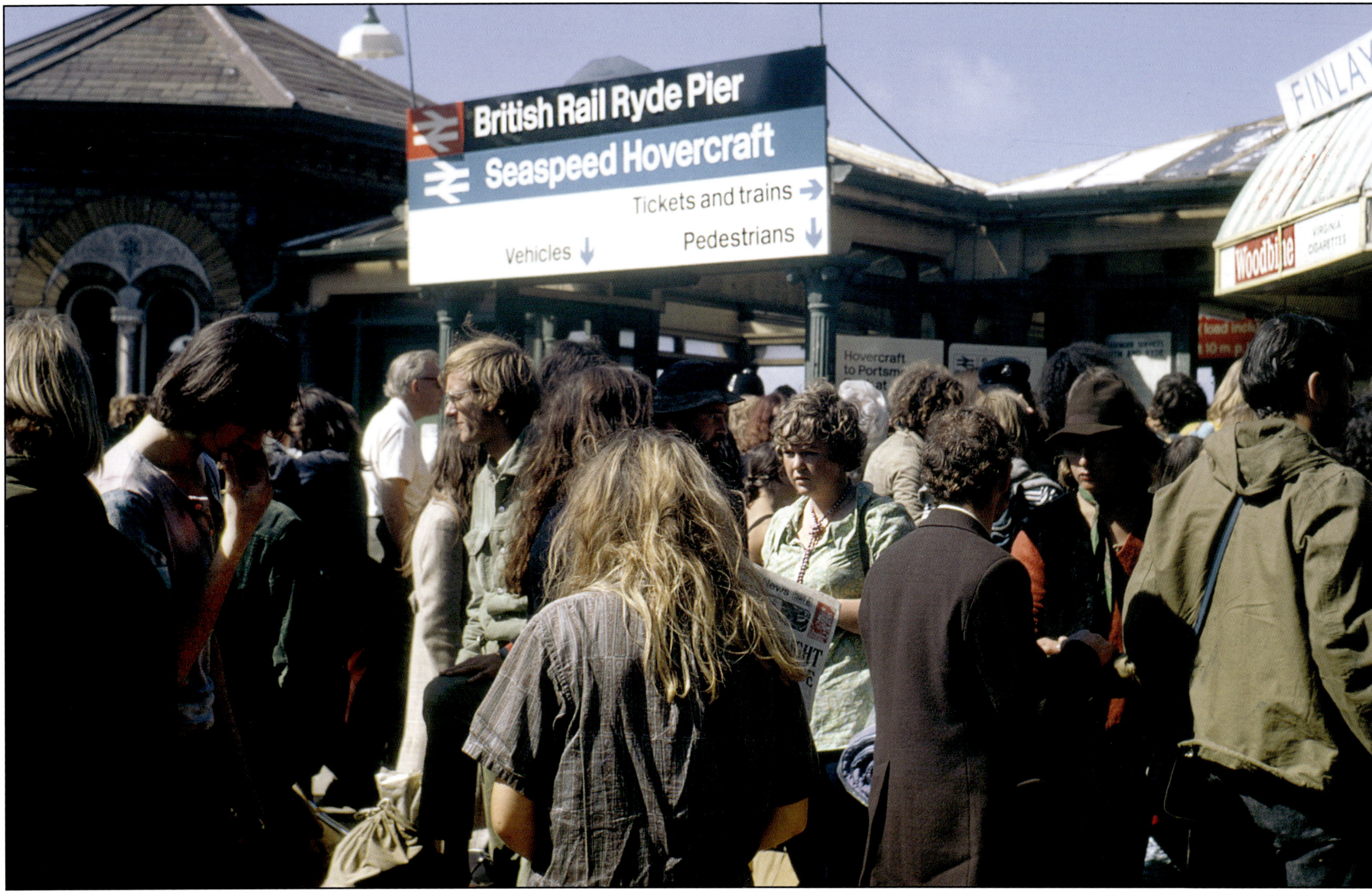

"For days now, garishly dressed individuals have been arriving at the various ferry terminals; from thereon it has been a question of reaching Freshwater by any possible means. Although many had the money to pay bus fares, there were equal numbers using the thumb. Some of those travelling to the festival have been 9 to 5 London office workers who changed from natty suits to pop gear in the train."
I.W. County Press, August 29, 1970.

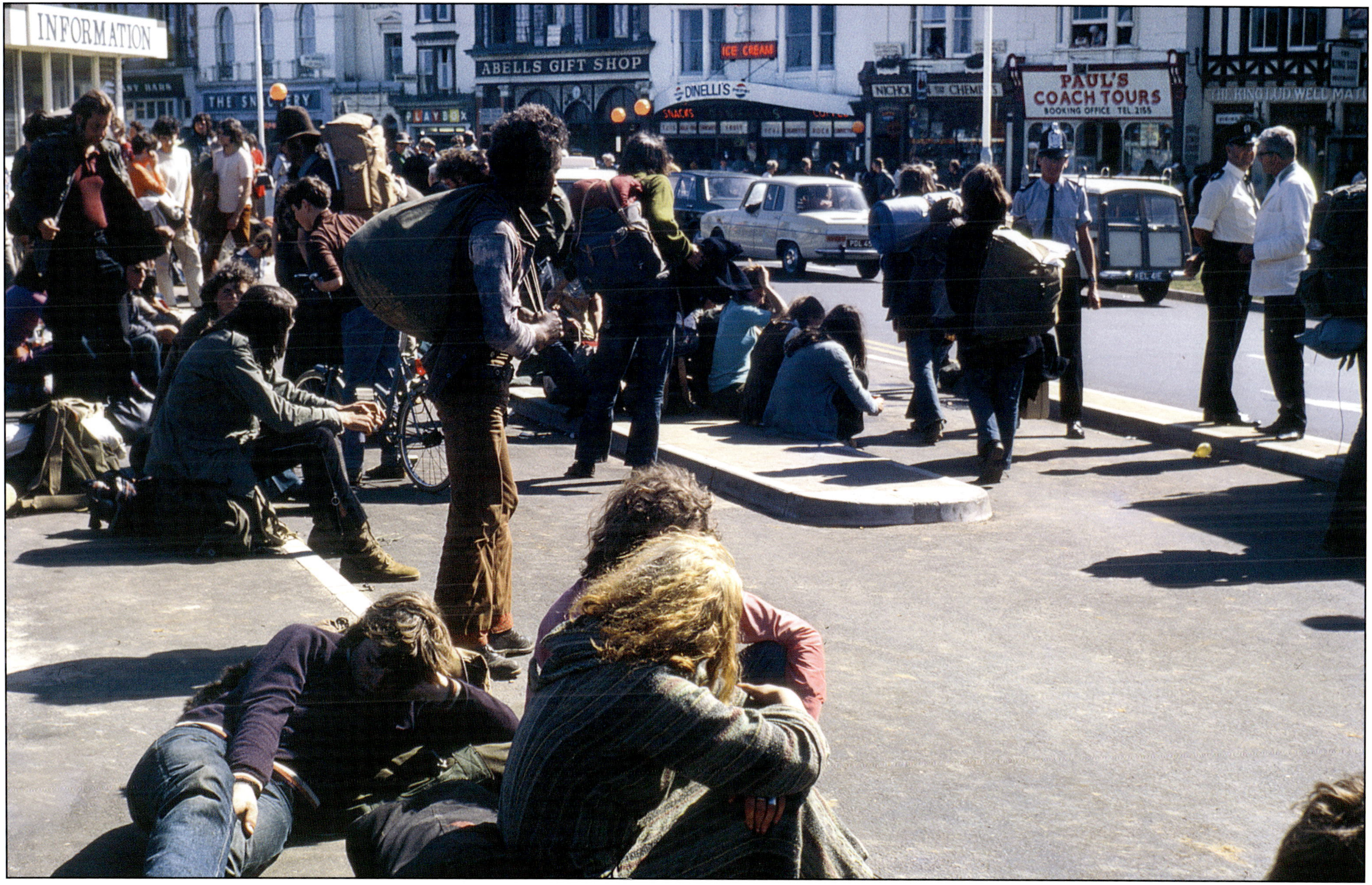

"During the festival it is expected that there will be a large influx of young people to Ryde with nowhere to sleep and with little or no money. The danger of Council properties being broken into or deckchairs being used for sleeping purposes is obvious. Staff are asked to take precautions to ensure the safety of Council property. Attendants are to stack all Esplanade deckchairs, and securely rope all stacks. Best chairs to be placed in centre of stack, oldest to outside." - *Internal memo, Ryde Borough Council.*

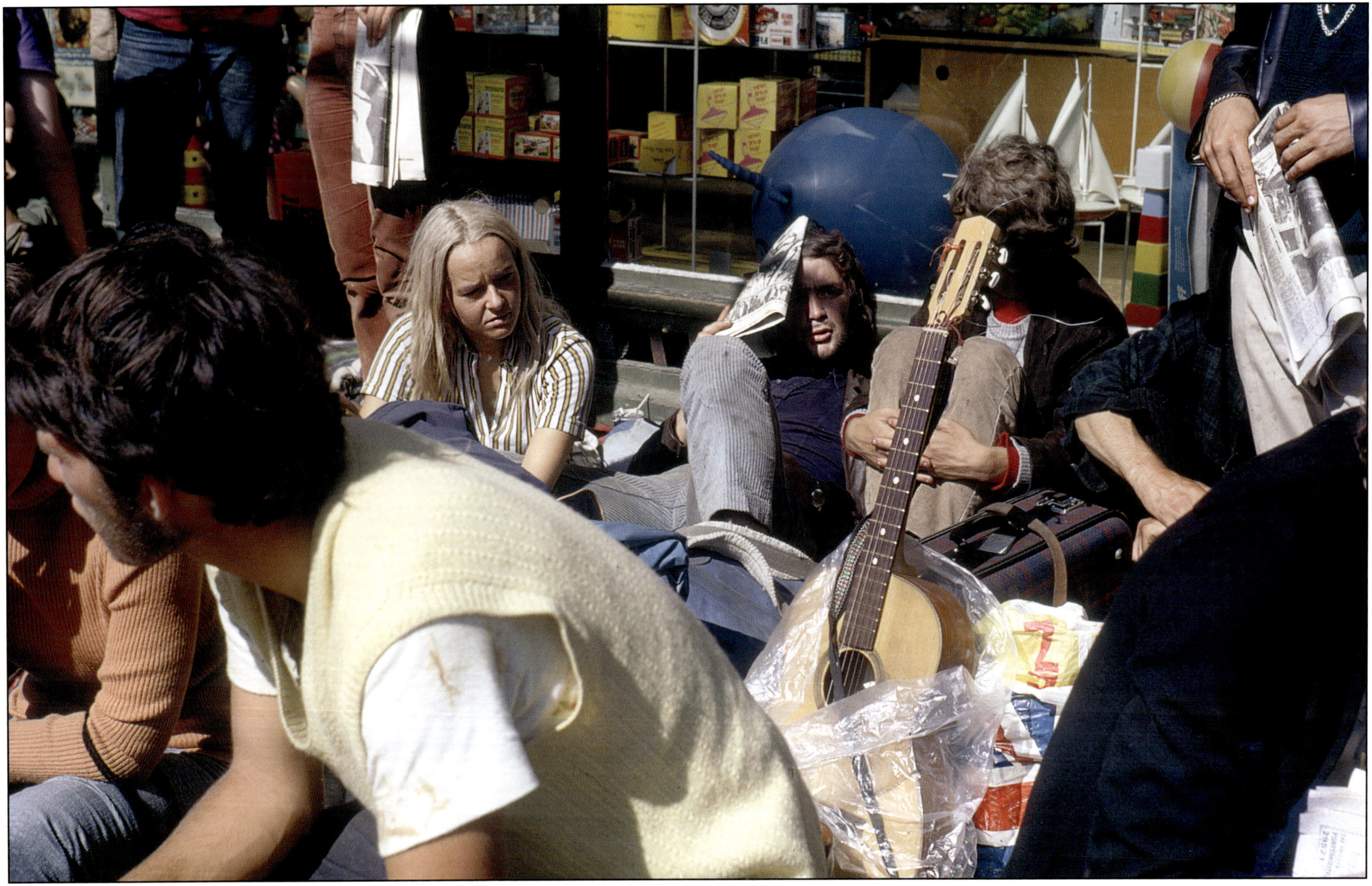

"Mr Pointing of Mobile Security Dog Patrols said that Ryde Esplanade shopkeepers had hired a dog patrol for 24 hours a day for eight days, and this would cover from the "Polka Dot", past Arcadia, up to the Cafe at the corner of Esplanade with Union Street."
Internal memo, Ryde Borough Council.

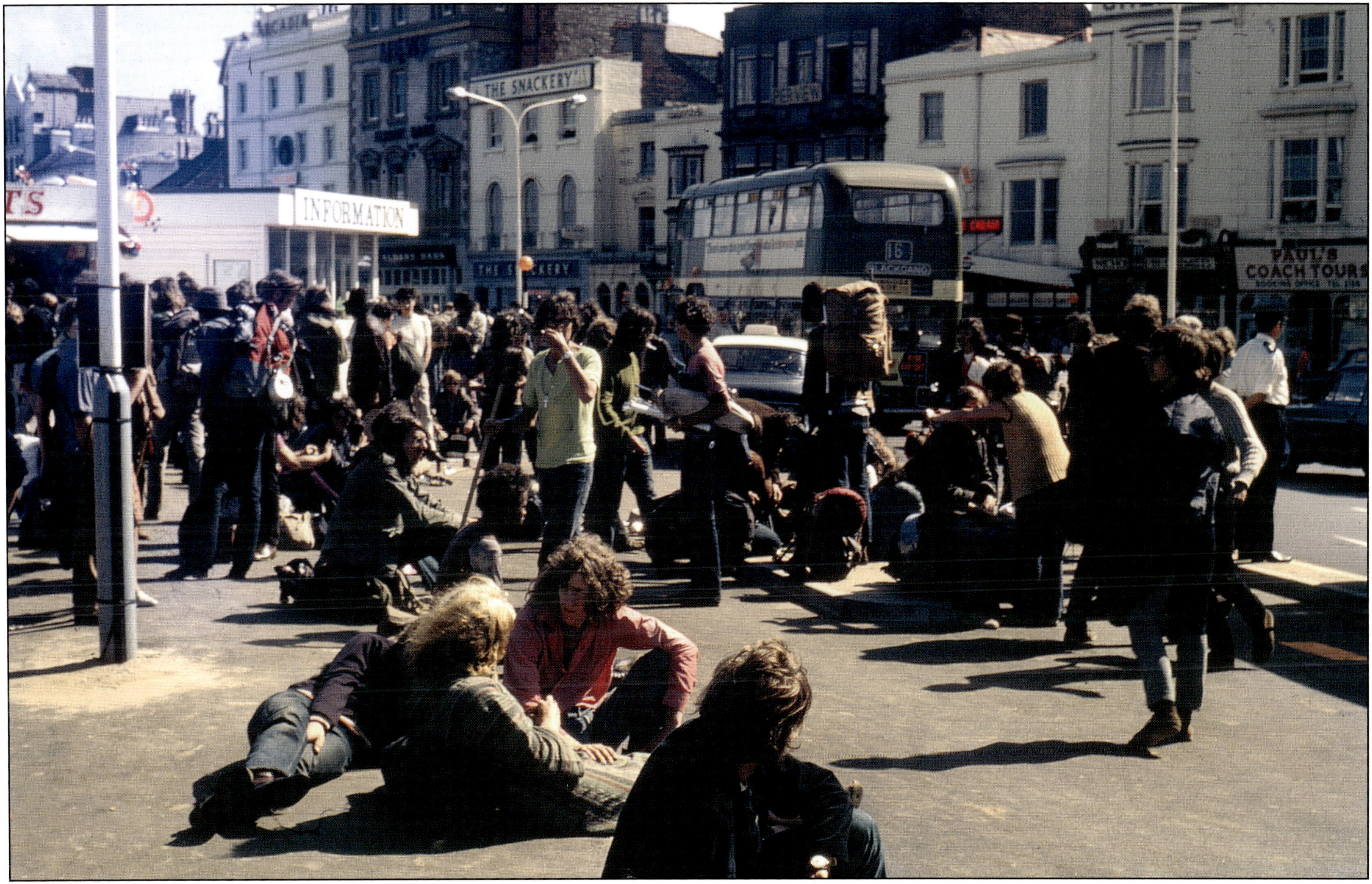

"Spoke to Mr Pointing of Mobile Security Dog Patrols, asking if security dog patrol could be doubled during the Festival Period. Mr Pointing said he would do his best but could not promise. Apparently his firm were doing all the security on the Festival Site. He would have 16 men engaged altogether over the Festival period. He was getting 25 dogs from the mainland."
Internal memo, Ryde Borough Council.

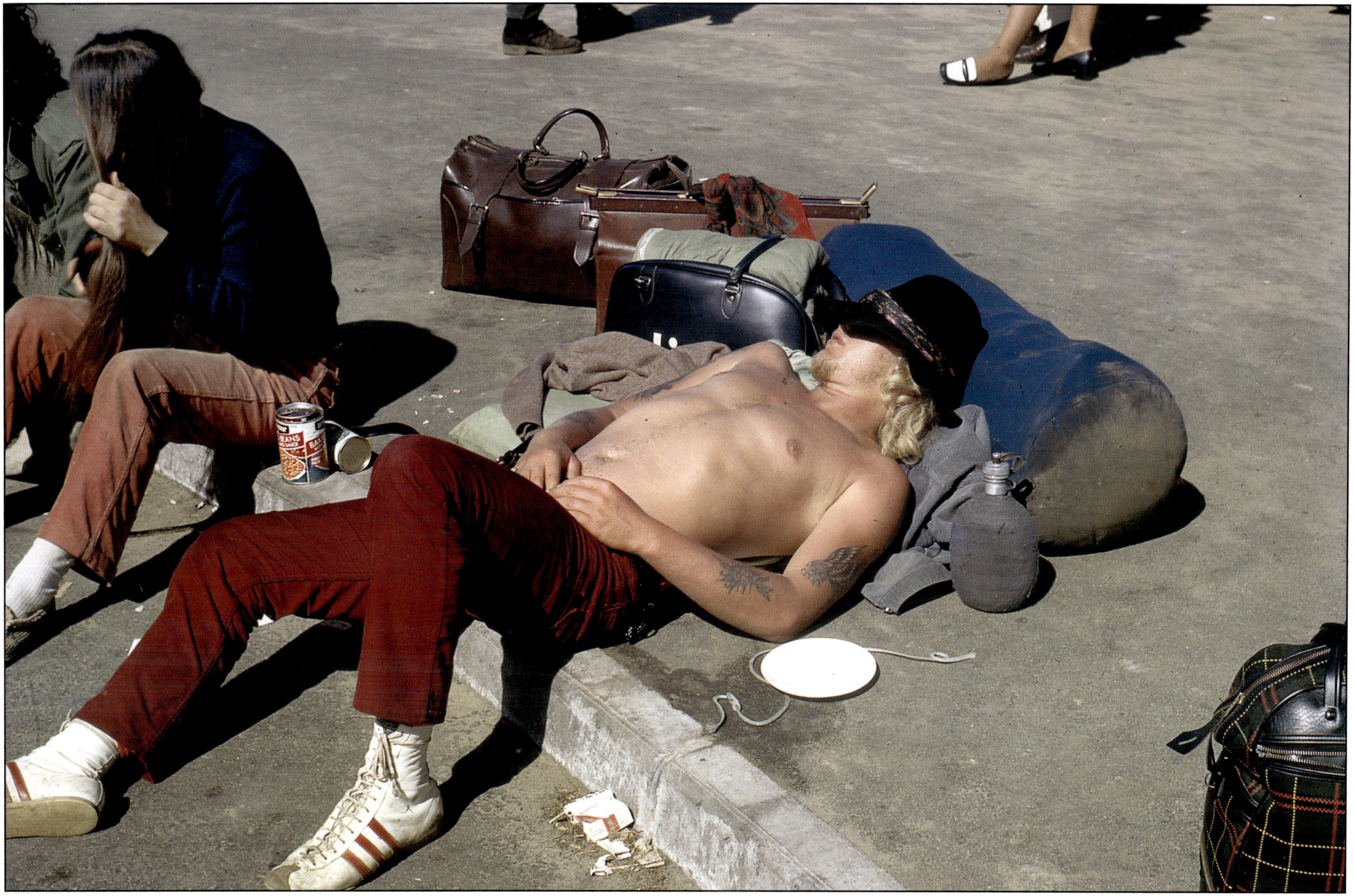

"I think the principal risk to Ryde Borough is a possible breakdown of public order which could arise should frustration build up amongst fans if the festival is a failure or the weather is bad." - *Ryde Public Health Inspector, internal memo, July 31, 1970.*

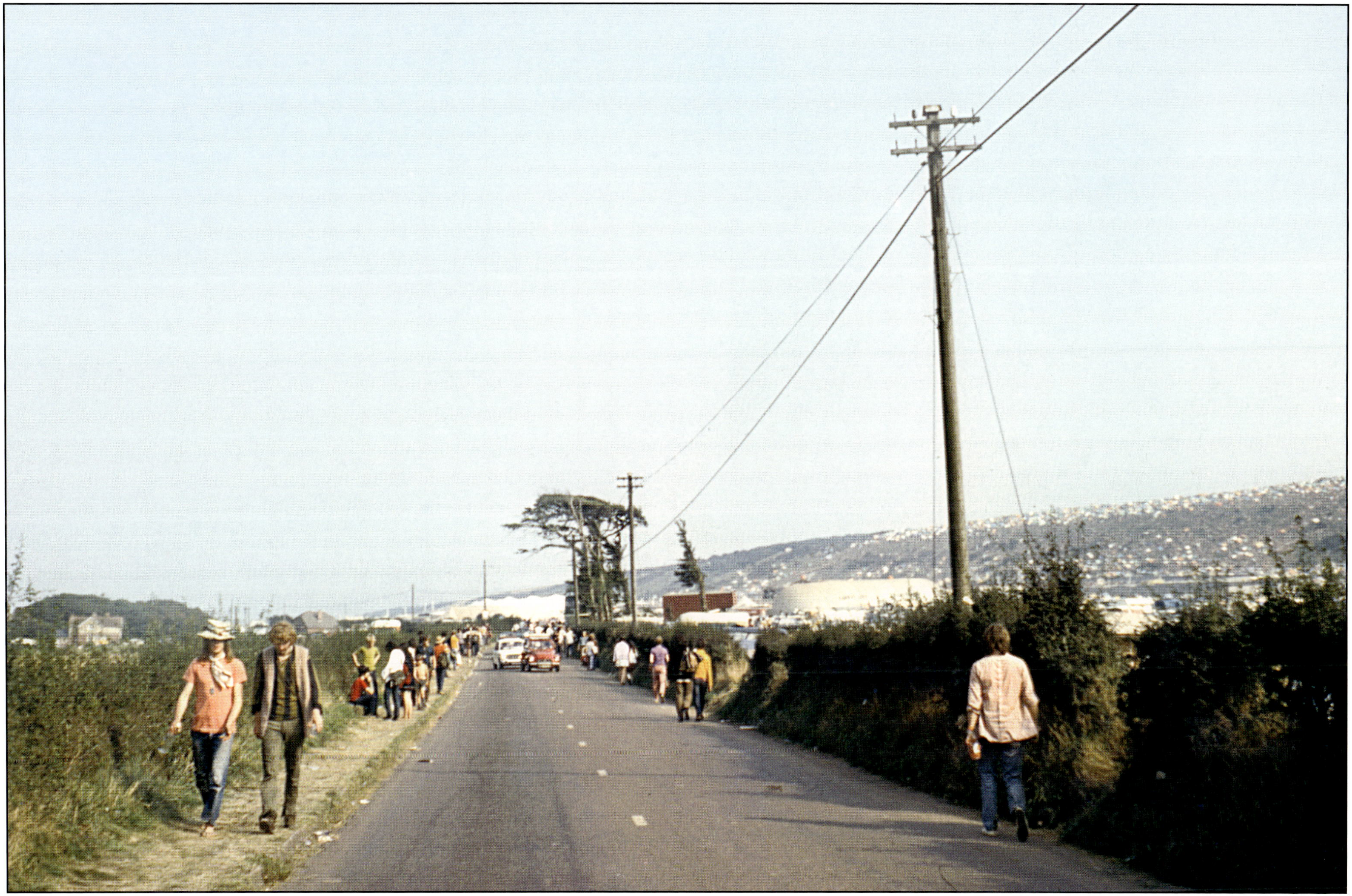

"Many remarked on the efficiency with which the roads were kept clear all around the site. Even on the peak day, Sunday, it was possible to drive freely out to Freshwater and after a 10 minute one-way routing and a bit of hassling, back in again. The police, in fact, were obviously extremely well organised, briefed and behaved." - *Friends Magazine, October 2, 1970.*

Harry Matthews

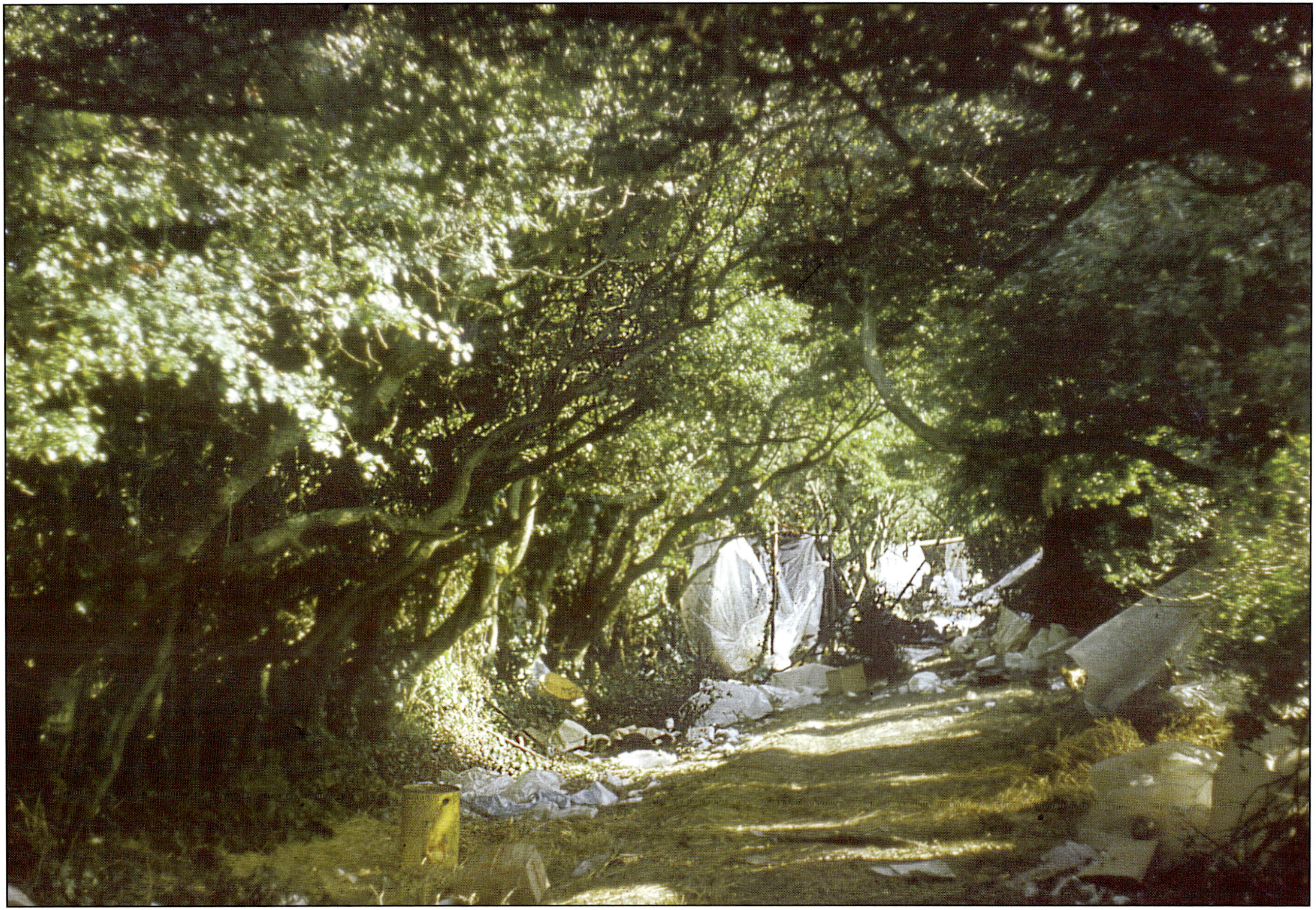

Desolation Row *Harry Matthews*

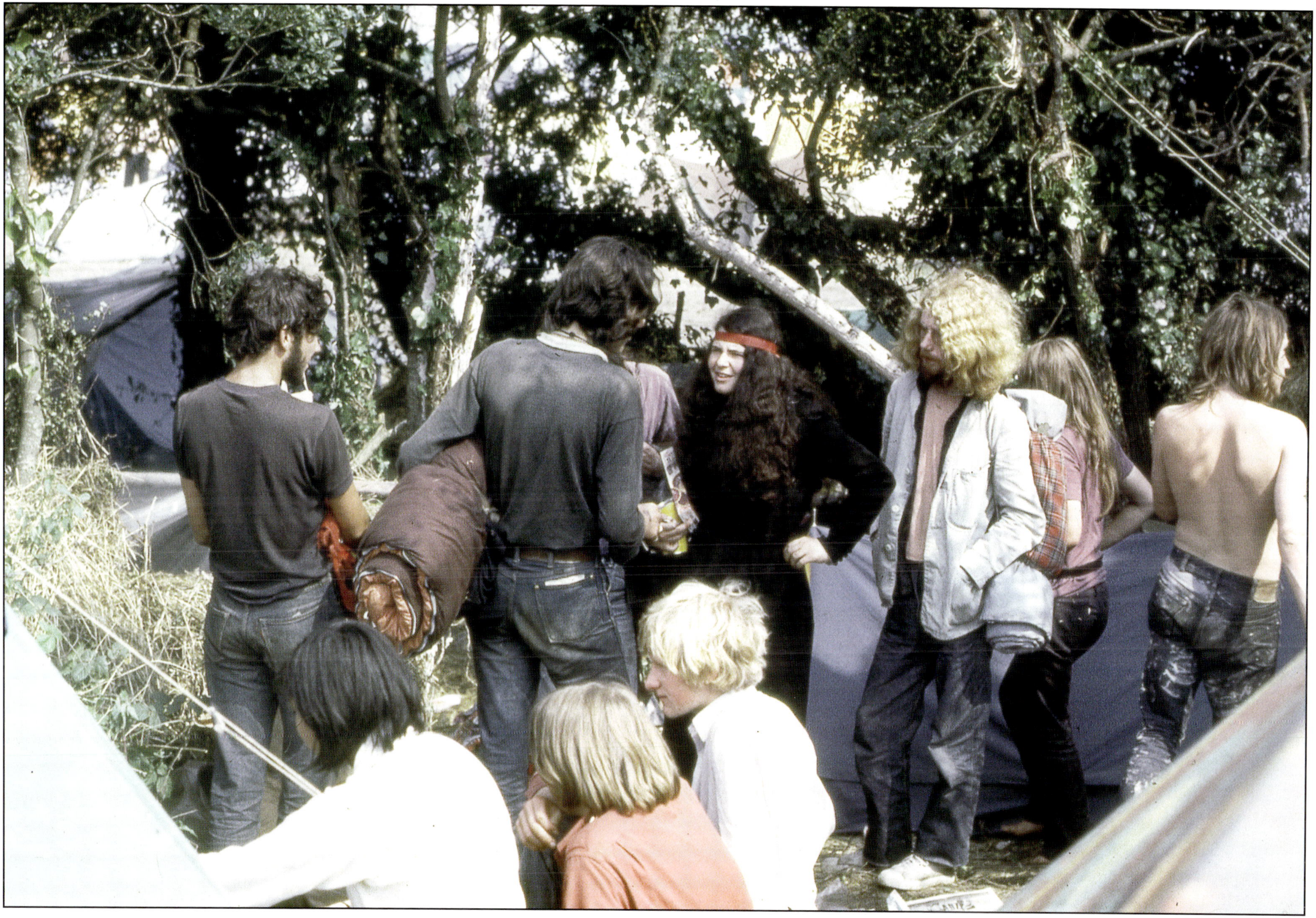

Desolation Row *Ken Box*

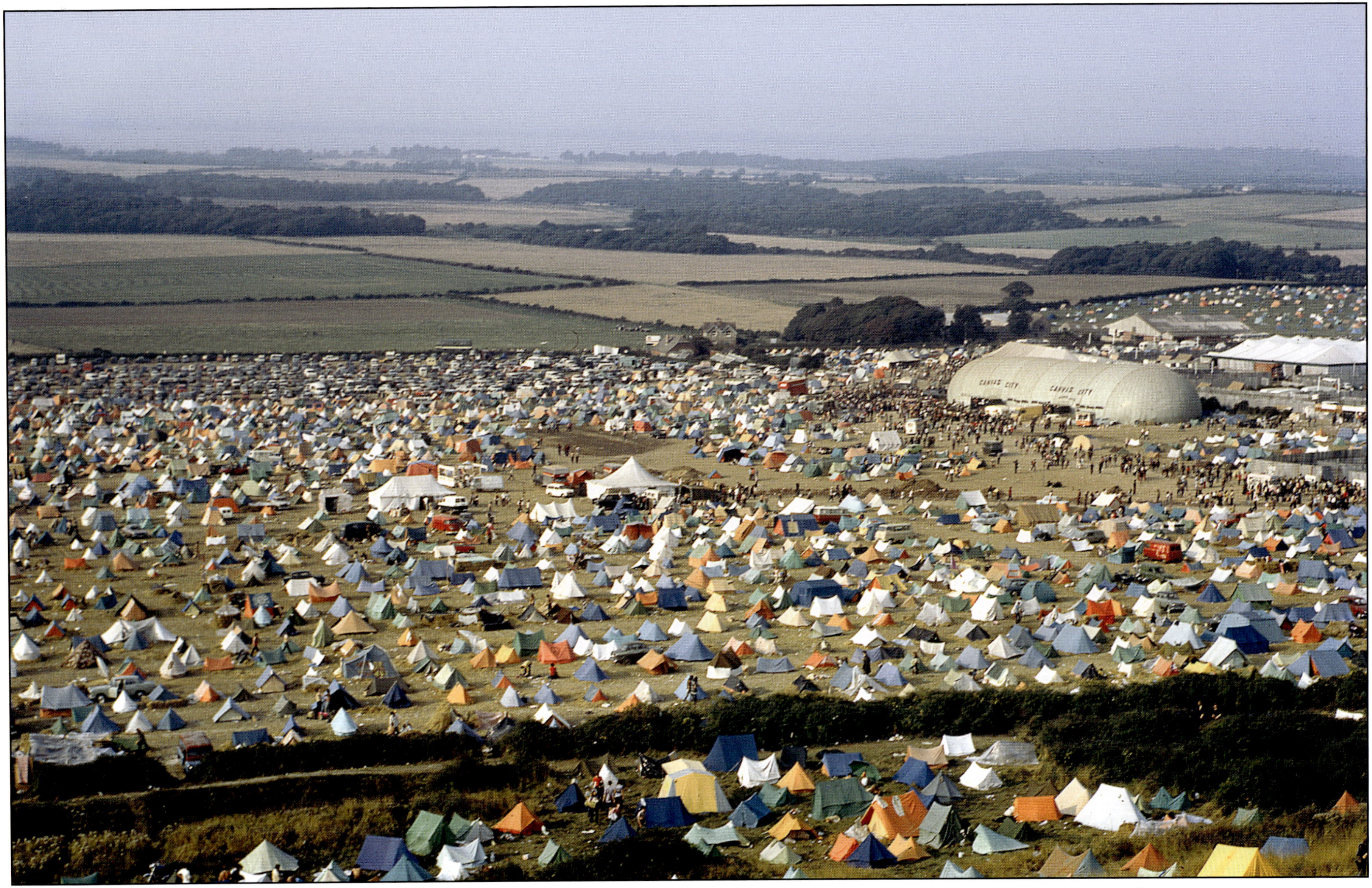

"It is fascinating to watch the proliferating hippy township. The cow towns in the Wild West or the gold-mining towns in the Australian outback would have sprung up like this, rough and rude, with the smell of frying food mingling with the smoke from the campfires, and the sound of people knocking together their makeshift homes." - *Michael Watts, Melody Maker, September 5, 1970.*

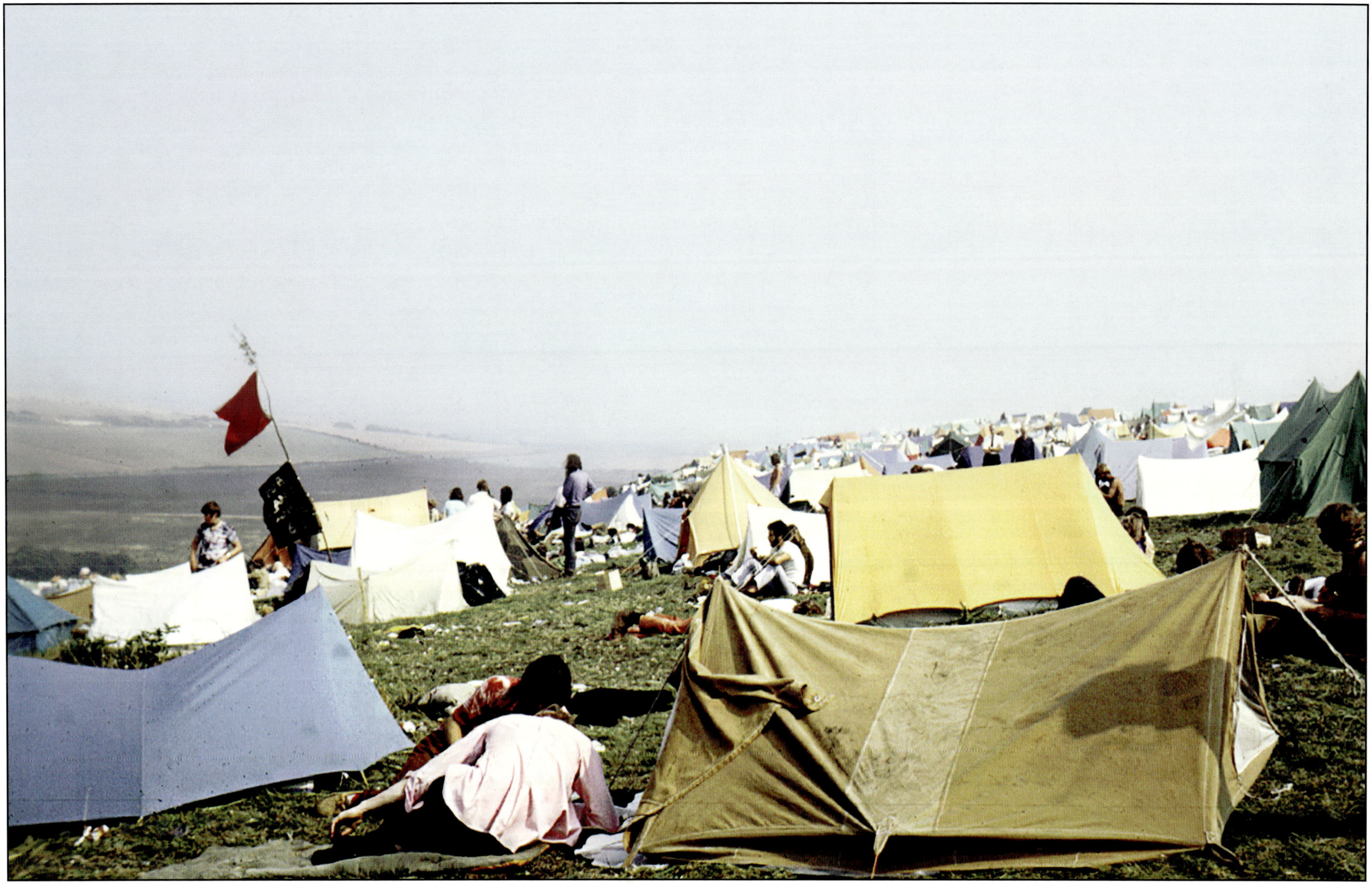

"Not since Attila and the Huns had a people been so taut with anxiety about an oncoming invasion, and not since last year's onslaught had they been face to face with such vast numbers of hairy holidaymakers. As shown them last year, there was relatively little to fear. "Hippie Types", as the daily papers described them, made their way peacefully and mysteriously to the little prefab settlement constructed near Tennyson Downs, erected their humble abodes and waited for the action." - *Lon Goddard, Record Mirror, 5 September 1970.*

Eric Moth

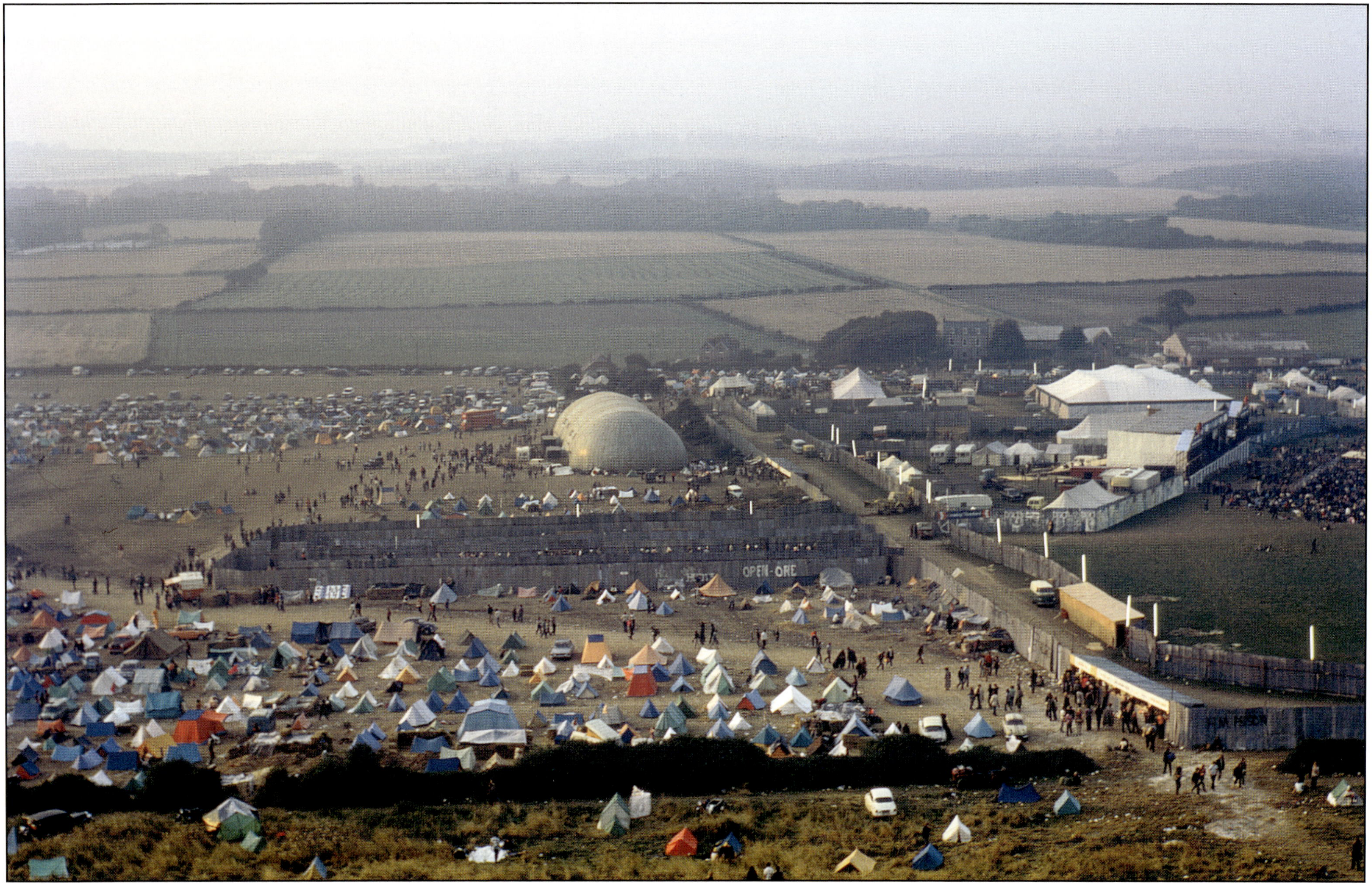

"The double wall system was a great idea because it serves a few things at once. One is that you got additional security, you've got two walls to get over rather than one. Secondly, you can have your security within the double wall zone so nobody sees your security unless they are in the business of trespassing and thirdly, you've got a roadway all the way around the site to service your shops and toilets and backstage."- *Ray Foulk interviewed by the authors.*

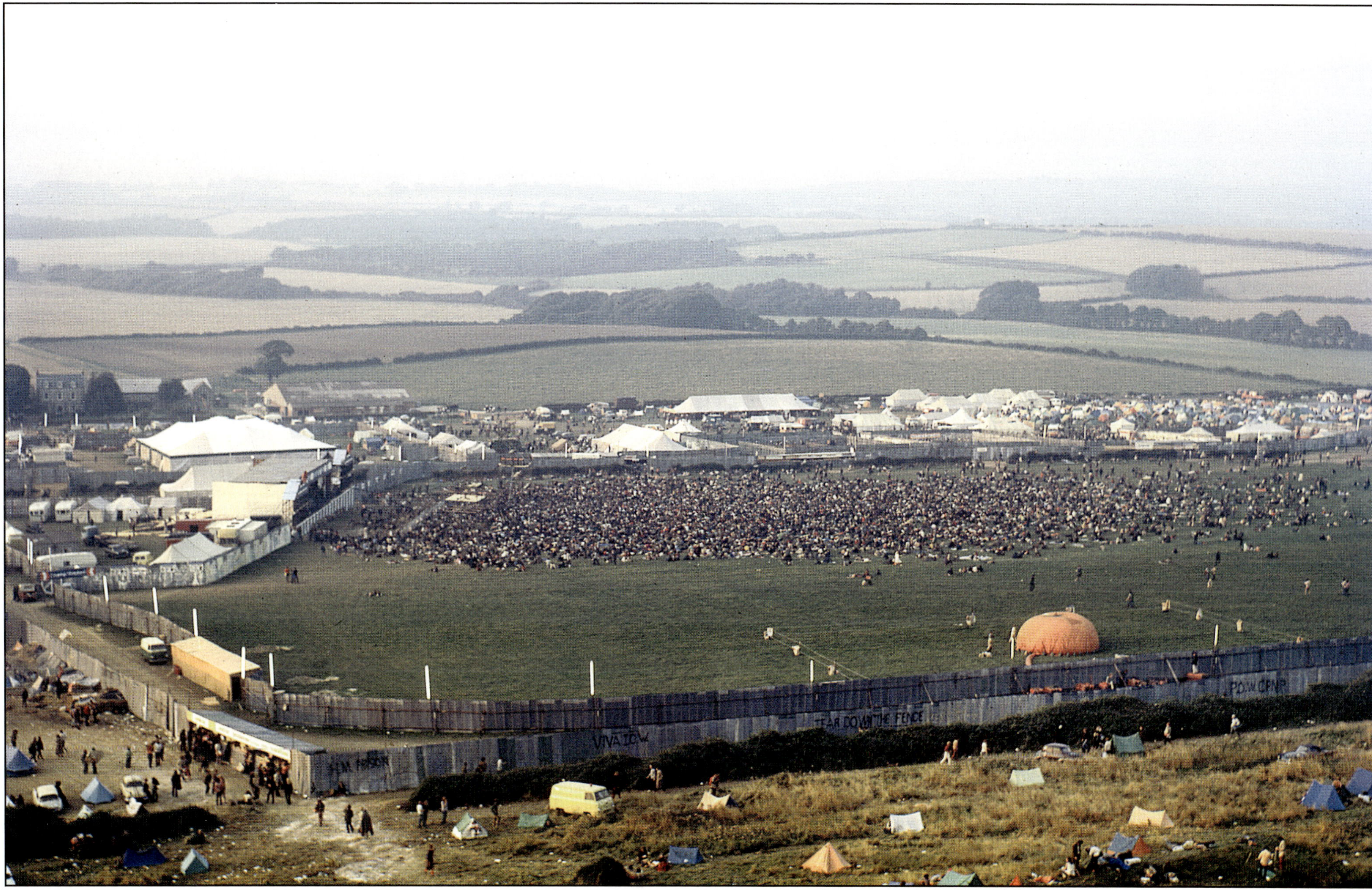

"This is East Afton Farm, the farm which over the next seven days will be reaping the pop harvest. There are already thousands of fans here, some under tents but many with no more protection than a paper sleeping bag. Caterers are preparing for what could be the biggest bonanza of their catering lives. 60,000 eggs, a quarter of a million cans of Coke, thousands of rashers of bacon, 750 gallons of tea and a million paper cups - and this is just the start." - *ITN News report, August 24, 1970.*

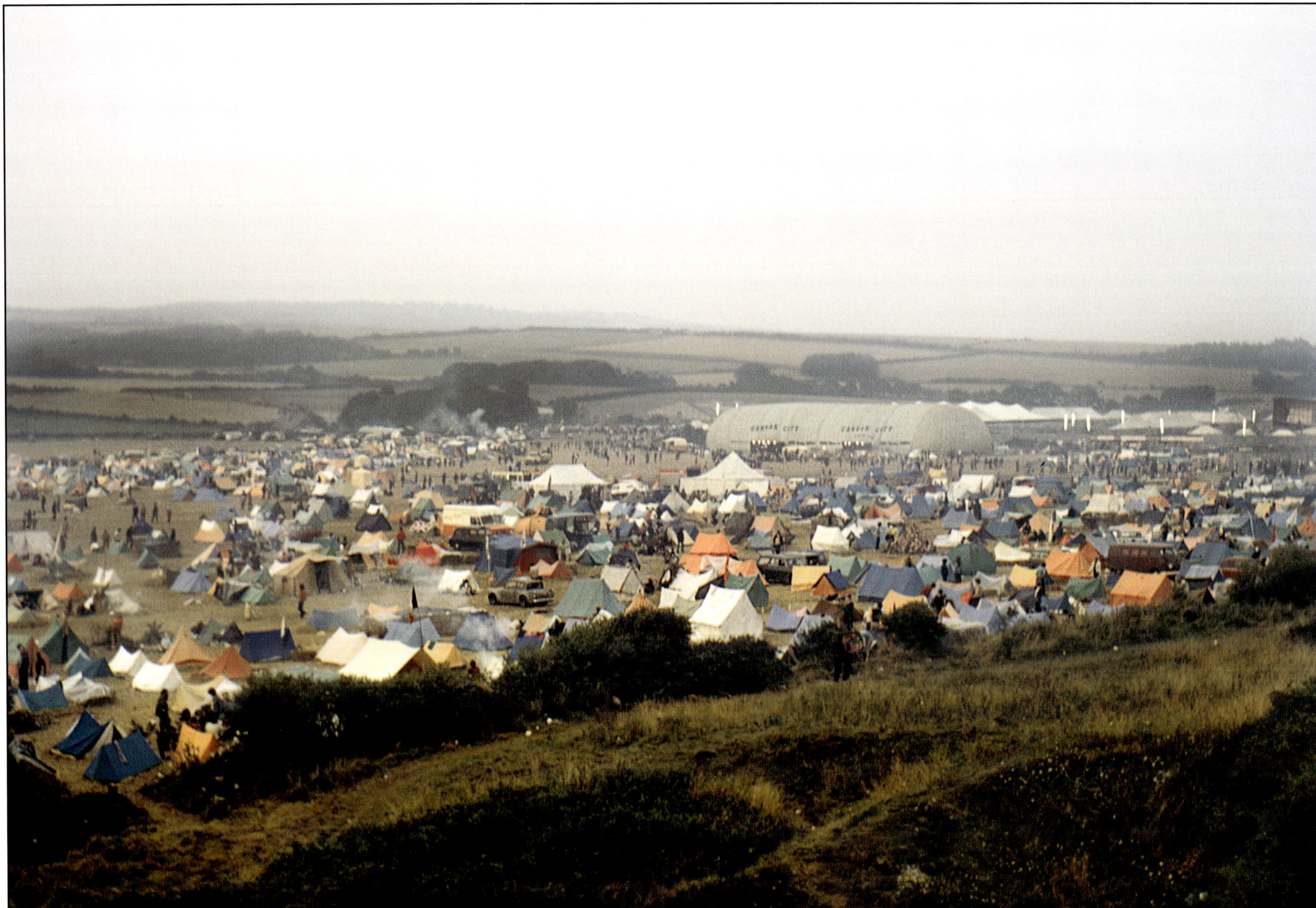

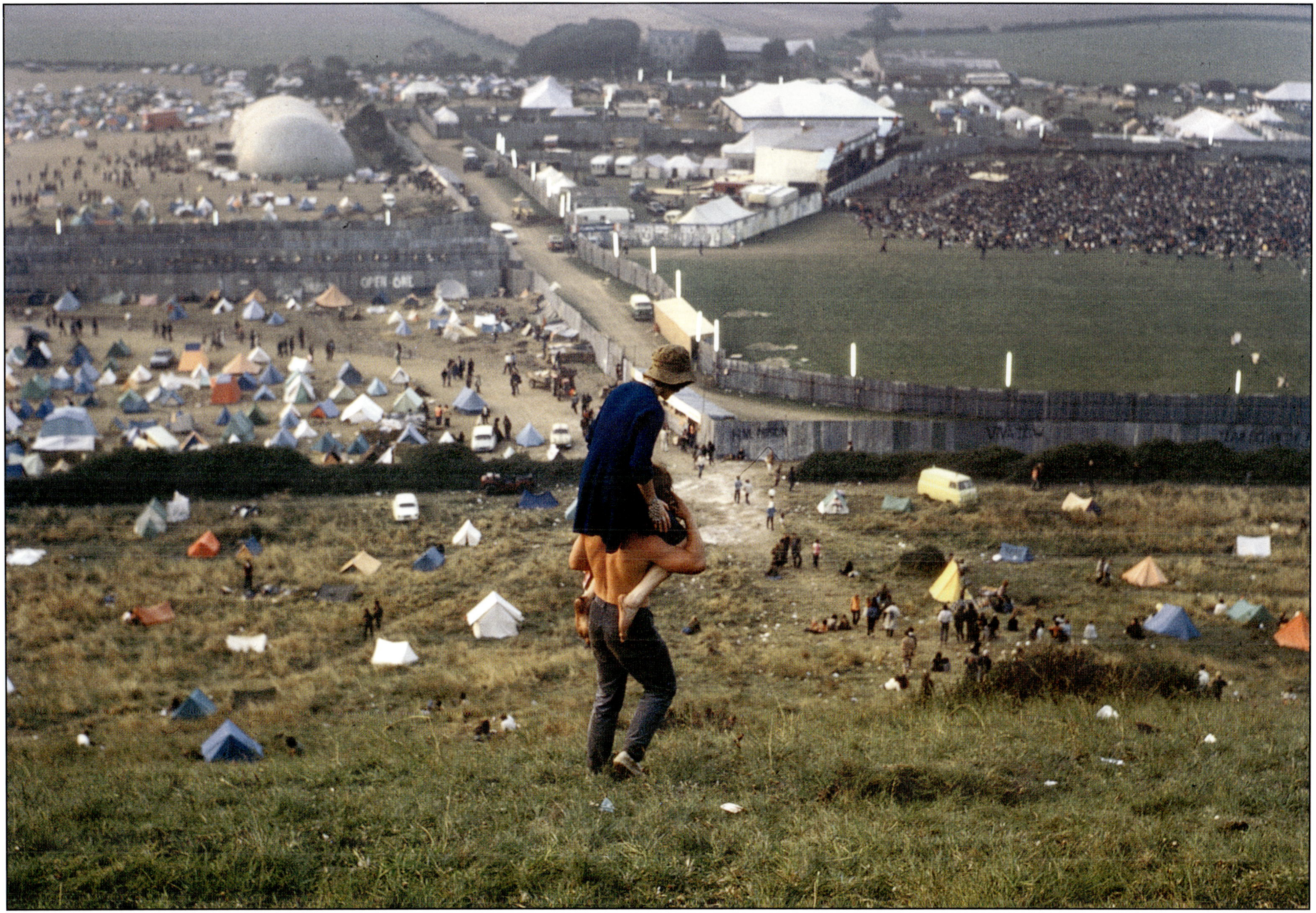

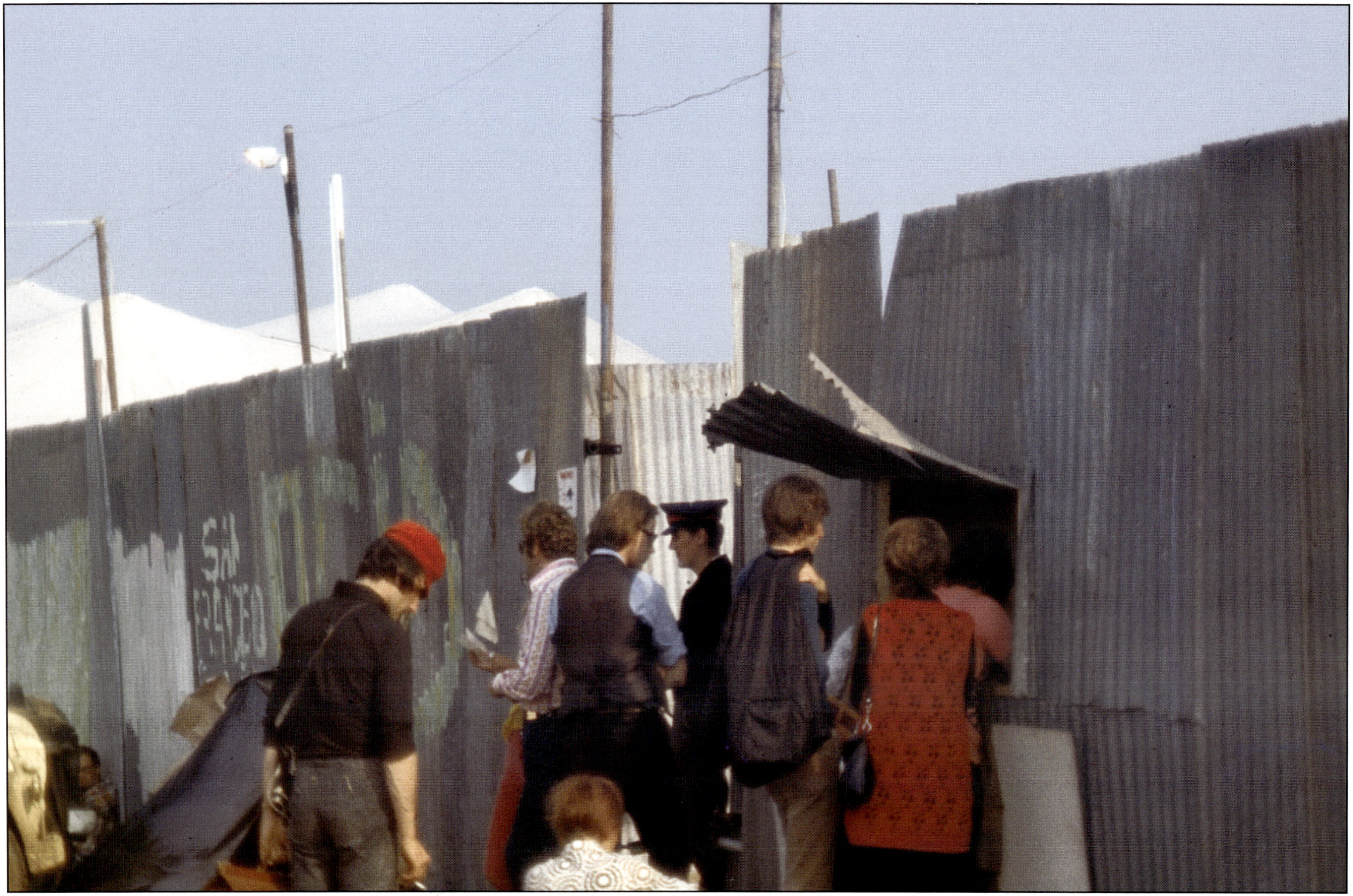

"The wall was eight foot high corrugated iron. It was a bit unfortunate that it didn't get properly painted. We had uniformed security guards and in those days it was the standard thing that they had Alsatian dogs. We didn't like the idea of these guards with dogs mixing with the public so the double wall system enabled them to be kept in a zone of their own and if somebody jumped over, the guards would be in a position to deal with them and escort them out. I think the dogs were unfortunate but we had to have them." - *Ray Foulk interviewed by the authors.*

Harry Matthews

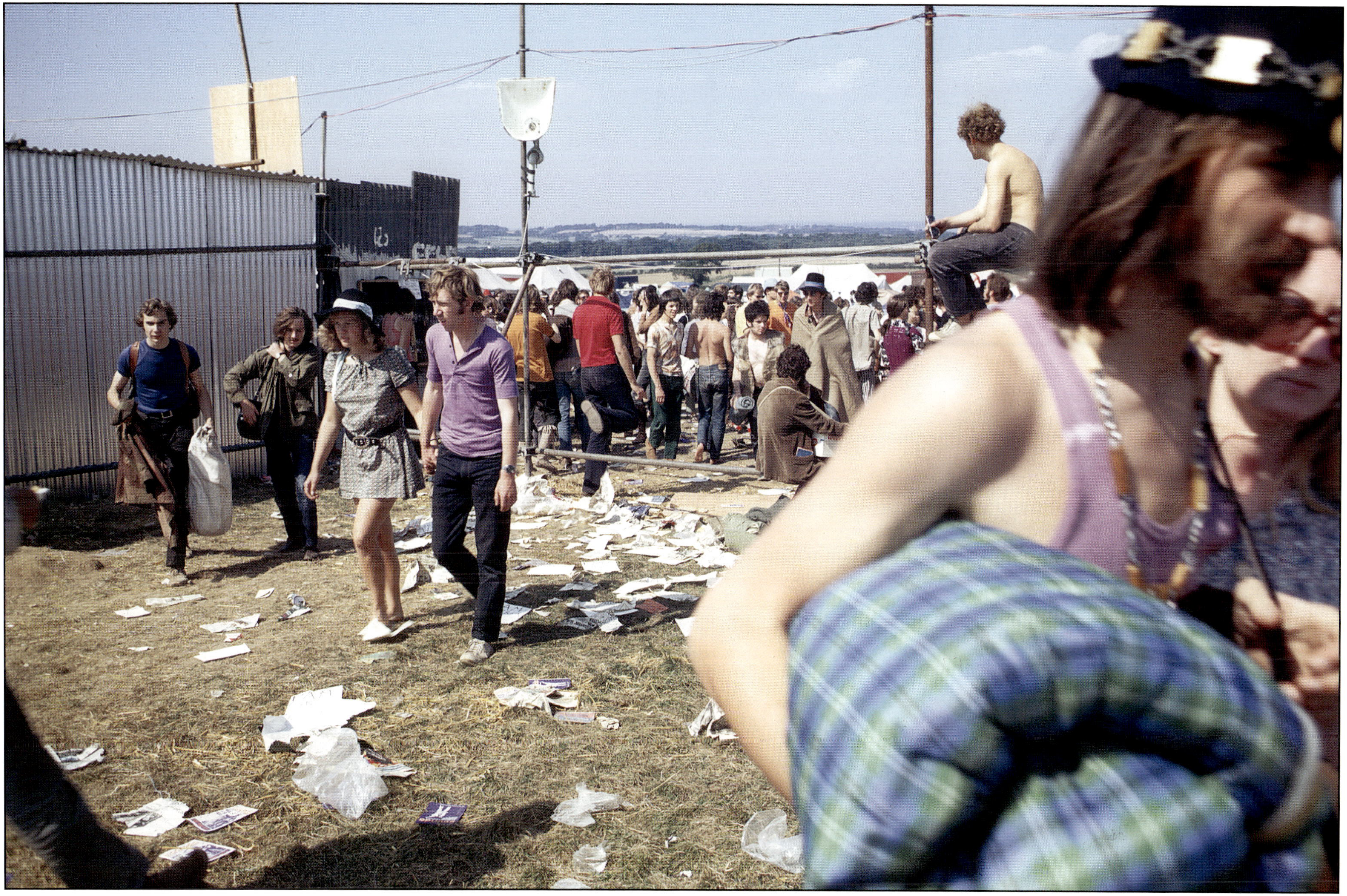

"On the 200-acre festival site the show is being put together efficiently behind a facade of controlled chaos. Food stores are rapidly being brought in ahead of time to cope with the unexpected thousands who have been arriving since last week. A huge canvas warehouse has been erected to store tons of tinned food, fruit and vegetables. Trucks arriving with new loads give part of the site a distinct flavour of Covent Garden." - *Michael Watts, Melody Maker, August 26, 1970.*

Ken Box

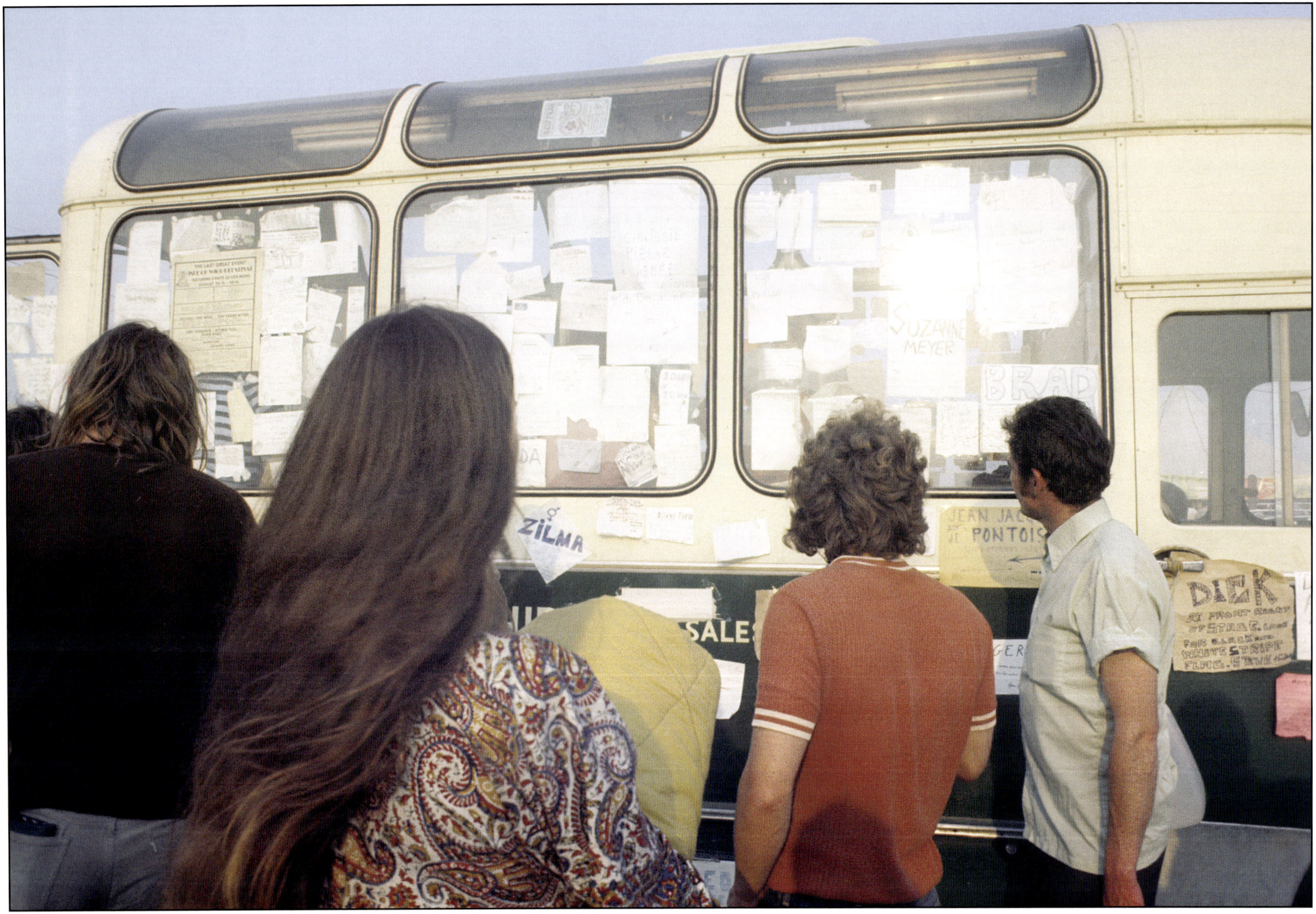

Ken Box

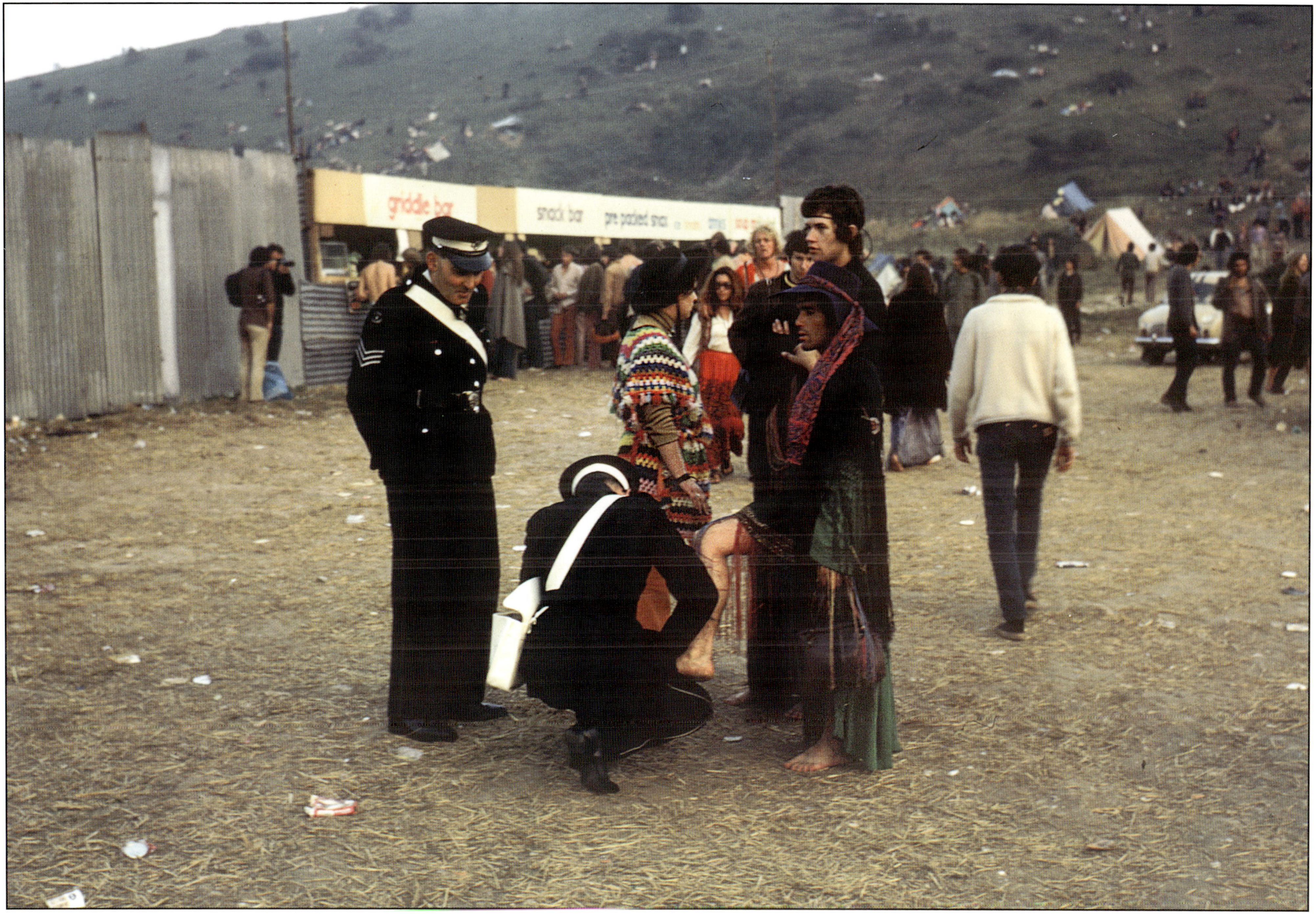
griddle bar
snack bar

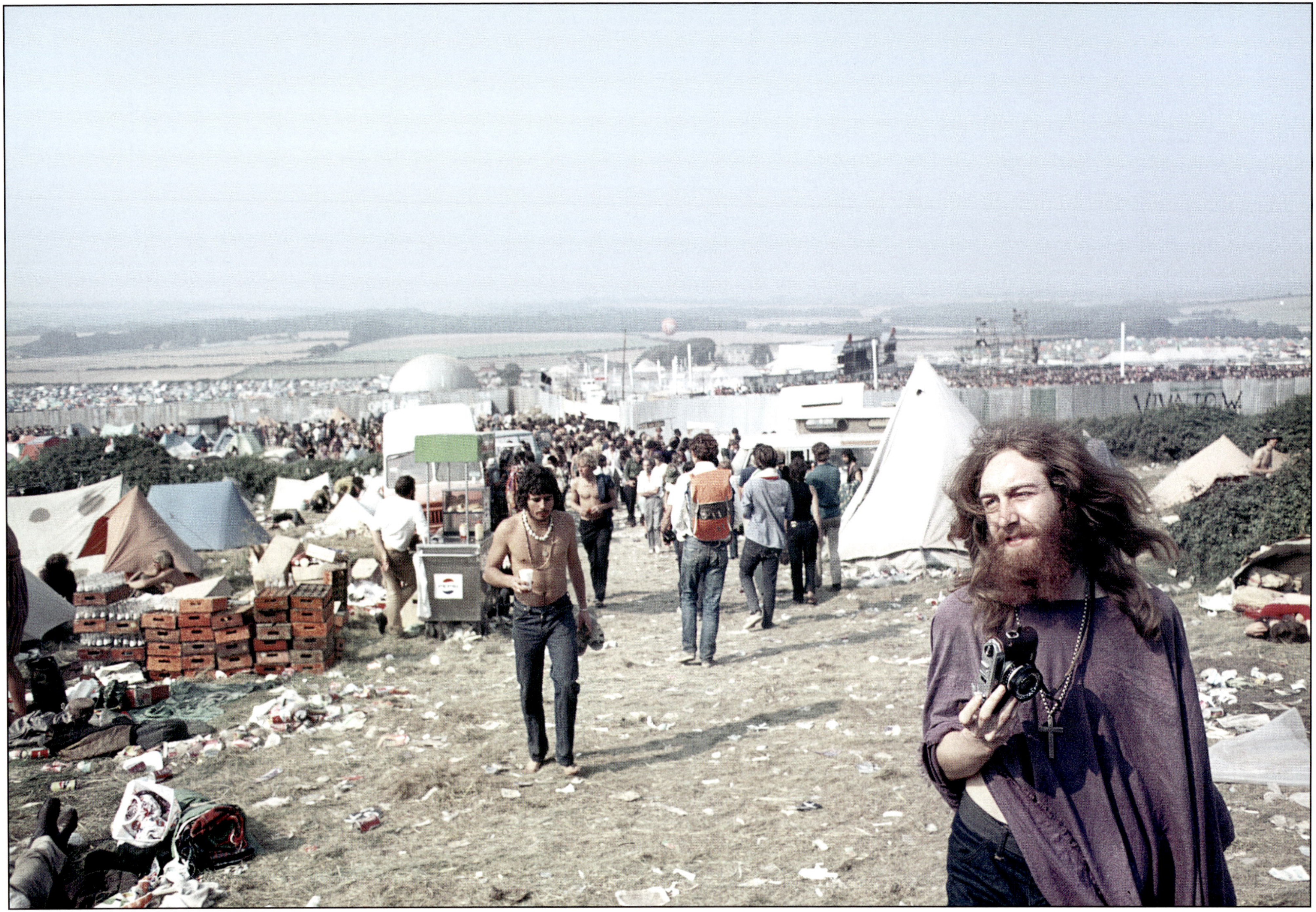

Ken Box

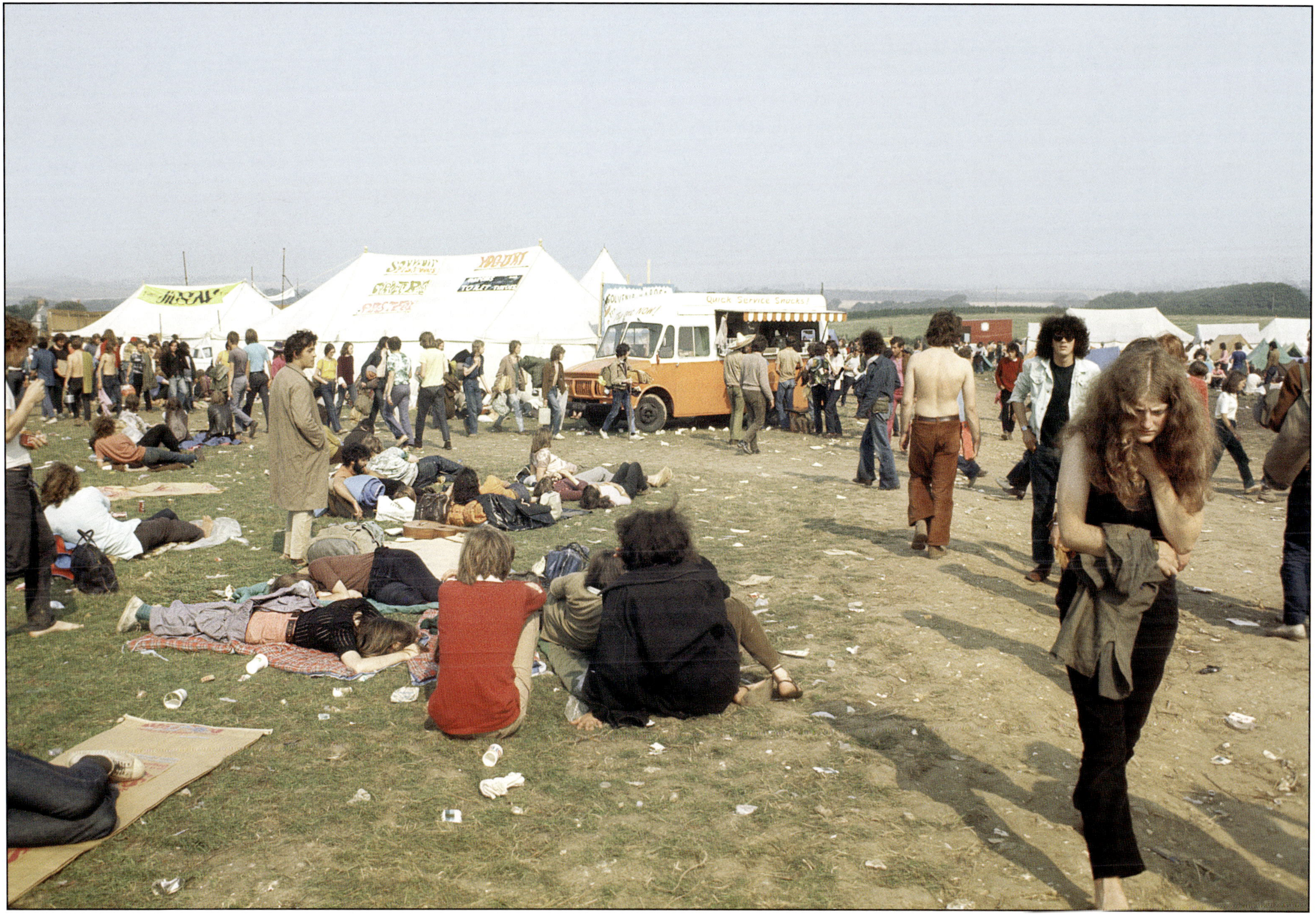

Ken Box

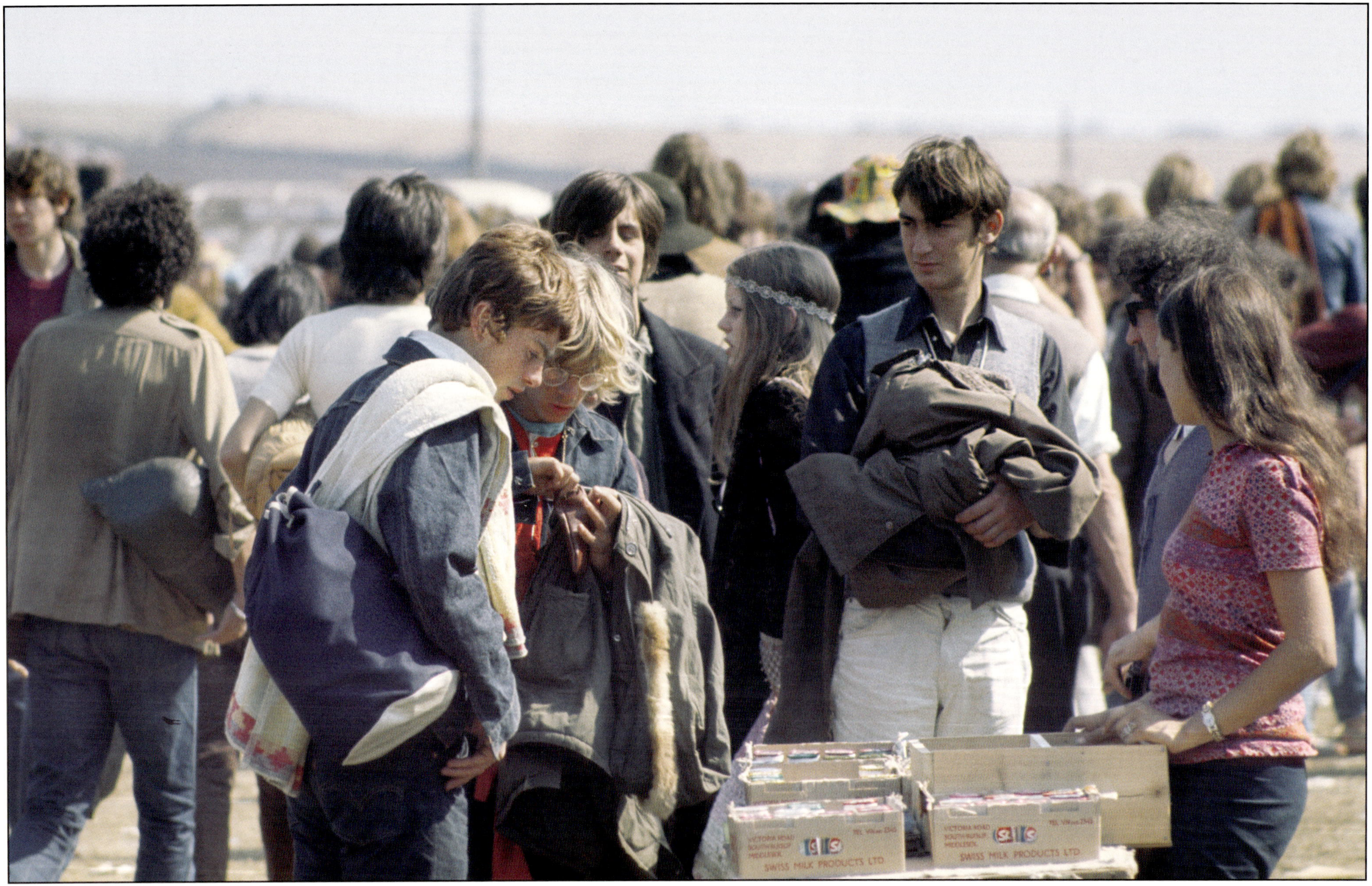

Ken Box

"Reports suggest that catering standards were generally good. Comment was made during the Festival and since, on the prices charged by vendors at the site. This was investigated at the time and price lists were obtained from the promoters and checked with prices actually charged by the official caterers on the site. Without exception these prices were found to coincide. There were, however, a large number of unlicenced vendors both on and off the site and there seems little doubt that some of the prices charged at these stalls were excessive." - *IW Council internal report, October 1970.*

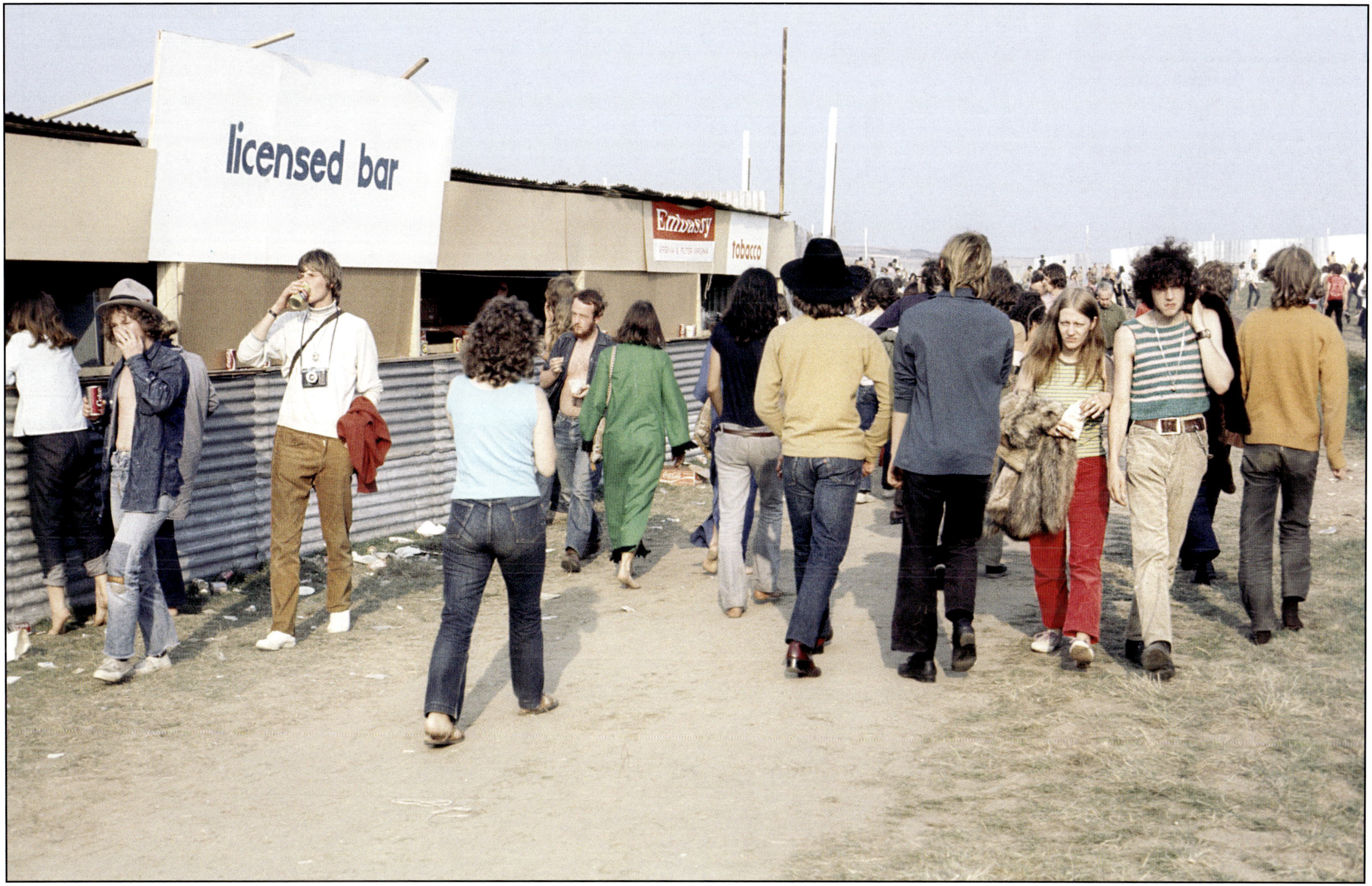

"There was a total bar staff of 40, with three bars in the arena - one for the Press, one for artists and one for staff - and two public bars in marquees. They sold canned beer and spirits in paper cups, there were no glasses. A lot of people were worried – but a lot of people were thankful after the week at the amount of money they'd made. About £40,000 to £45,000 was taken over the bar, which was a lot of money then."
John Webster, Site Licencee.

Ken Box

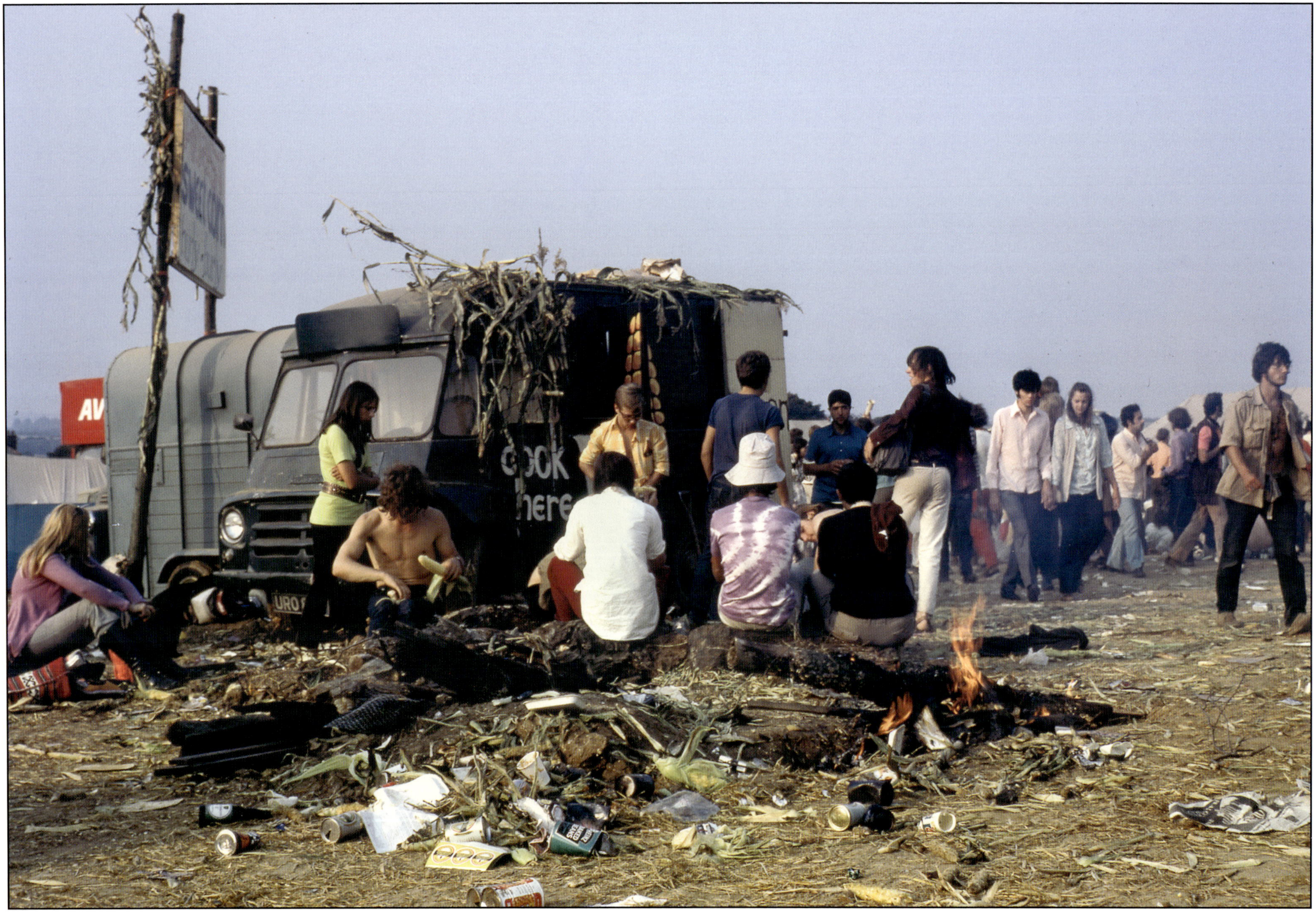
cook
here

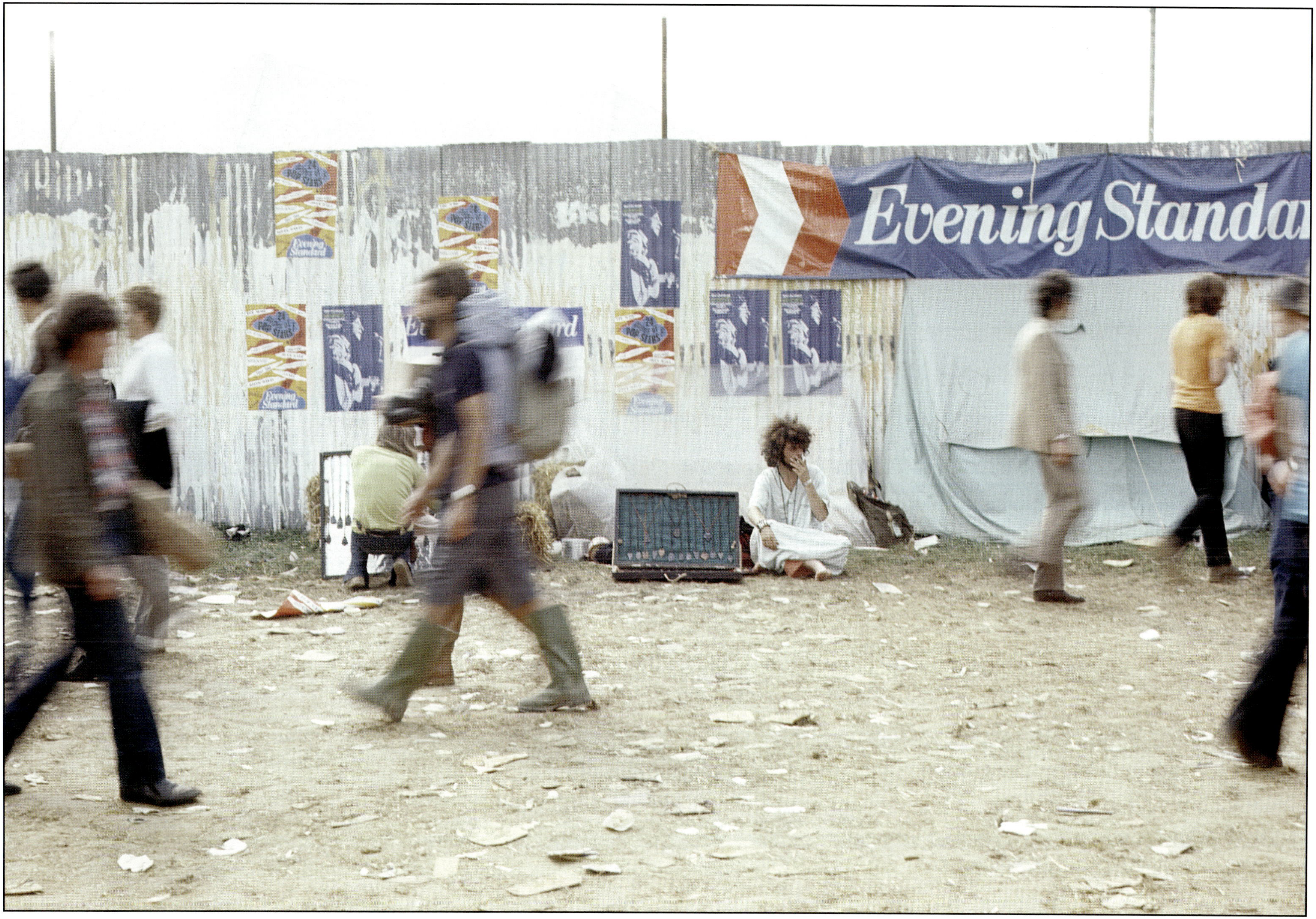

Ken Box

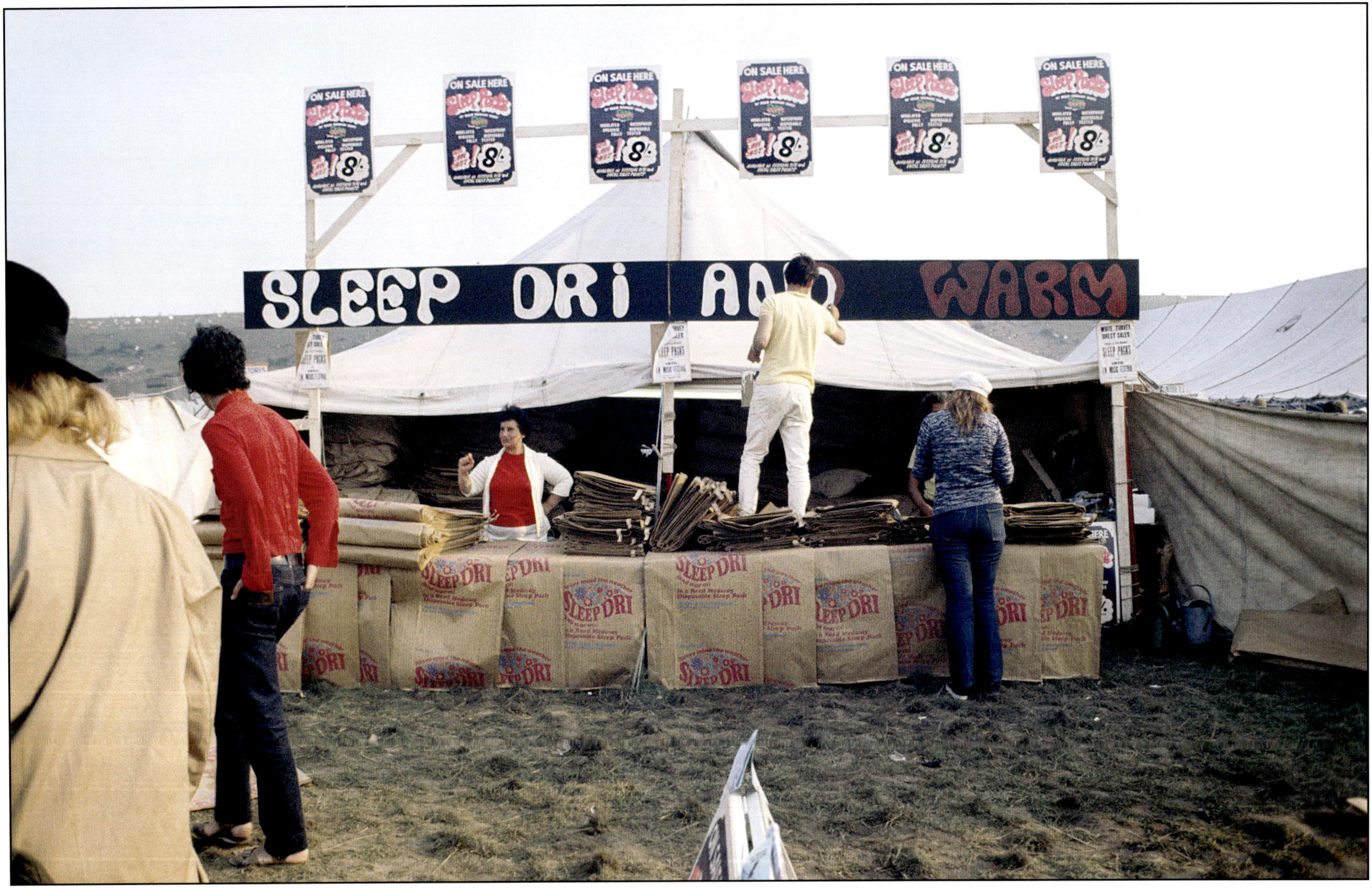

"Visiting the Festival? Stay overnight and sleep 'dri and warm' in a White Turvey Supplied Sleep Pack. Proved beyond doubt in a demonstration by White and Turvey, who slept Friday night in their Sleep Pack on desolate No Man's Land Fort. Both slept 'dri and warm.'. Waterproof and Insulated. Available on Festival Site For Only 8/-." - *Advertisement, I.W. County Press, August 22, 1970.*

Ken Box

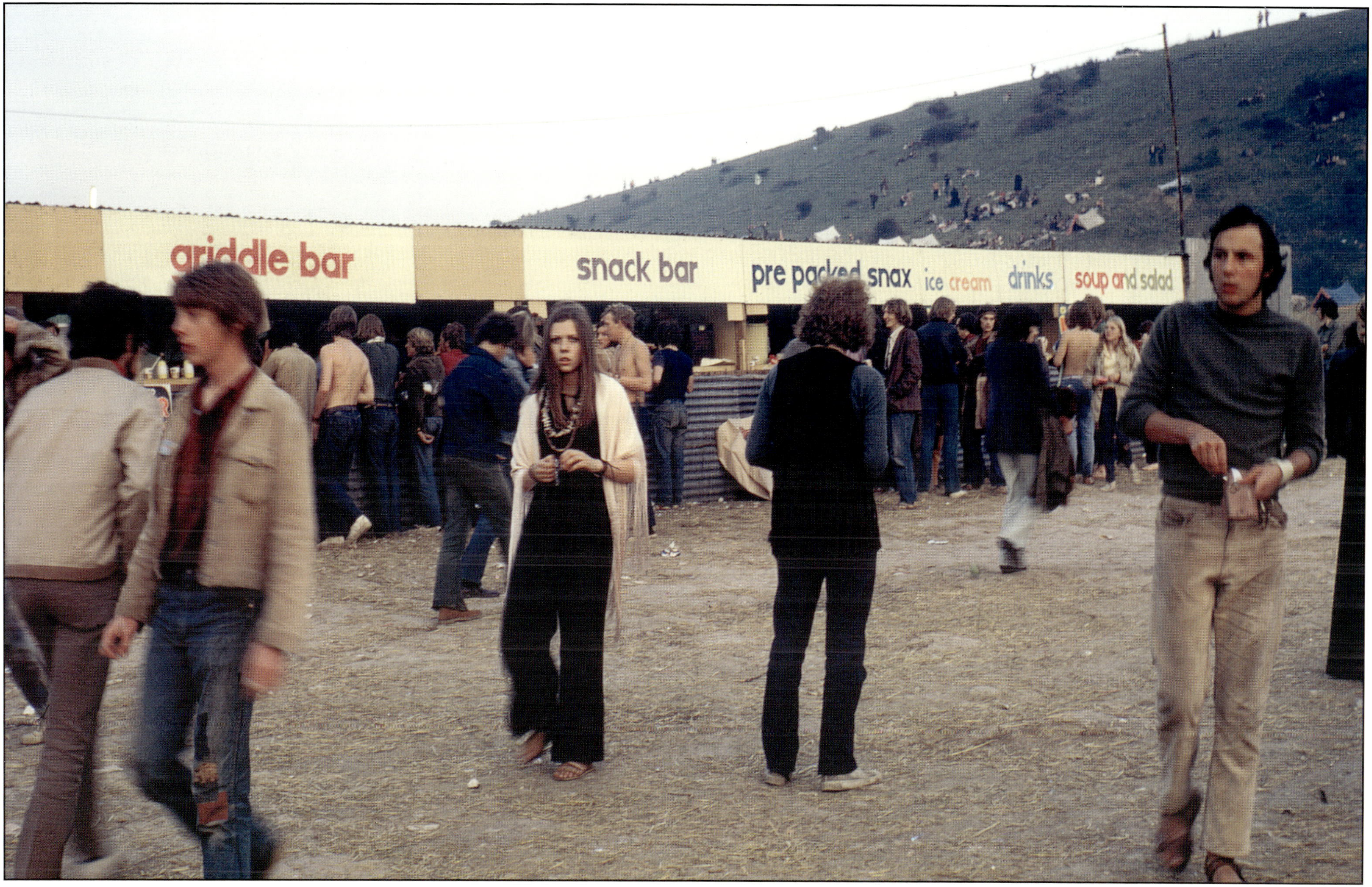

"Once you have pitched your tent, thoughts turn to food. If you have brought a little stove, then tins of beans can be heated, but most people line up in the queues for the fish and chips, which cost three shillings, or hotdogs, two bob. The prices are quite reasonable: tea and soup are ninepence and a shilling respectively, and it is even possible to buy mutton biryani for five and sixpence." - *Michael Watts, Melody Maker, August 26, 1970.*

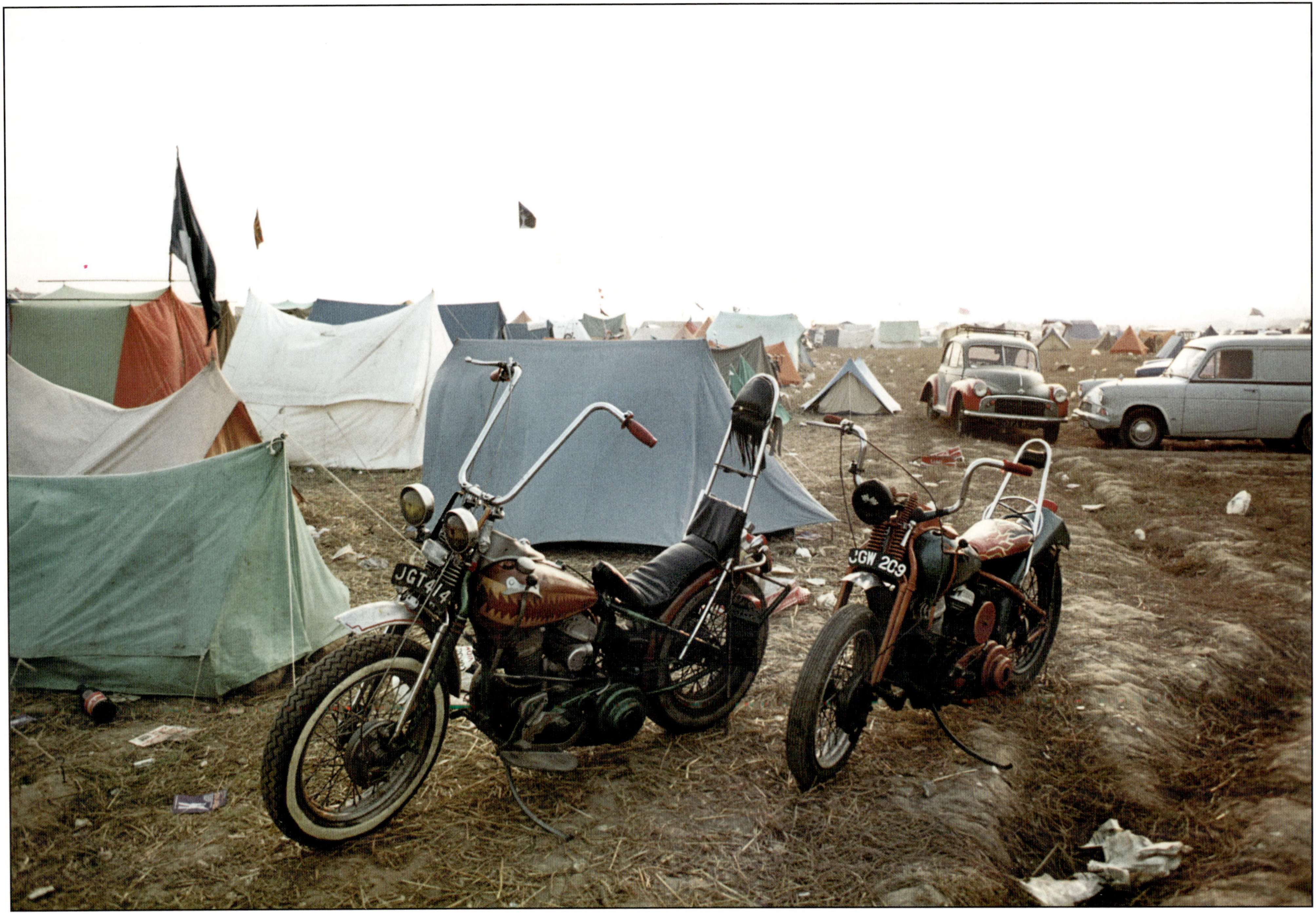

Ken Box

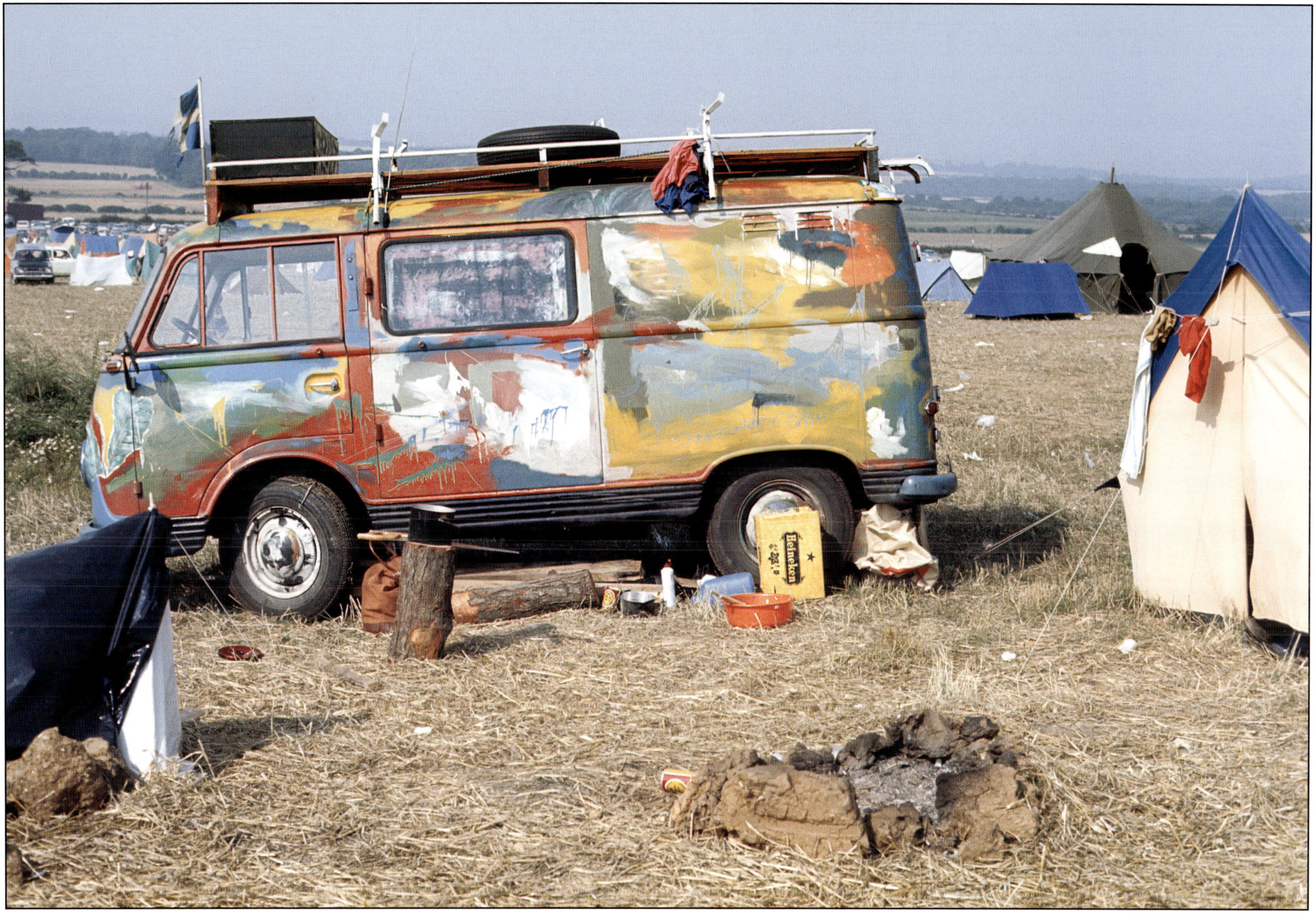

Ken Box

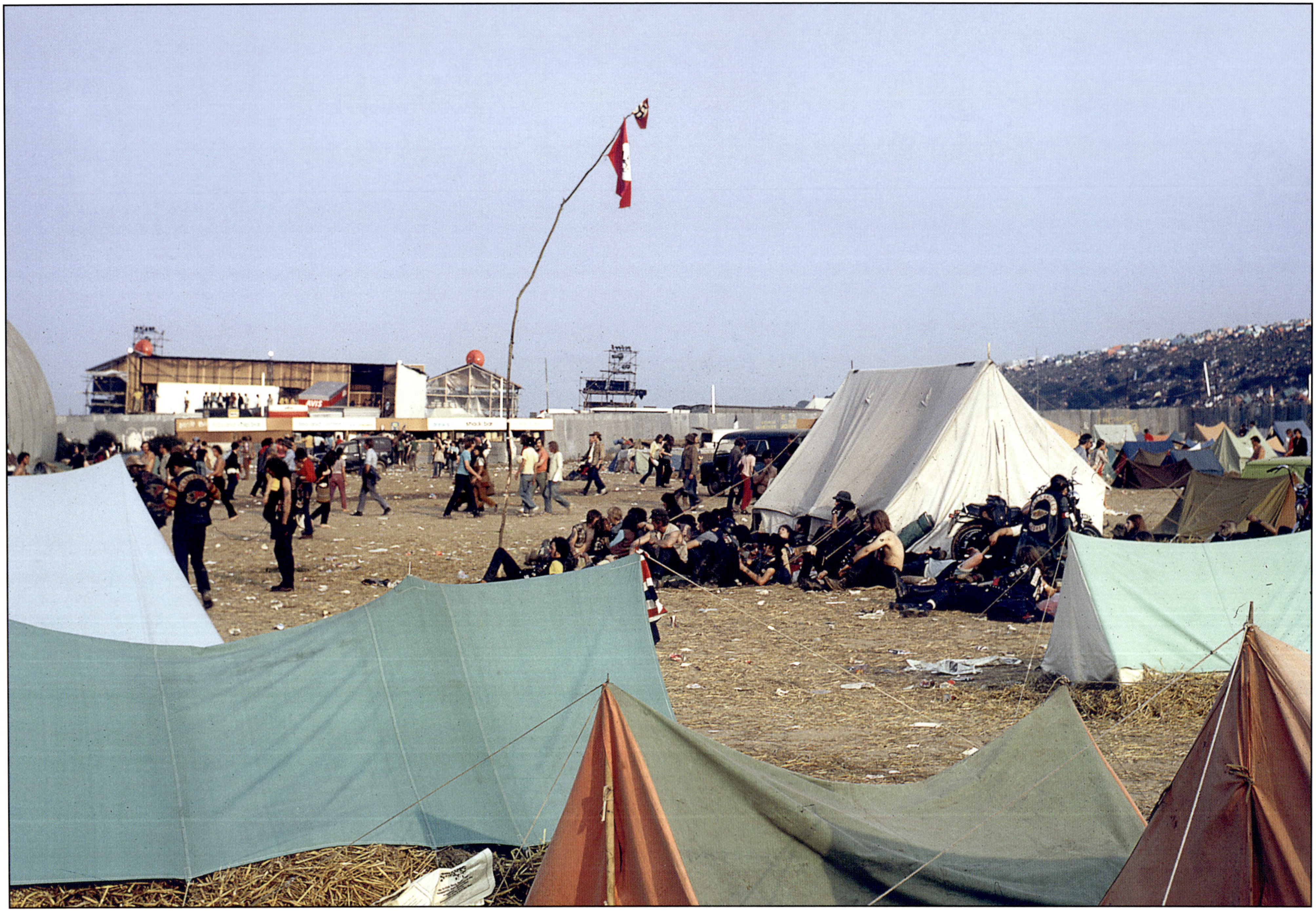

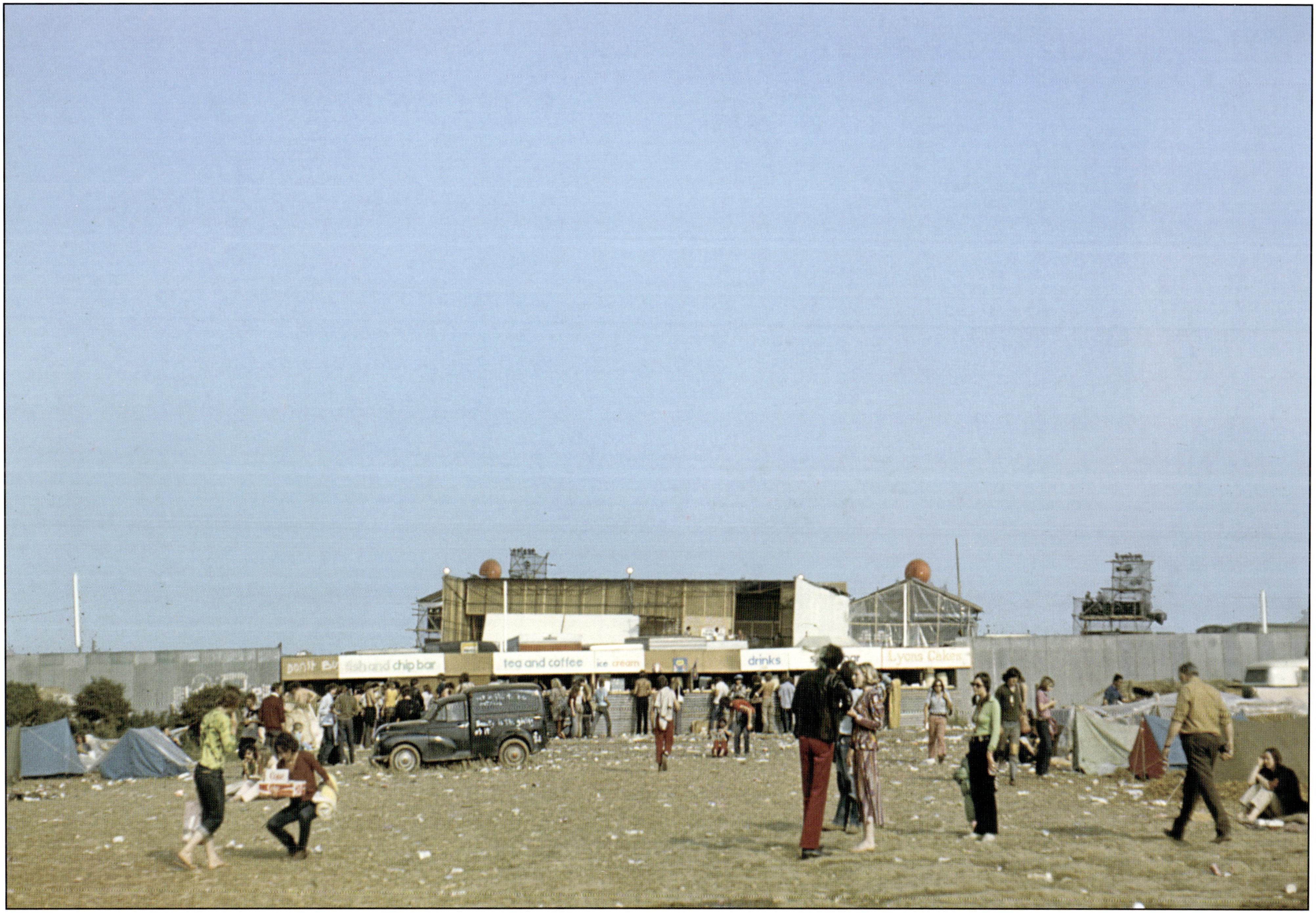

Harry Matthews

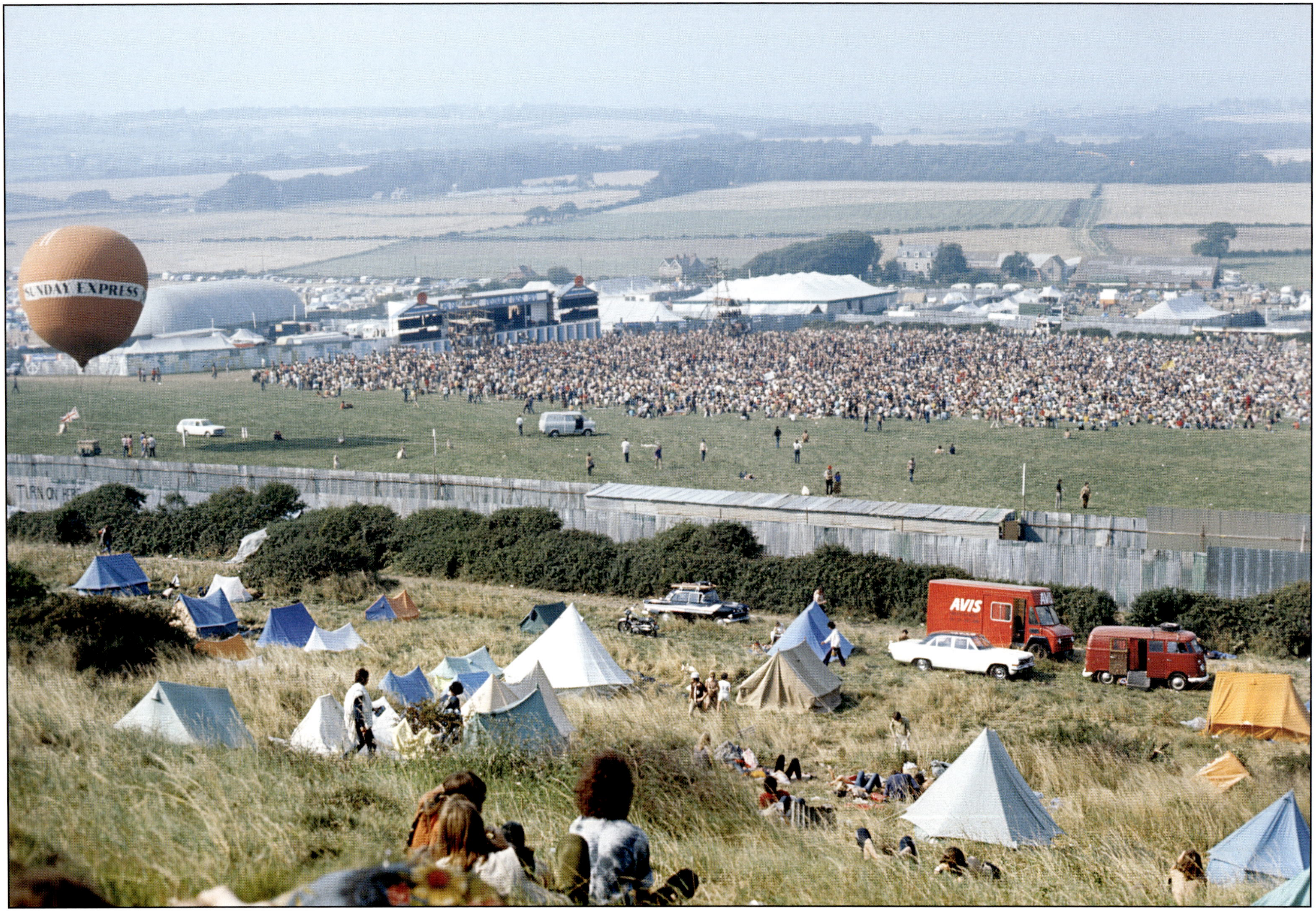

Ken Box

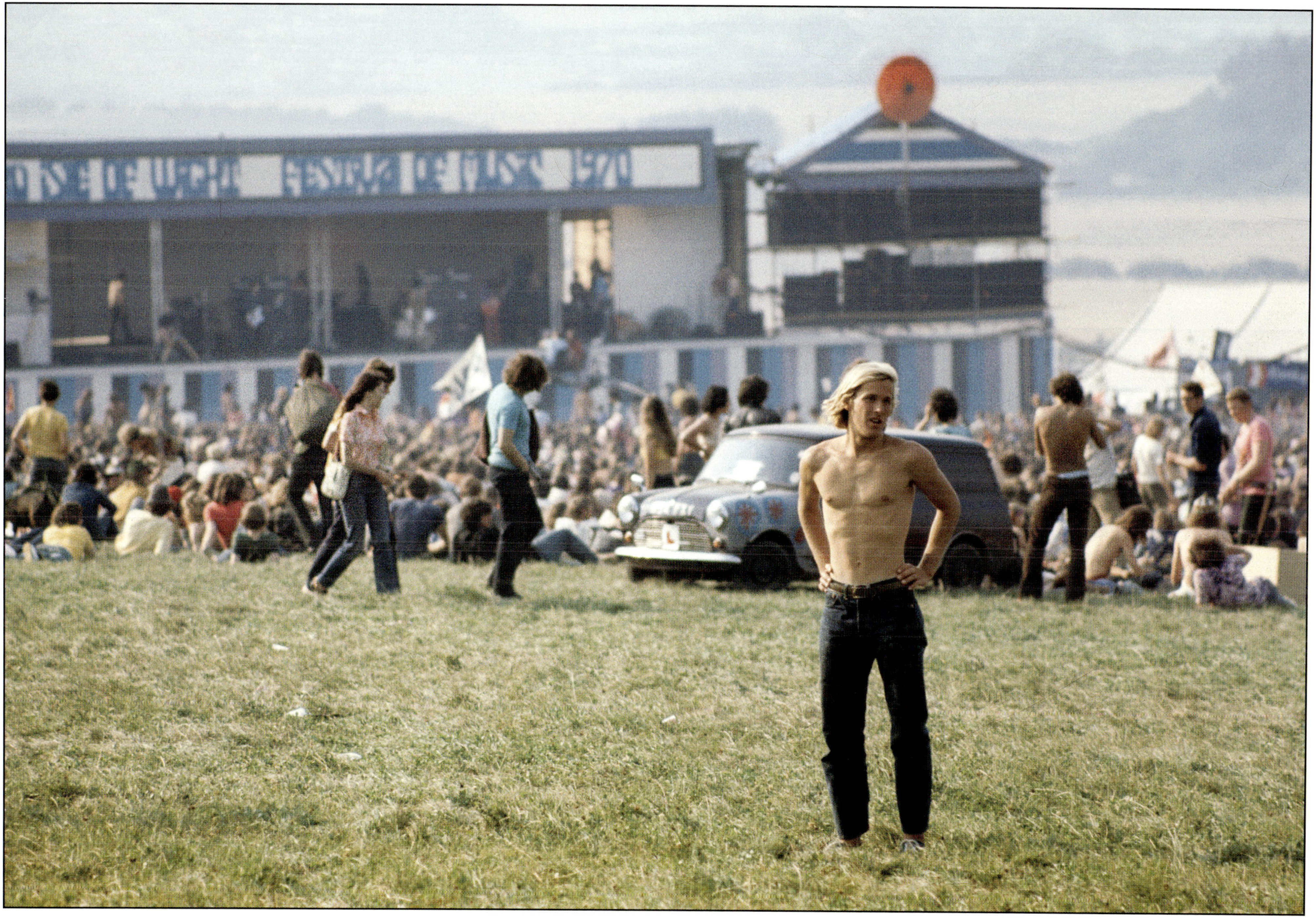

Ken Box

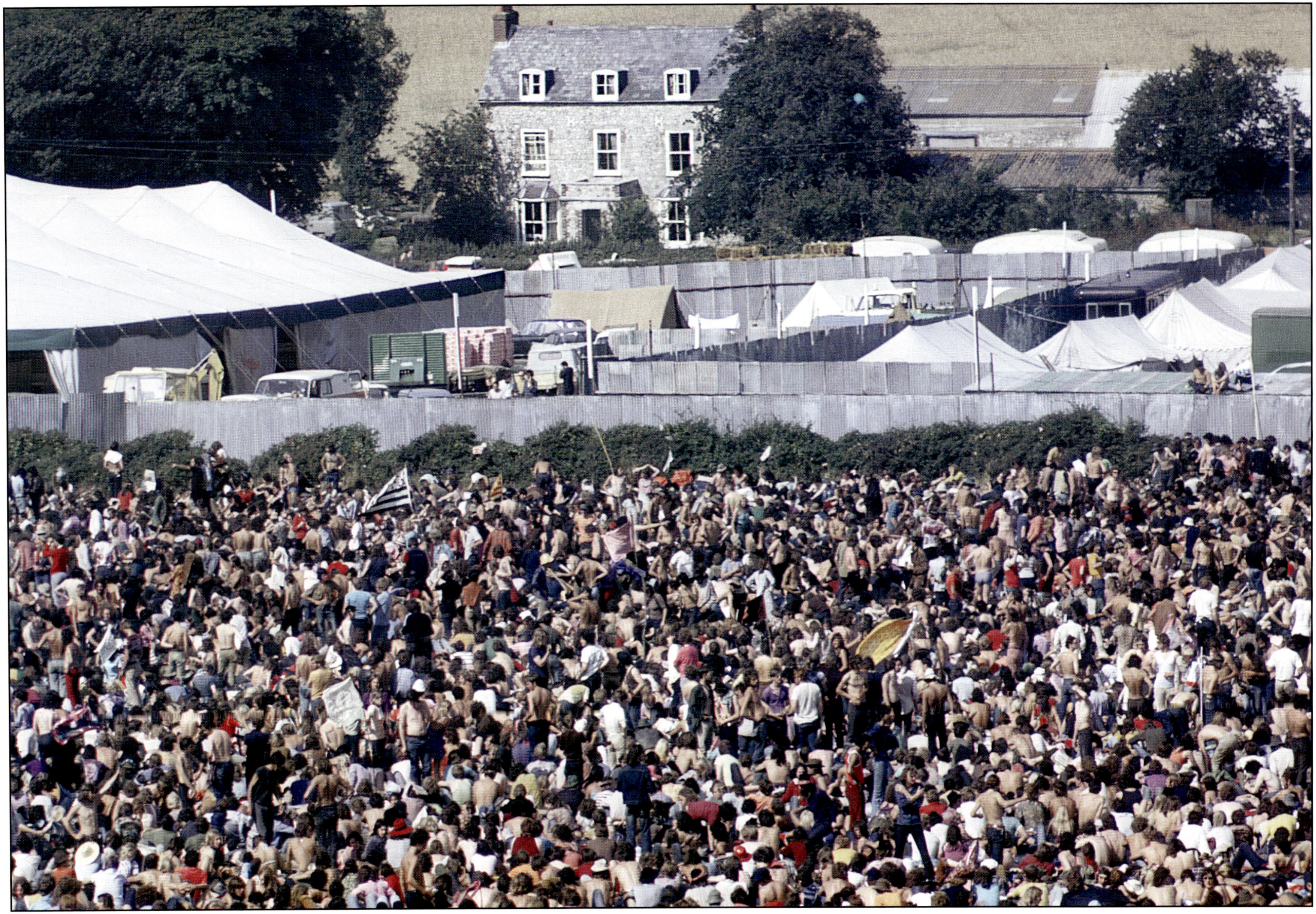

Ken Box

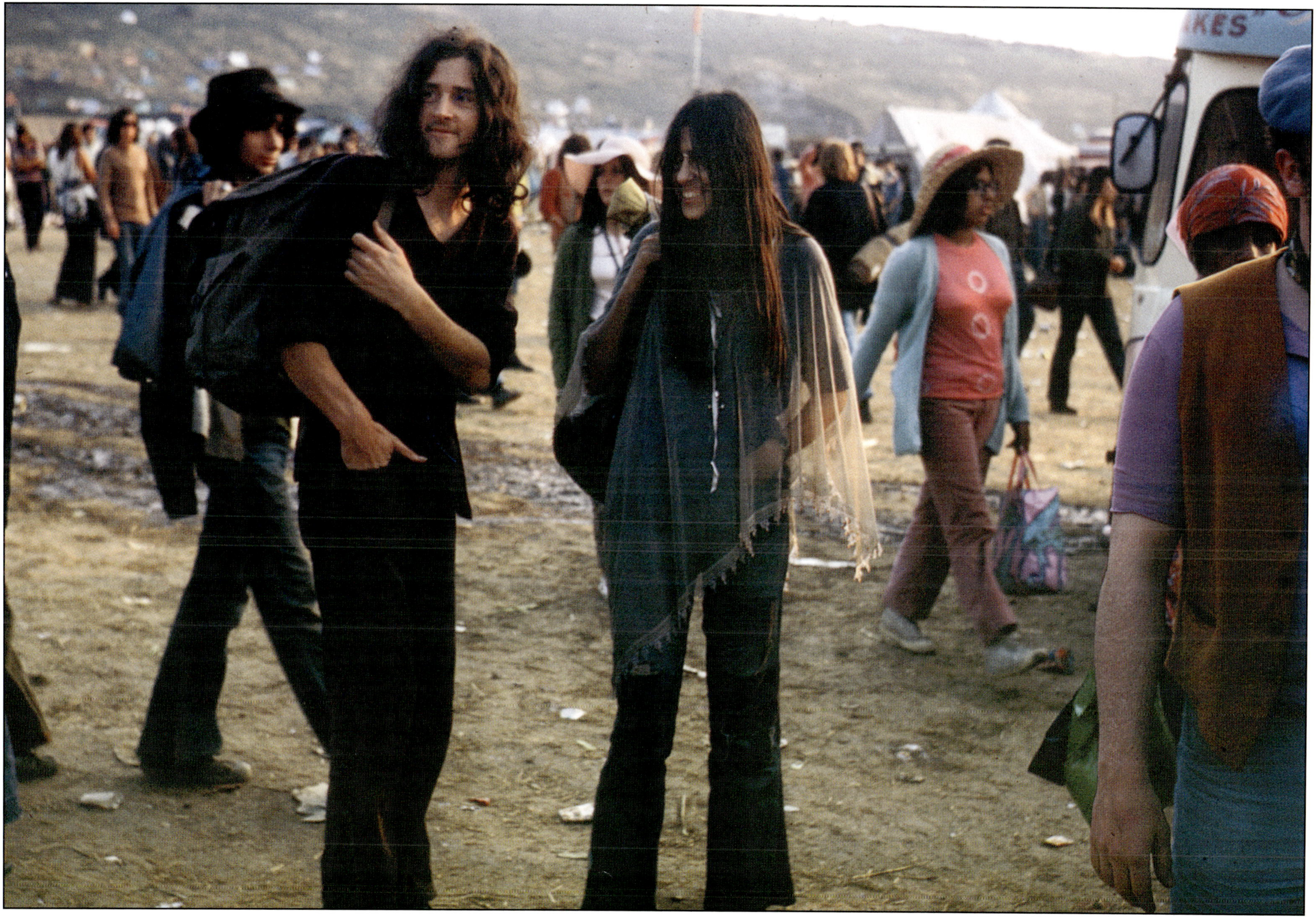
KES

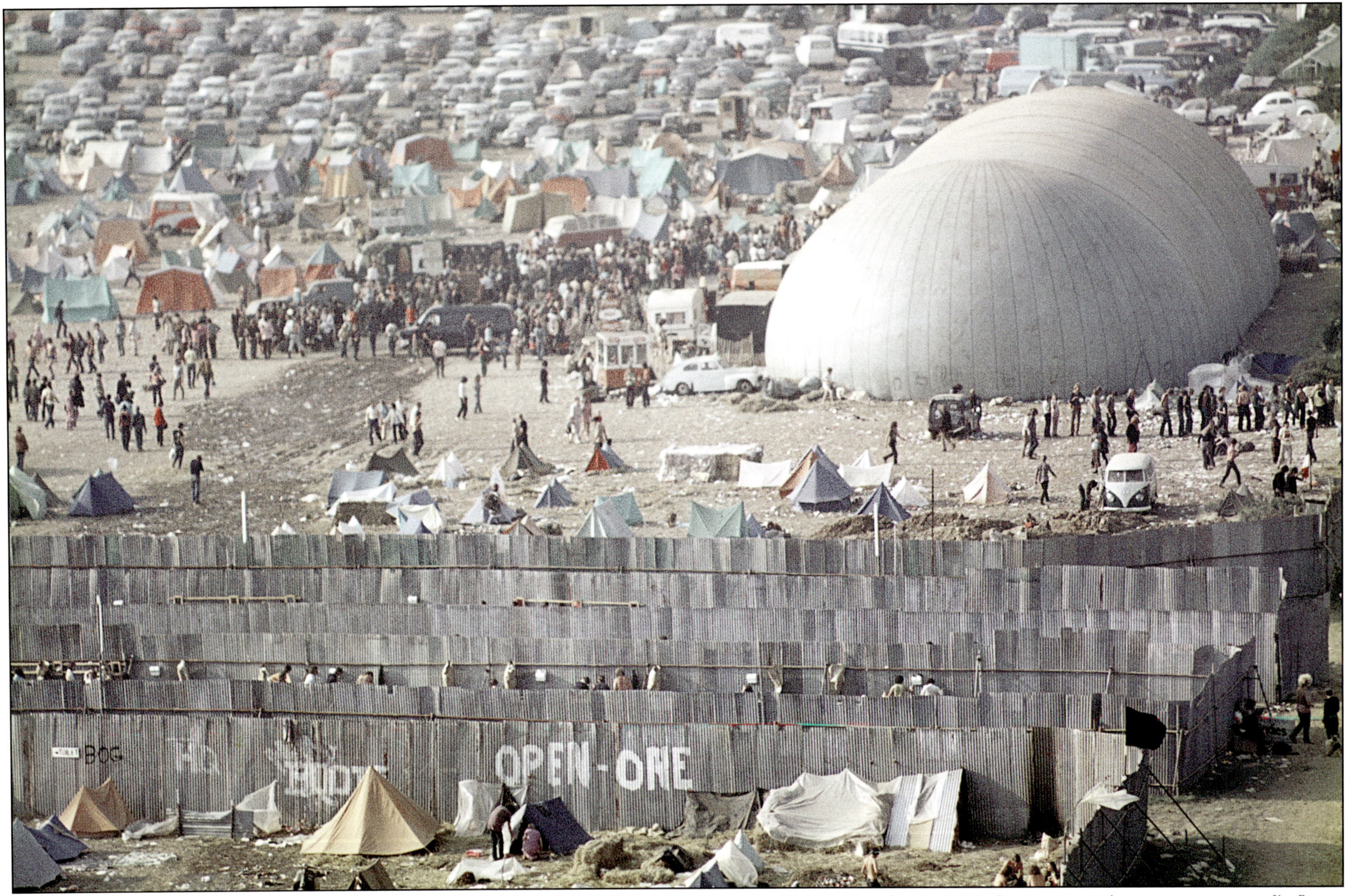

"We provided over a thousand closets and 1800 feet of urinals. Doctor Quantrill said, 'There is no known disease that you can get from urine.' He didn't want doors on the toilets. He said, 'That's not a health issue, you don't need doors on there,' and we said, 'Well, we're going to put doors on anyway, because we're sure people will want them!' " - *Ray Foulk interviewed by the authors.*

Ken Box

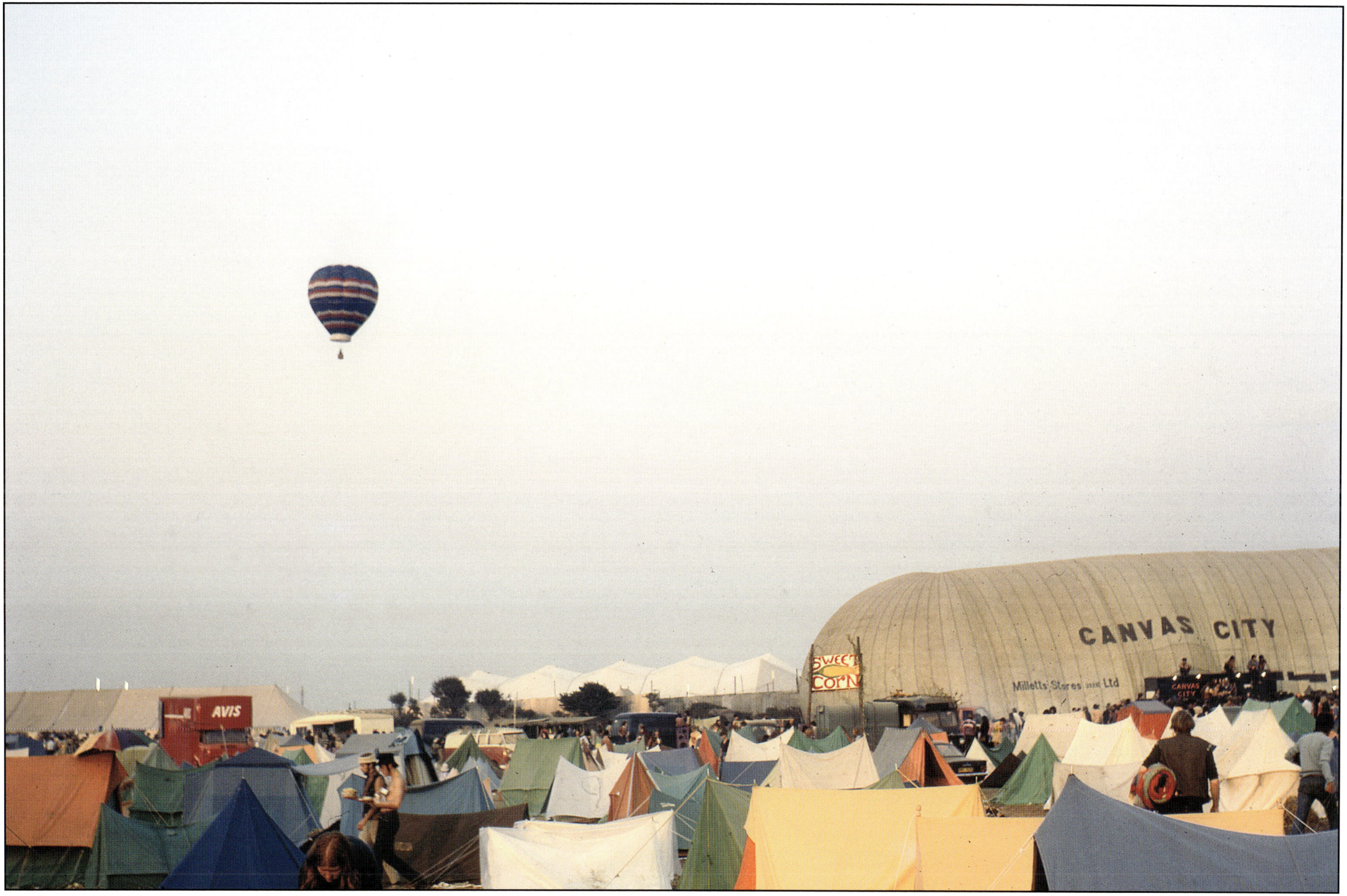

"British hippies are a race of masochists. Hedonism - implicit in the festival concept - is apparently unacceptable unless laced with discomfort, pain and misery. The typical Woodstock nationals, British variety, were those who chose to sleep in the bogs. The contented UK festival goer - curled inside a paper sleeping bag, dozing to the continuous hiss of piss on corrugated troughs."
Friends Magazine, October 15, 1970.

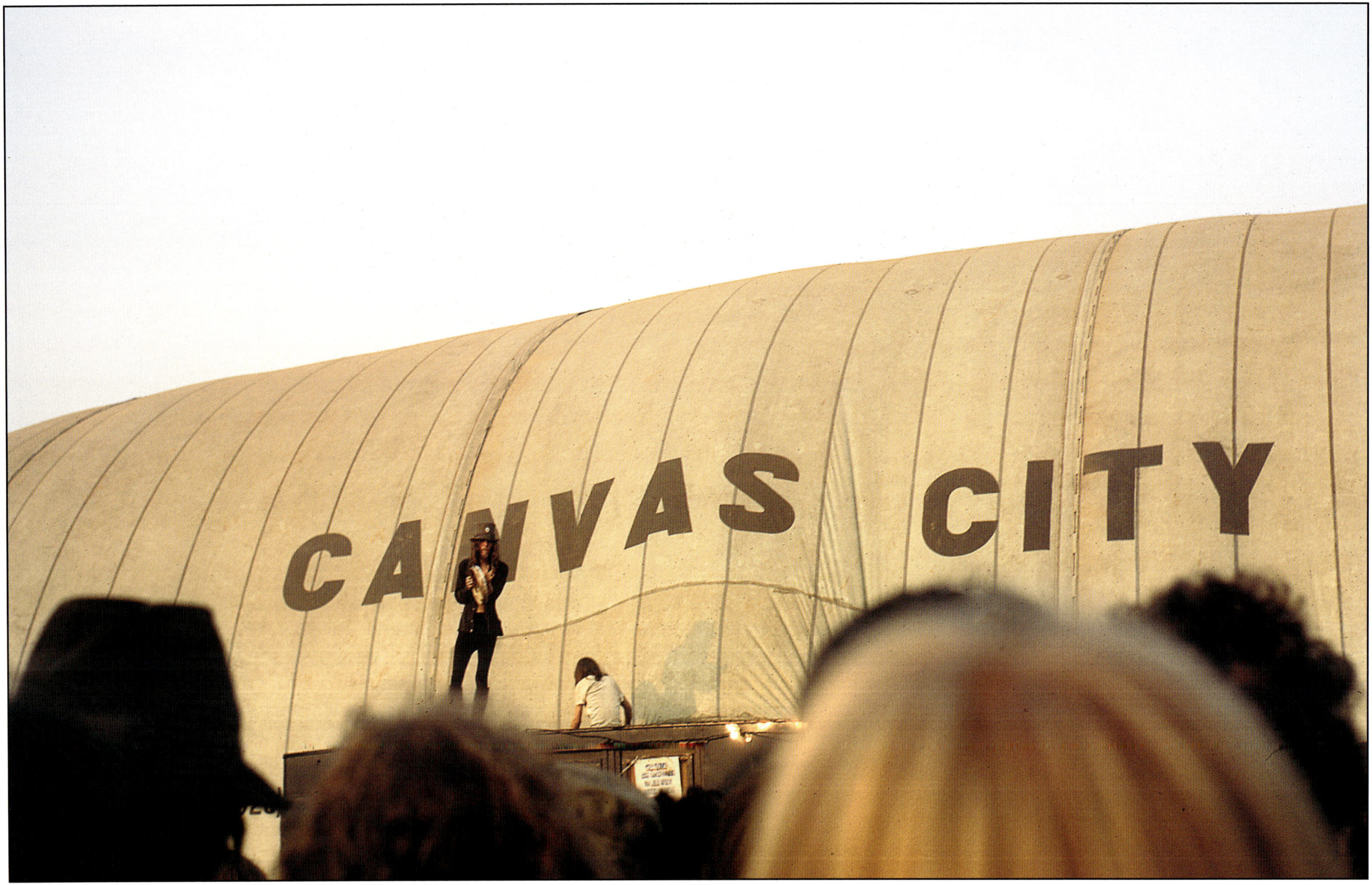

"We arrived at the site on Wednesday evening and after unsuccessfully hustling for a gig on the main stage, proceeded to set up our equipment in an inflatable tent called 'Canvas City', the owner of which, so it seemed, had kindly put at our disposal. Things went quite smoothly, we played rather a bad set but the spirit was there. Next day, the Fairies arrived and in the afternoon we set up all our equipment outside the tent, and had a nice blow, good vibes all over." - *Nik Turner of Hawkwind, Friends Magazine, October 15, 1970.*

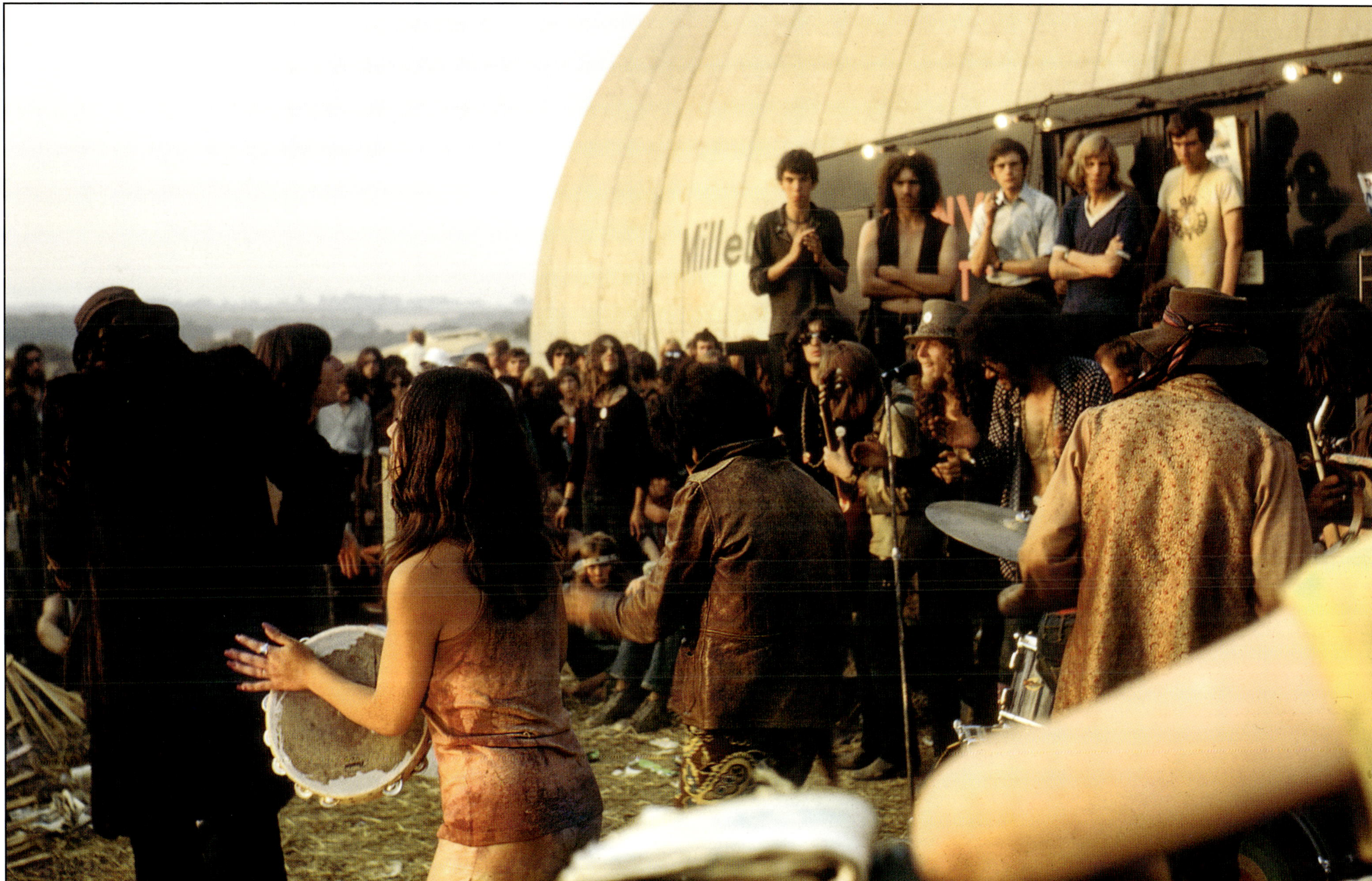

"That evening, both bands played too many sets in Canvas City, and the owner was now starting to apply pressure. He would pay both the bands £35. We agreed to this but we suggested that we play for nothing in order that he bring his entry charges down. He tried to convince us that to lower his charges was not a viable proposition even if we played for nothing,"
Nik Turner of Hawkwind, Friends Magazine, October 15, 1970.

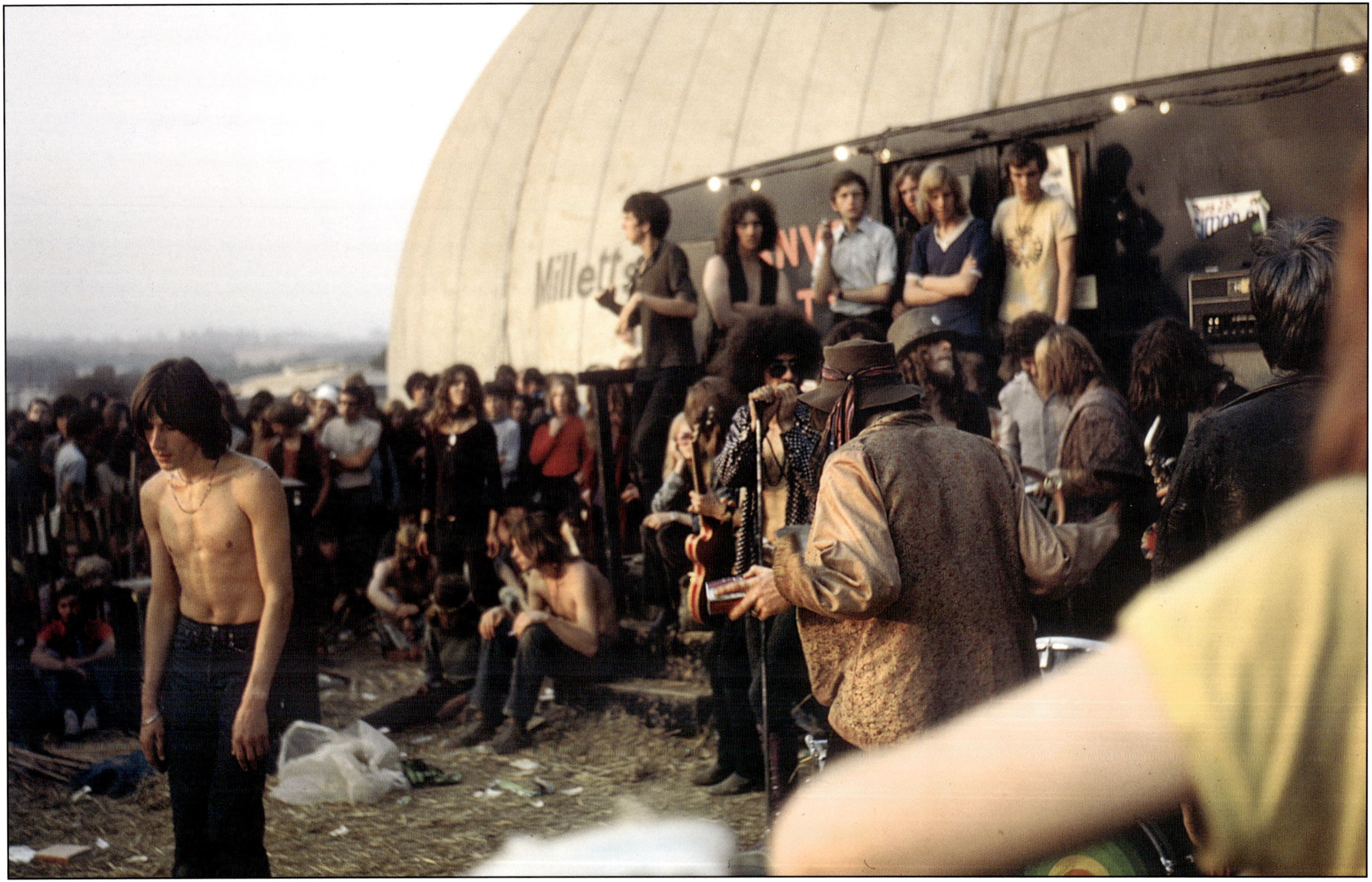

"Monday, Festival over, afternoon jam, all-comers, a collection was made to contribute to the fares of the needy and to the minds of band and friends. Gig in evening inside Canvas City, for £10 on condition entry charge was three shillings. Net result, Hawkwind played very spaced out space rock. That's all I remember. Zonk!! Tuesday we split from the Island."
Nik Turner of Hawkwind, Friends Magazine, October 15, 1970.

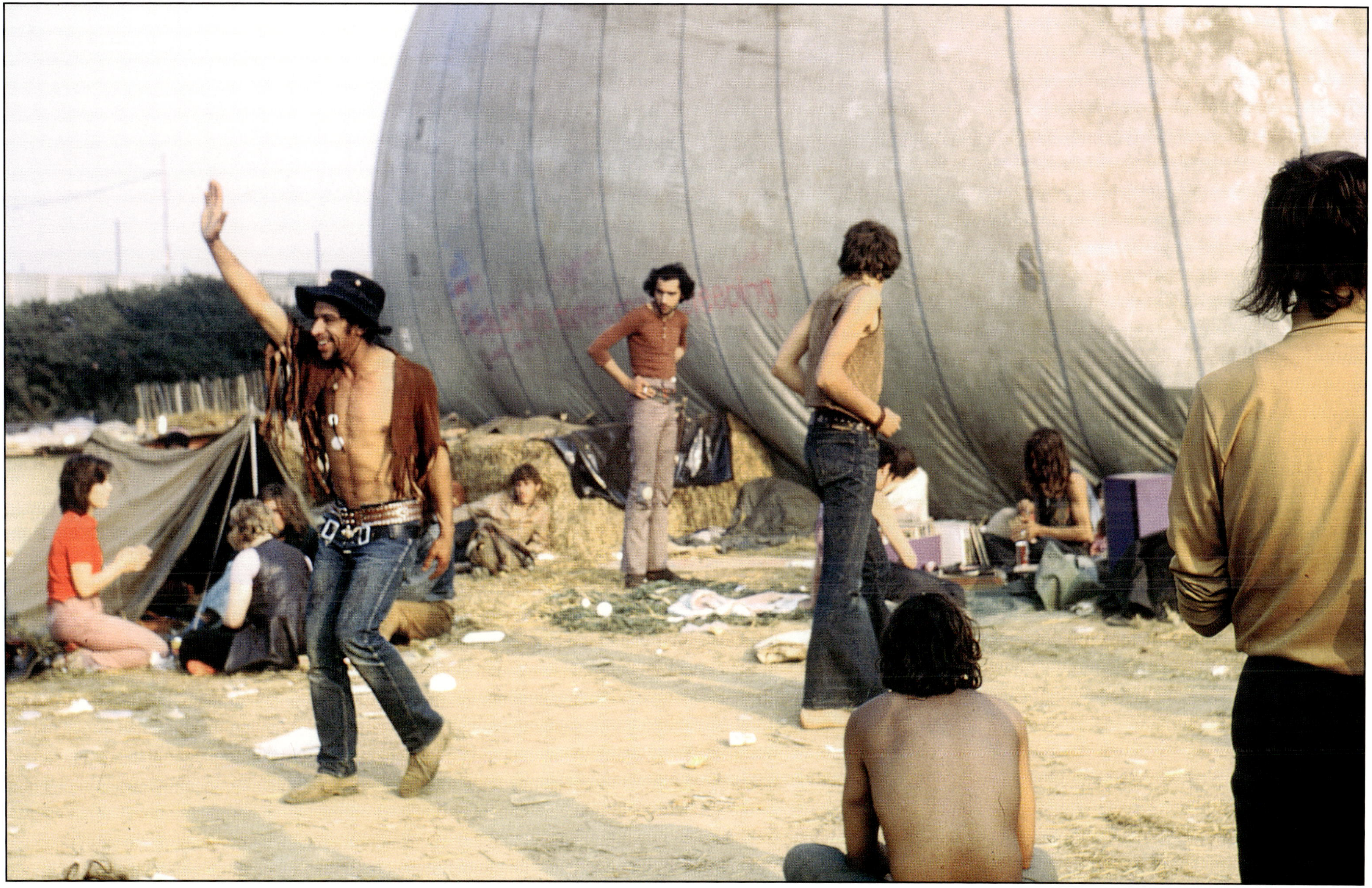

"We arrived at the site on Thursday afternoon. Went to a large inflatable dome which we had been invited to play in, called Canvas City. We found Tony inside, who had brought along a monstrous purple disco system which was set up outside the Dome. They had already collected a large listening and dancing audience, led by a black hatted guy, looking much like a Western baddie, who danced and mimed almost non-stop for three days." *Member of Pink Fairies, Friends Magazine, October 15, 1970.*

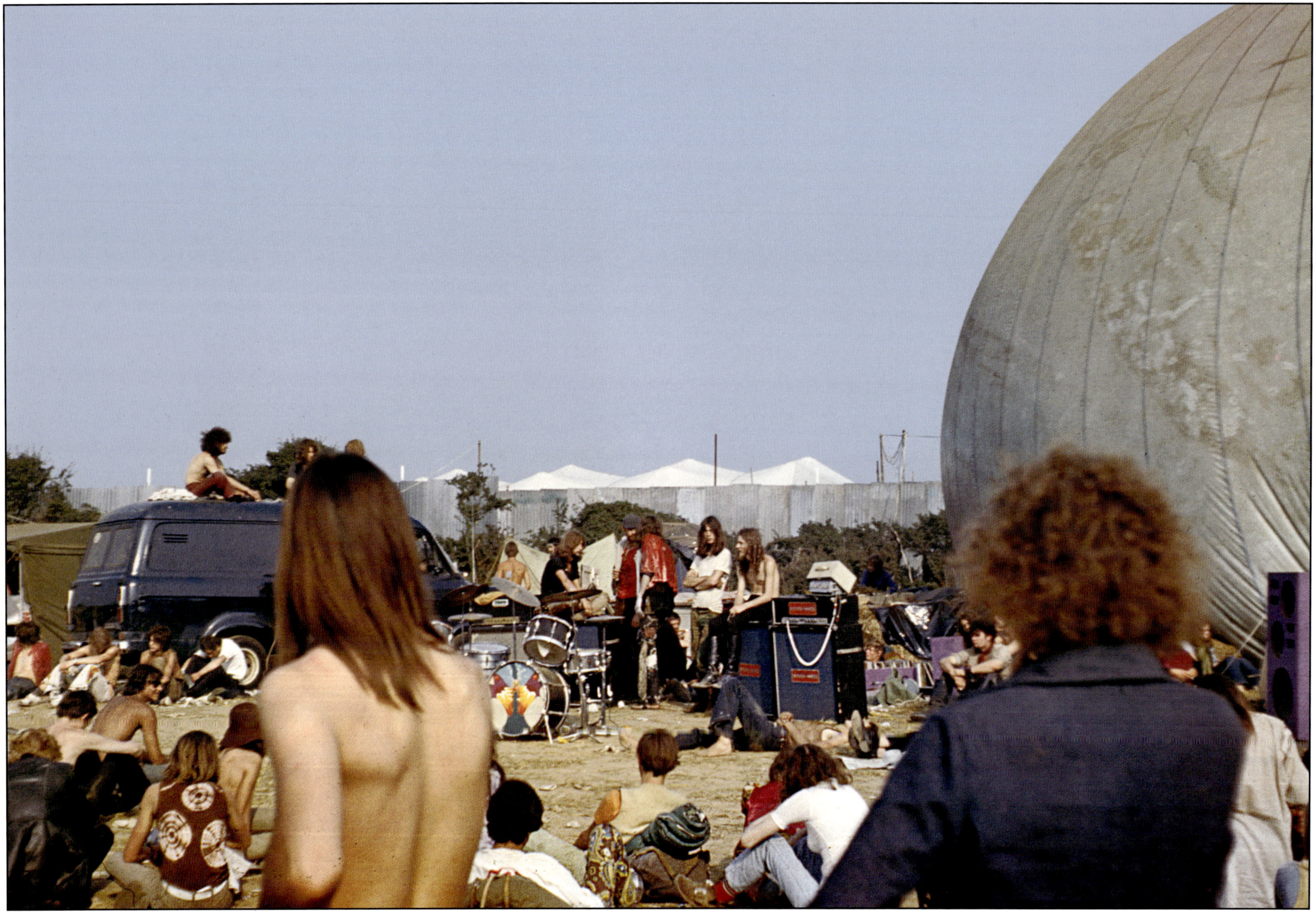

Harry Matthews

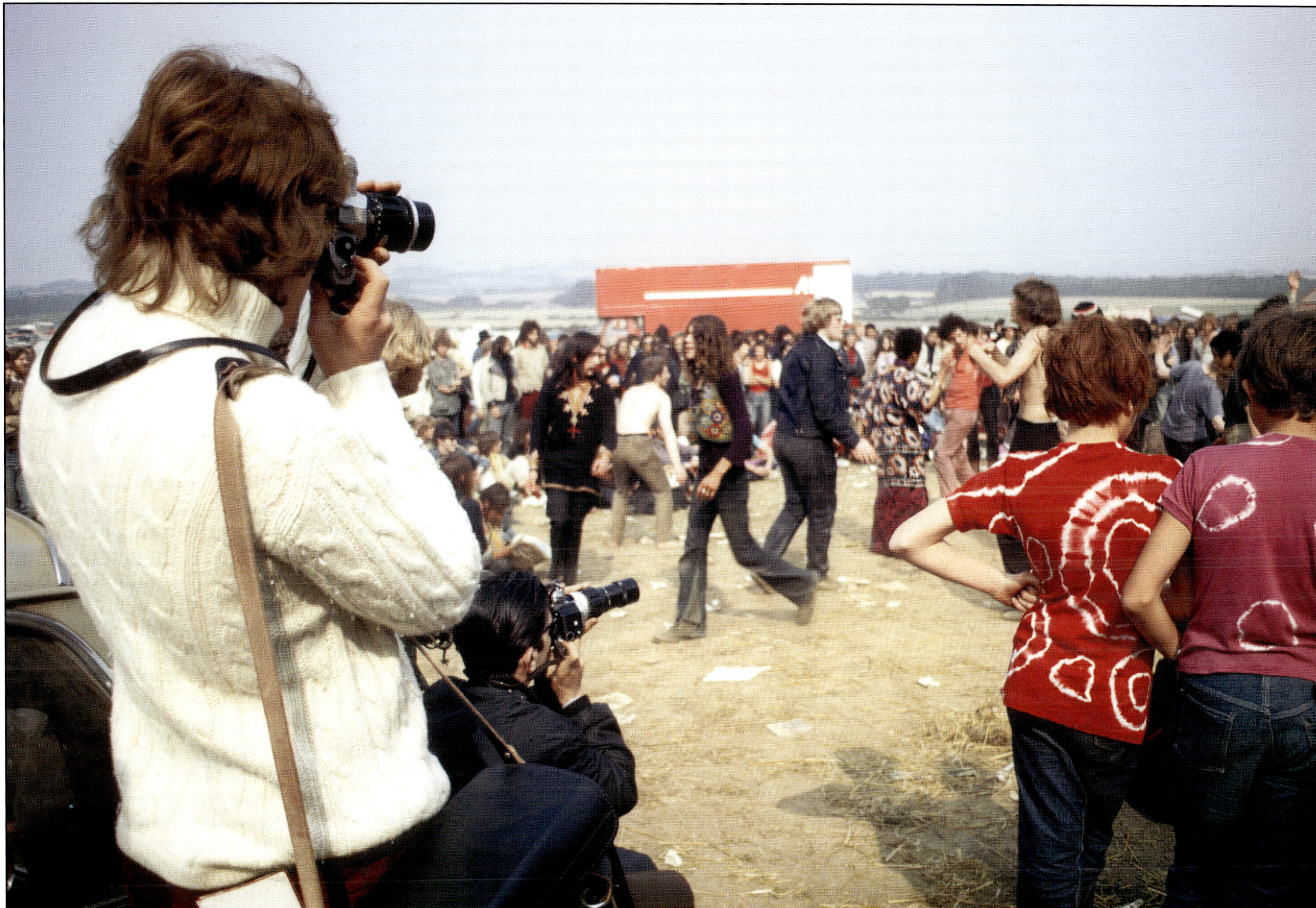

Ken Box

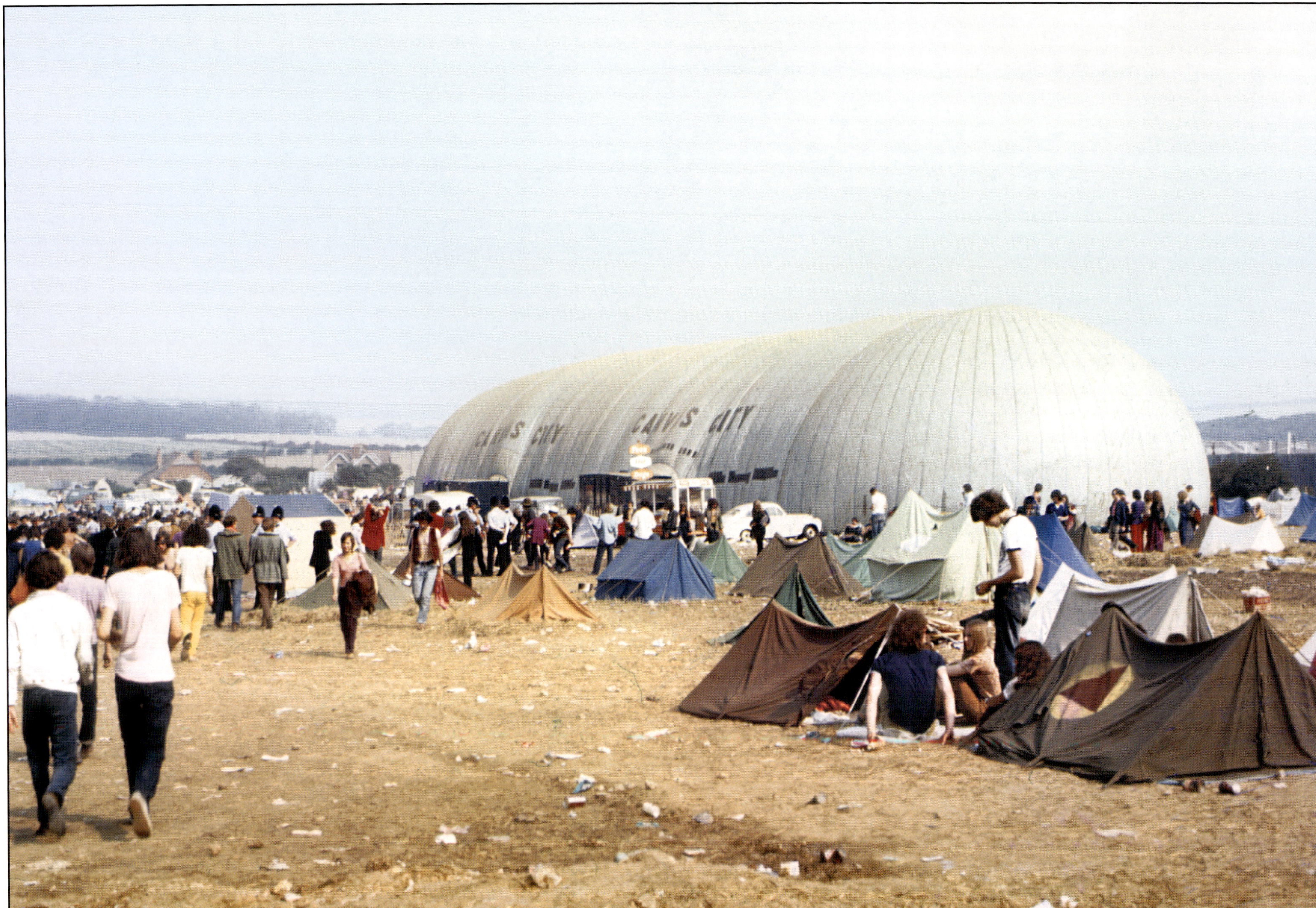

Eric Moth

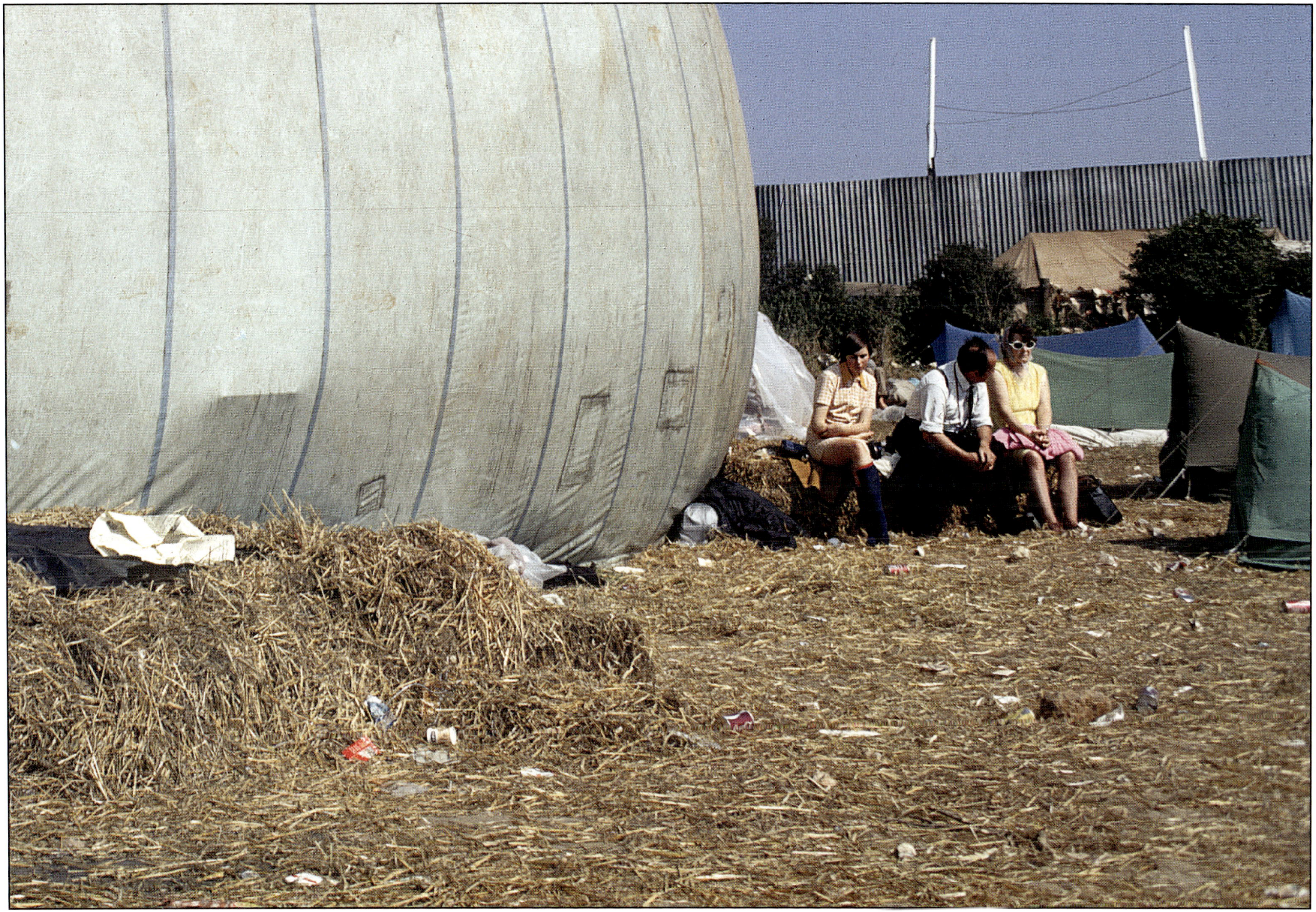

Ken Box

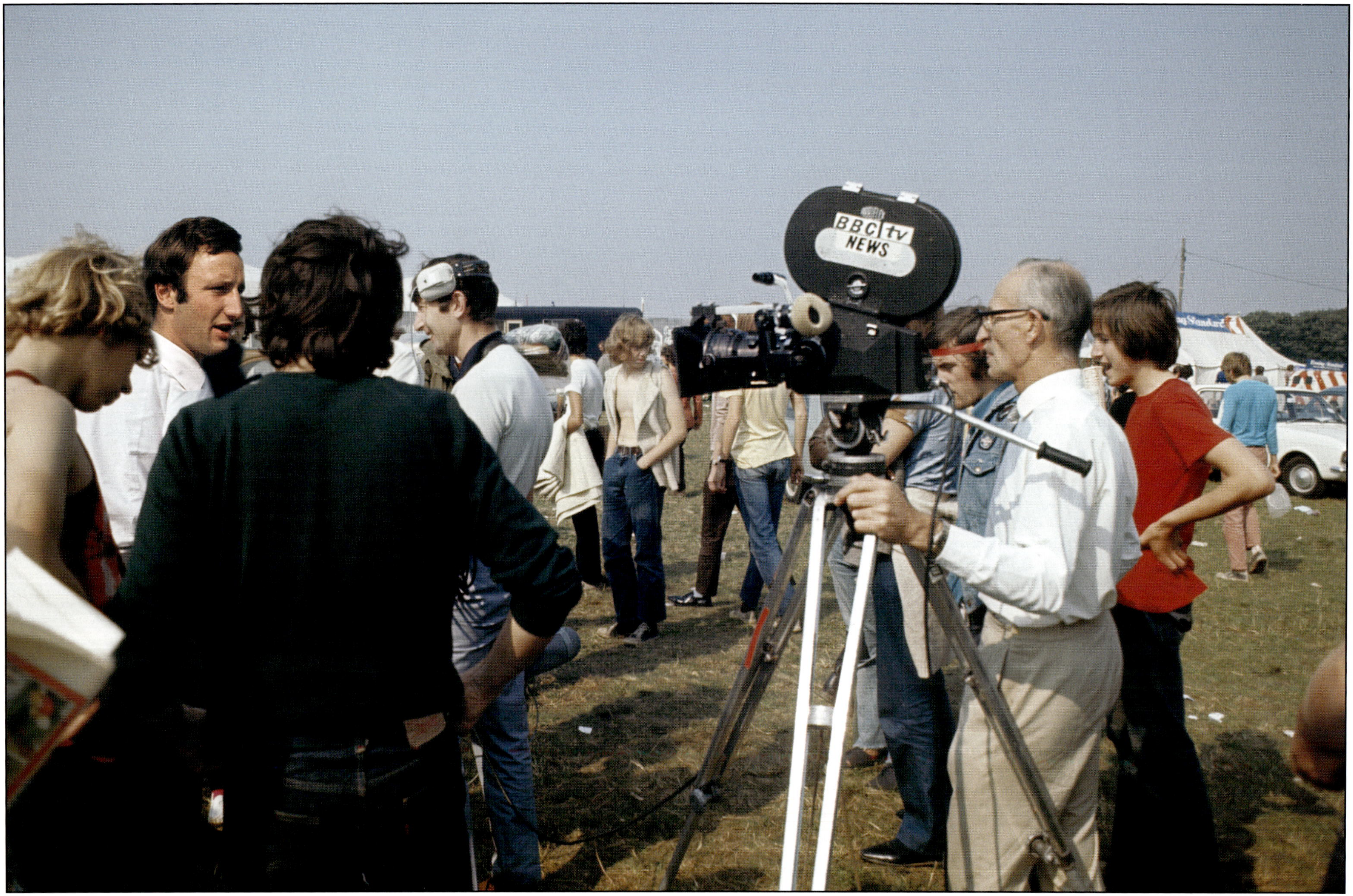

"As the fans stream into the concert arena for the first of the paying concerts, the organisers are worried about militant pop fans storming the fences. They believe that pop music should be free. Last night they tried to tear down some of the fencing, hurling stones over the wall at the security officers and their dogs." - *Andrew Harvey, 'BBC South Today' report, August 29, 1970.*

Ken Box

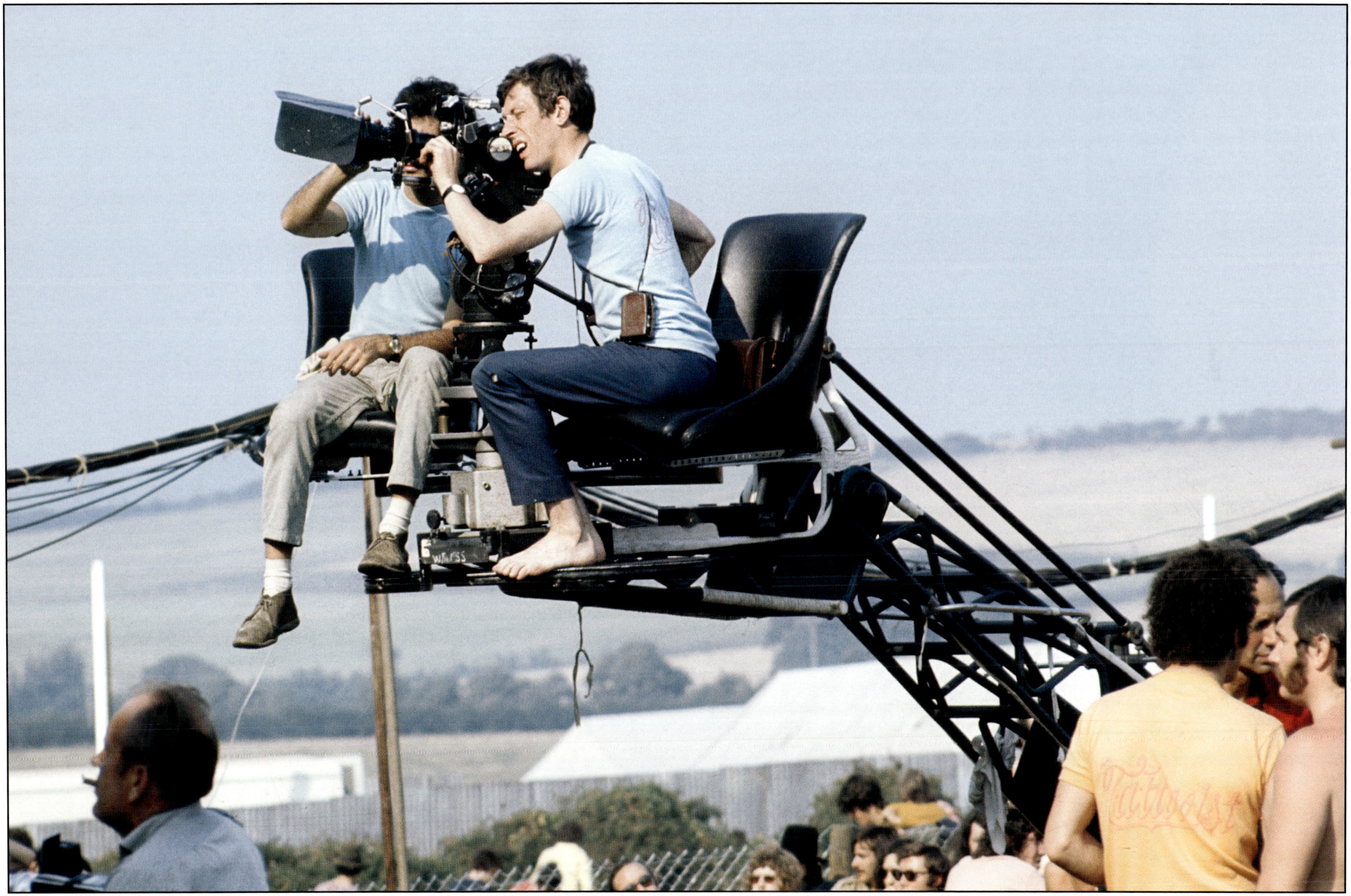

"Weeks before the Festival started, 'The Film' seemed to be the end Fiery were aiming at. Eight film crews worked on the Island under 'heavy' Hollywood director Murray Lerner and captured over 200 hours of footage. They also filmed at Fiery's headquarters, an old mansion. Visitors were grabbed for interviews and the old 'complete documentation' technique was applied." - *Friends Magazine, October 15, 1970.*

Ken Box

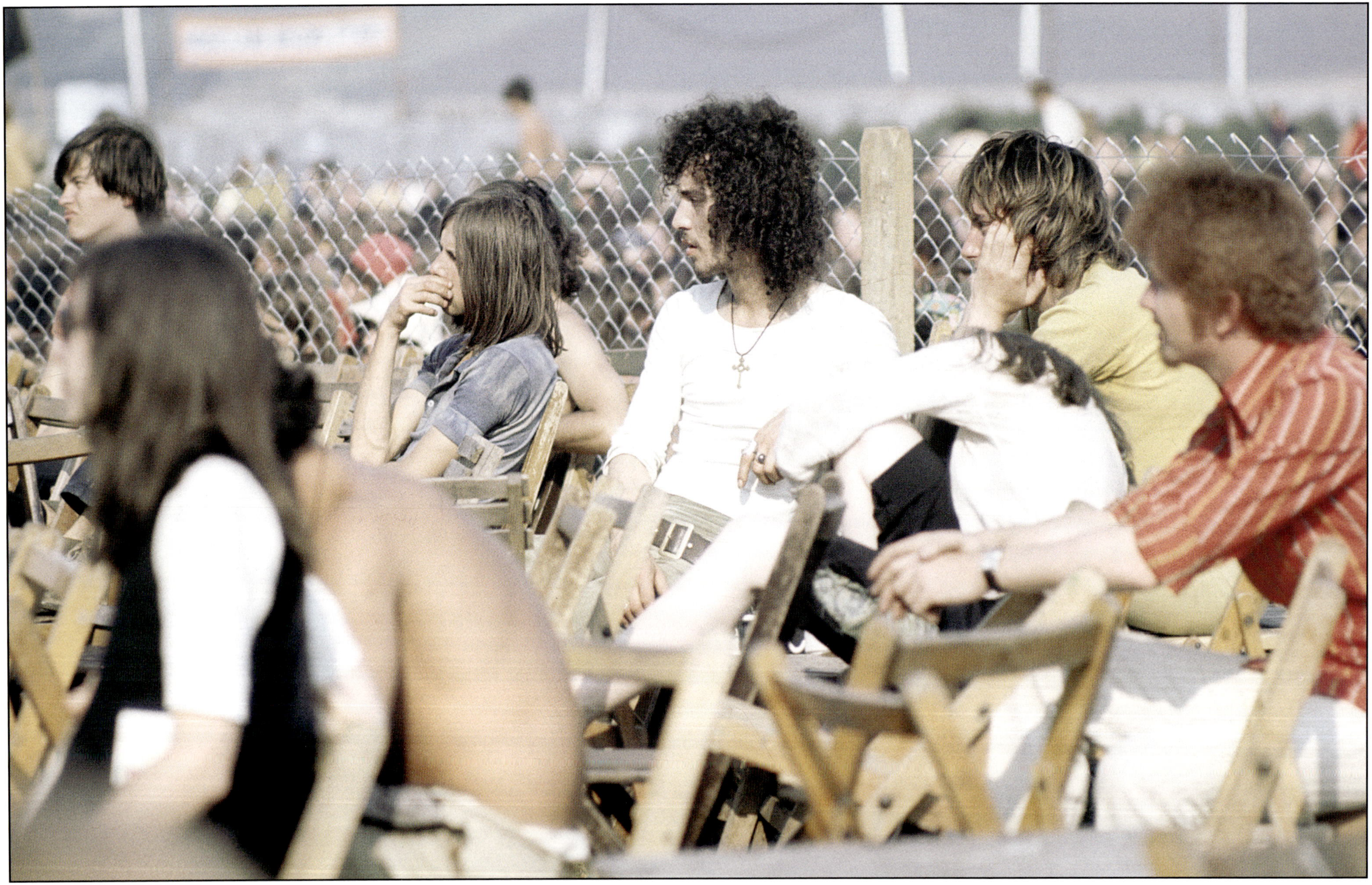

Ken Box

"Getting into the press arena, before chaos set in, was like getting into Fort Knox. Press tickets were handled by Charles Everest, an ex-ITV cameraman. A deal with Fiery guaranteed his firm, Press Lines, (two reporters and one photographer), exclusive onstage and backstage coverage, which would then be filtered out to the news agencies - at a price. Each newsreel cameraman was charged £150."
Eithne O'Sullivan, Rolling Stone Magazine, September, 1970.

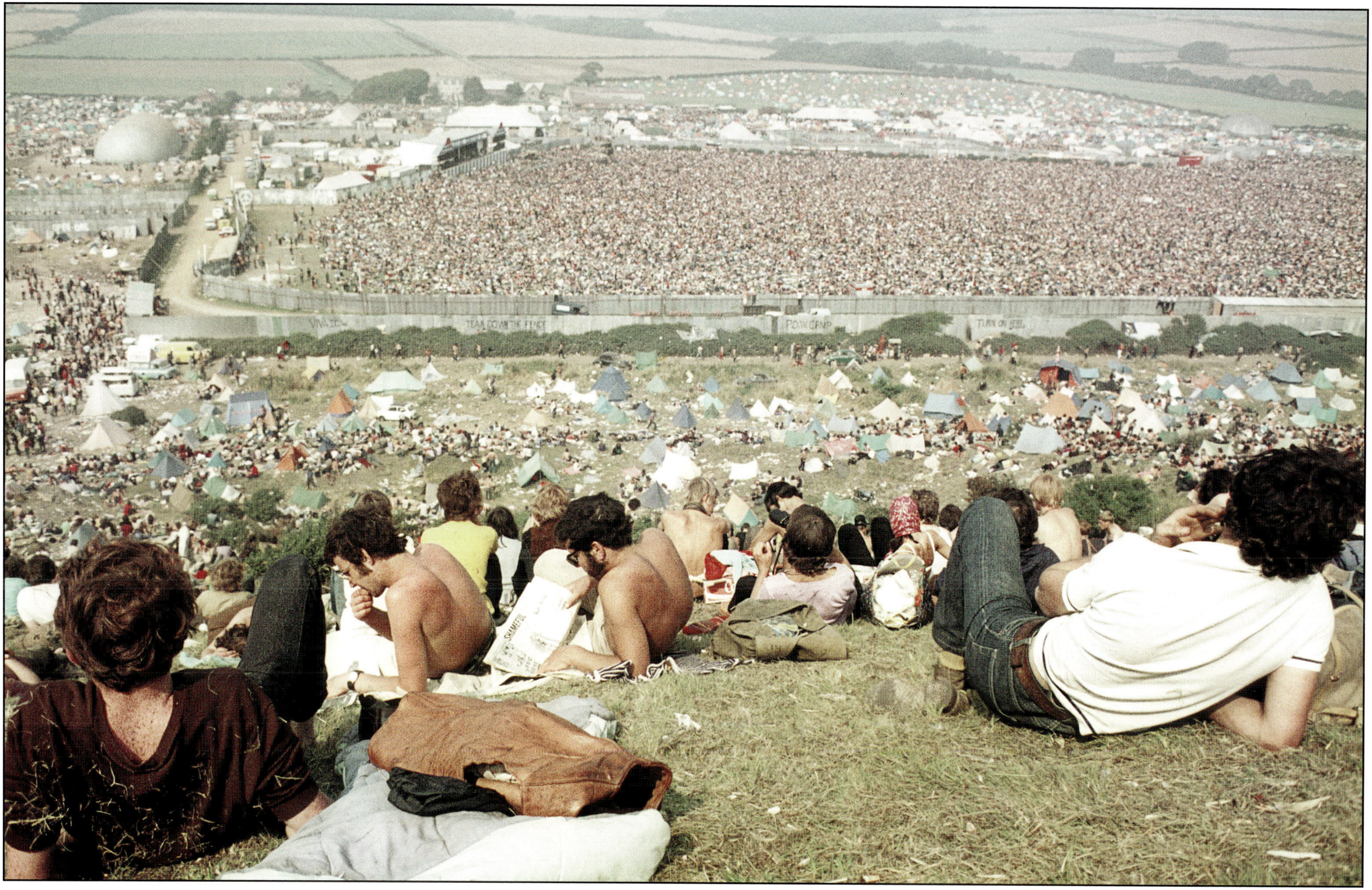

"Devastation Hill became the 'good vibes' area of the festival and even members of the straight press were attracted out of their privileged enclosure to sit among the anarchists, and the greens of the golf course provided the softest ground for tents anywhere in the festival." *Friends Magazine, October 15, 1970.*

Ken Box

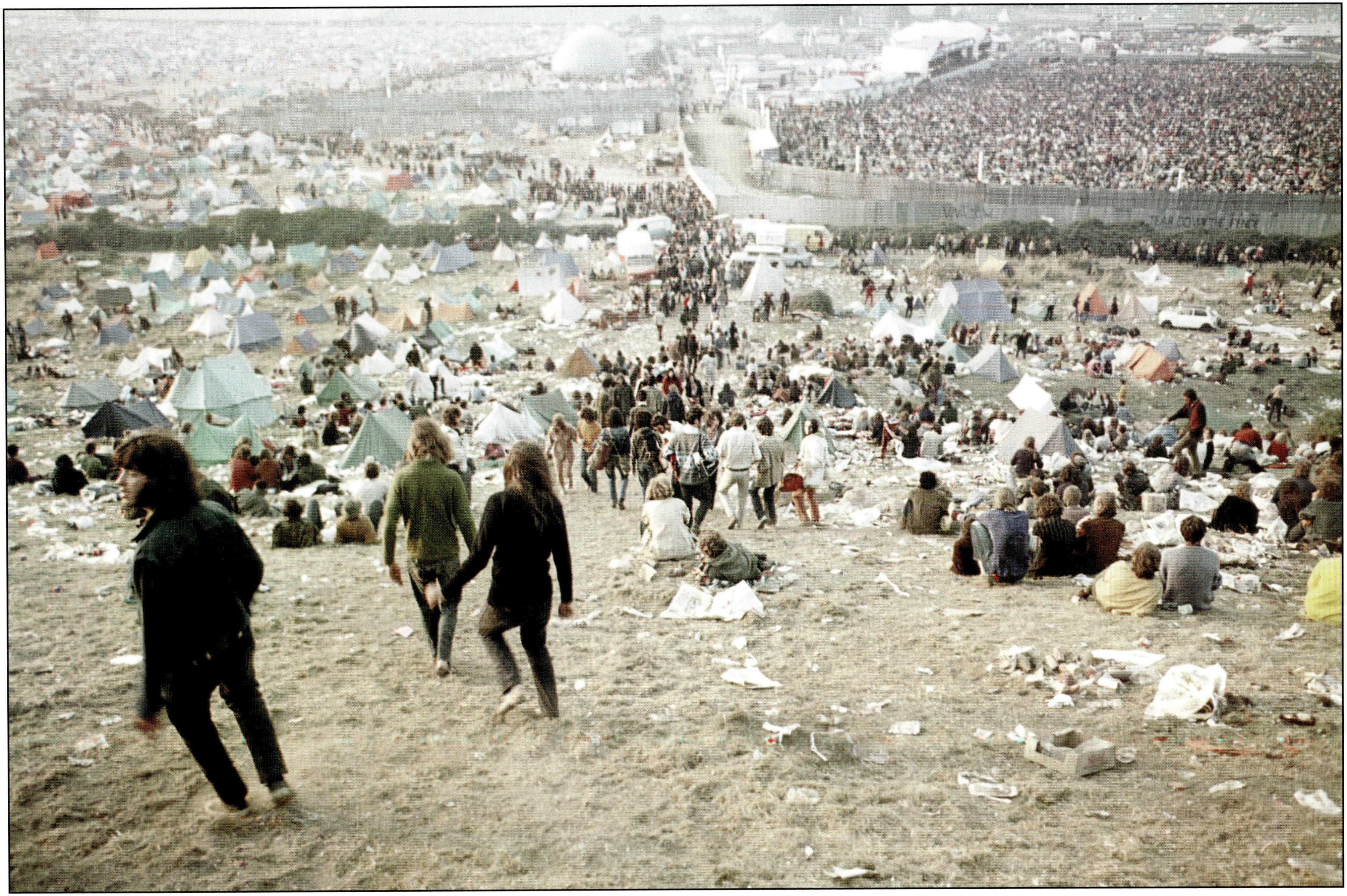

"As part of the usual festival arrangements, 'Release' had a trip tent for anyone on a bad trip, and aid and advice for the lost and unhappy. One German marched up to the Release tent, clicked his heels, saluted and commanded, 'I want to be taken off zis trip immediately.'"
Friends Magazine, October 15, 1970.

Ken Box

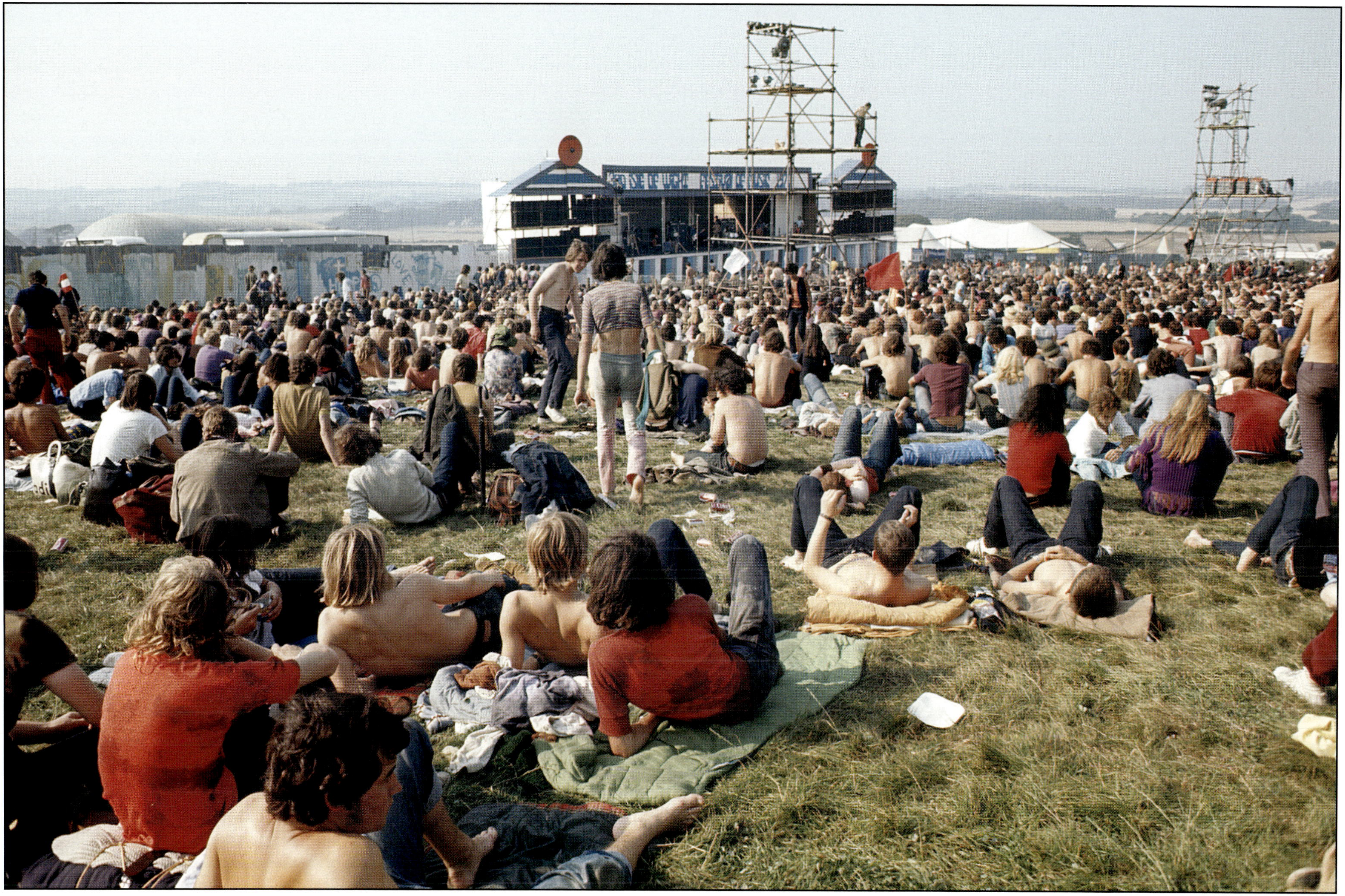

"Just who do these promoters think they are and why should we be invaded by a quarter of a million weird fanatics? They reject our way of life, they are contemptuous of our achievements, and our laws. Equally I am contemptuous of their non-achievement, their permissiveness and lack of discipline. I do not want them here and neither do the vast majority of Island people." - *Reader's letter, I.W. County Press, August 8, 1970.*

Ken Box

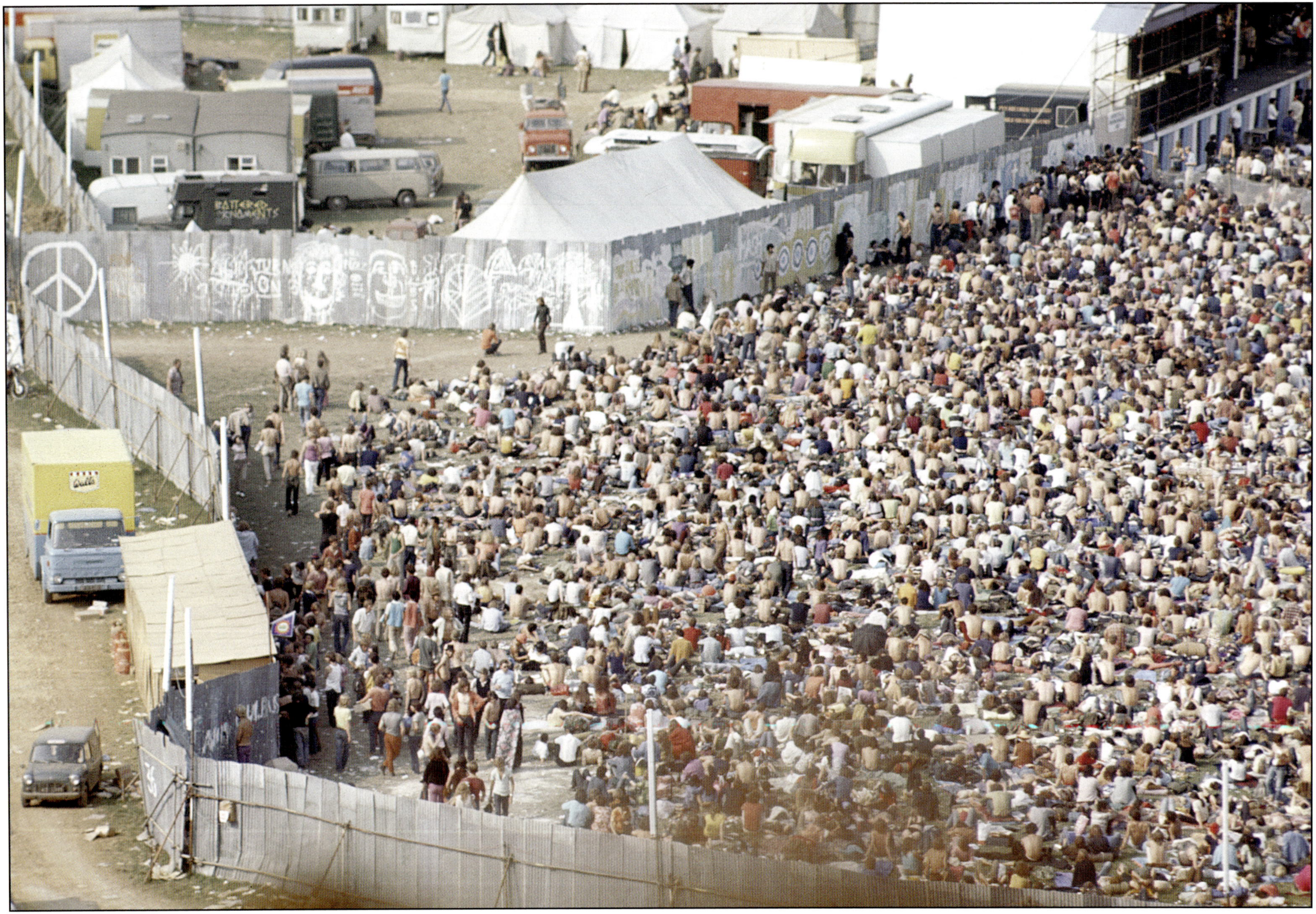

Ken Box

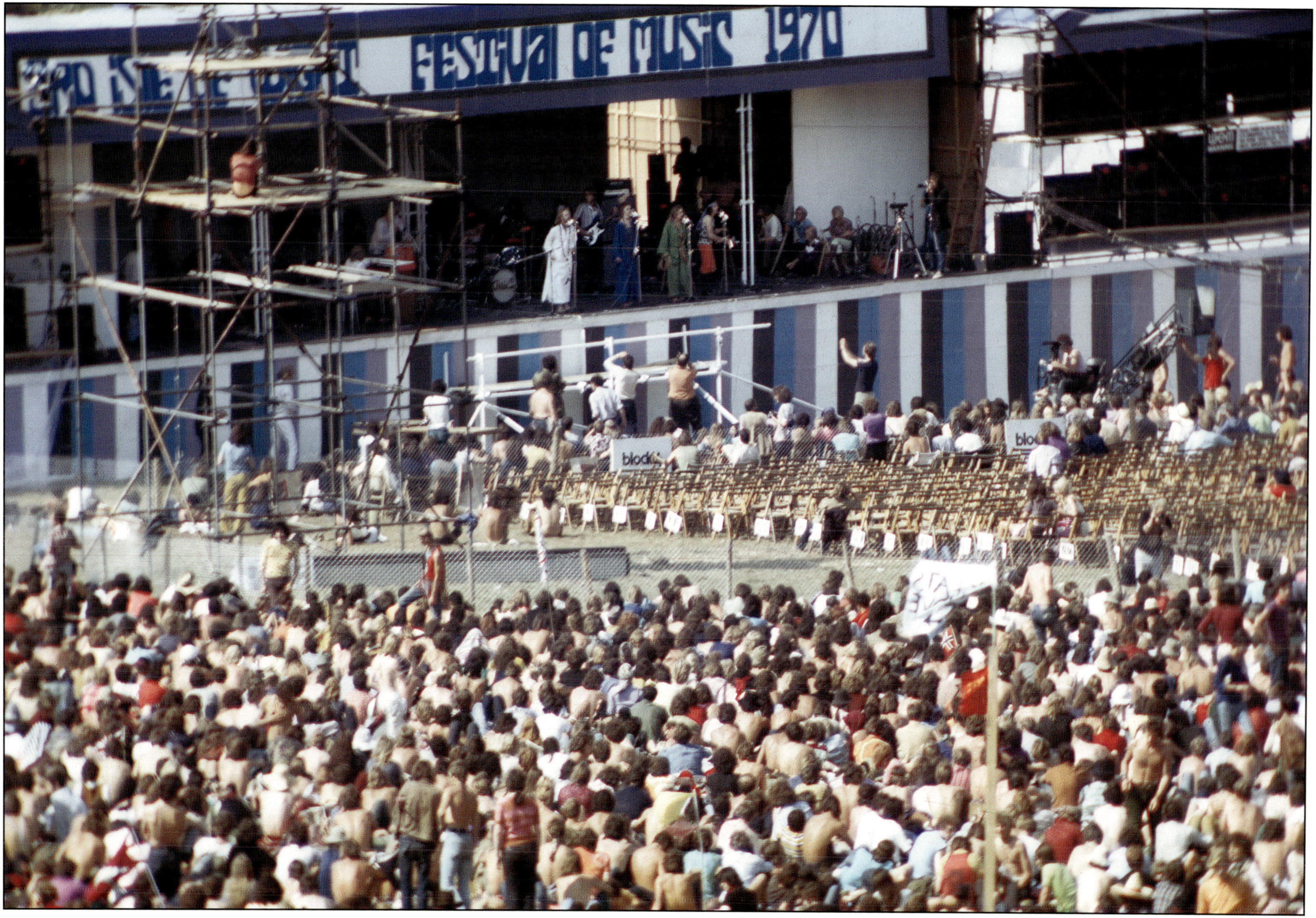

Ken Box

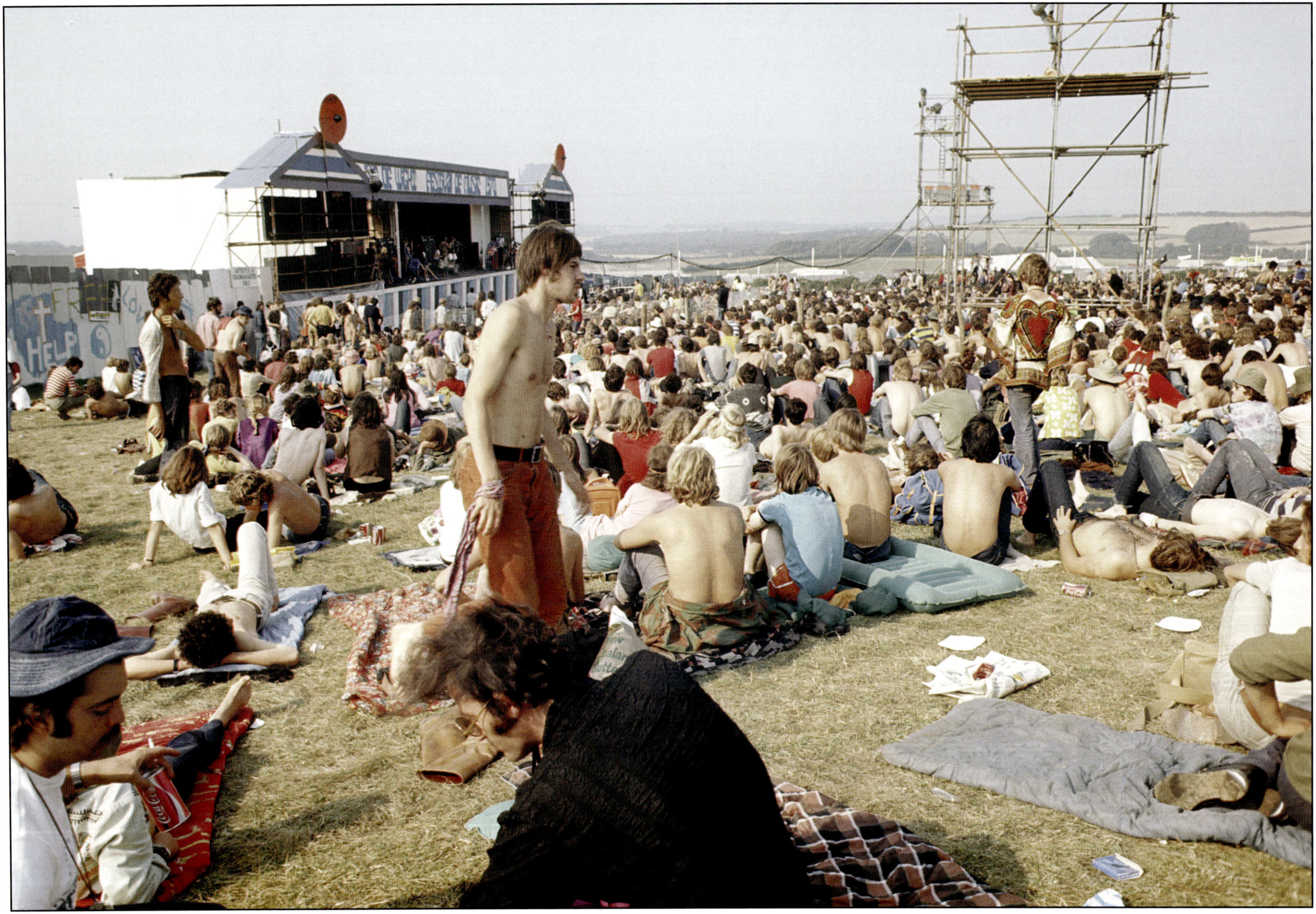

Ken Box

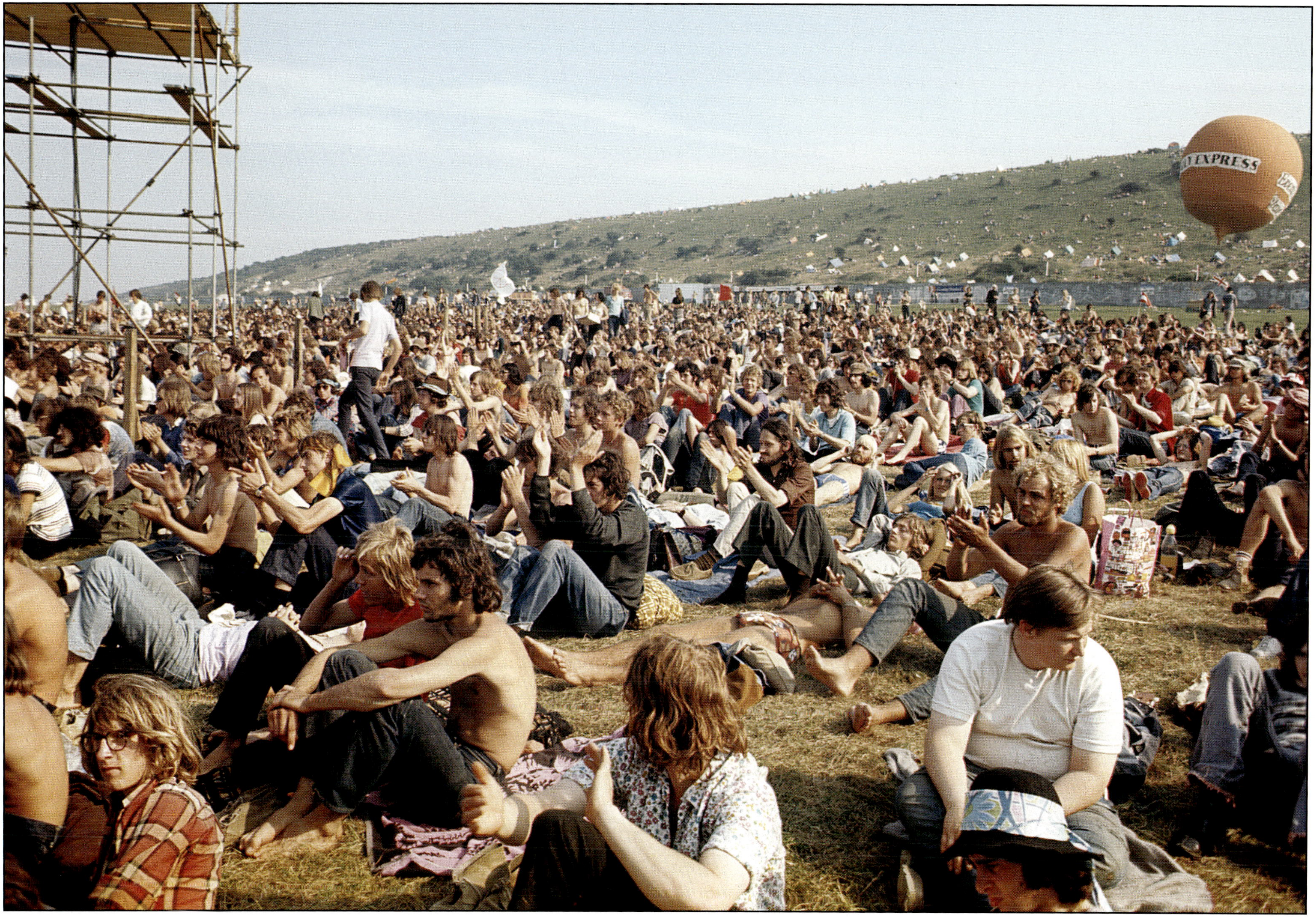

Ken Box

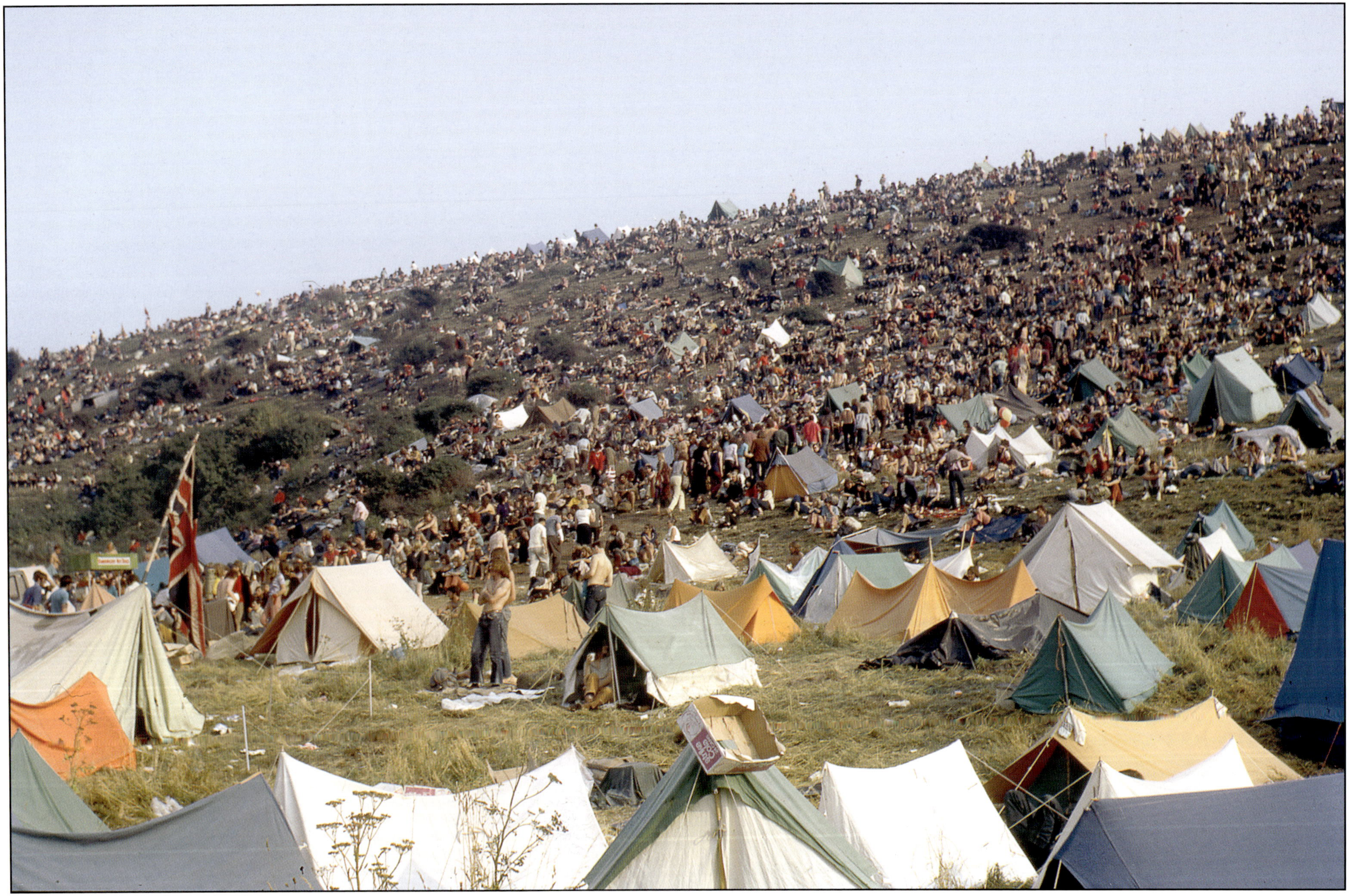

"There has been a lot of tripe and nonsense talked about epidemics. The only epidemics are outbreaks of prejudice and intolerance."
Dr. Douglas Quantrill, IW Chief Medical Officer, Daily Telegraph, August 23, 1970.

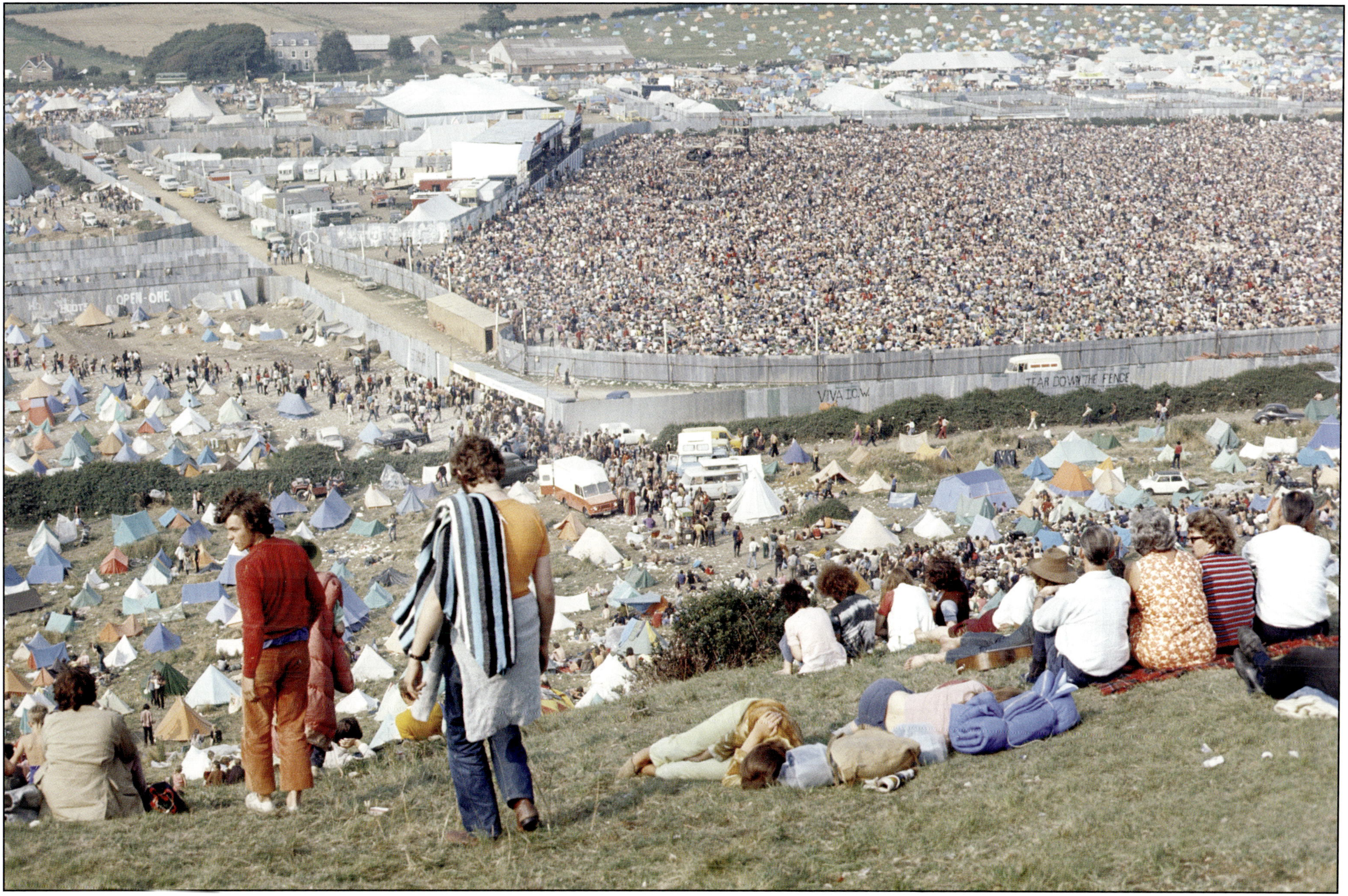

"I personally have never gone along with the 600,000 figure. I think that's absurd, it couldn't have been 600,000. It's a myth which has been built up much further by the Murray Lerner film that came out in 1995. These figures are exaggerated at all events."
Ray Foulk, interviewed by authors.

Ken Box

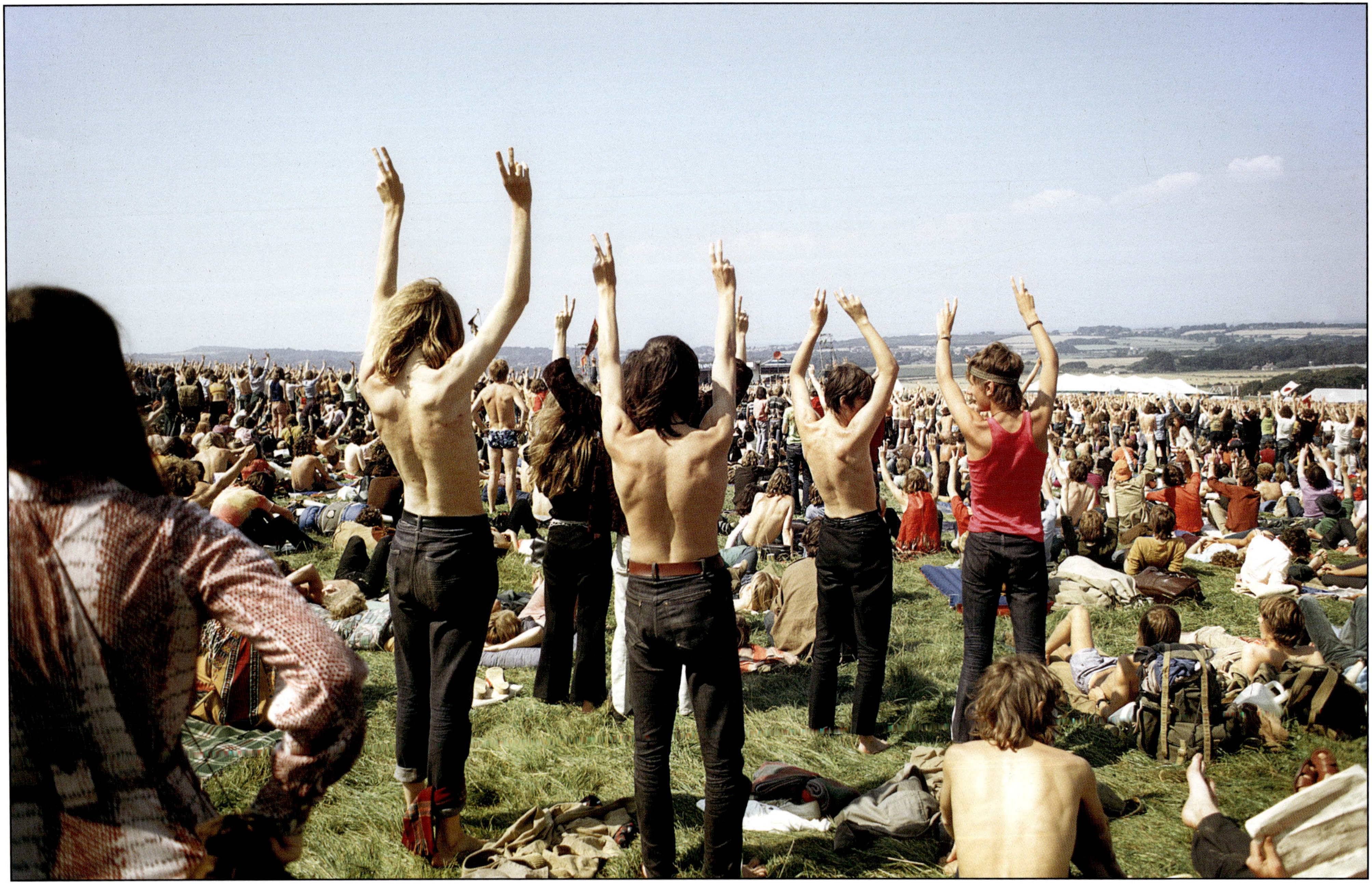

Ken Box

"This frightfully distorted thing appeared in the *Daily Telegraph* one morning, 'Vicar Supporting Hippies Against the Council,' I complained to them but they didn't take any notice. The pre-publicity, not by the organisers, but by the media, was that we were going to be invaded by a lot of drug addicts and louts and promiscuous people – our daughters would be in danger and our sons would be in danger. It wasn't so."
The Reverend Robert Bowyer, on-site minister.

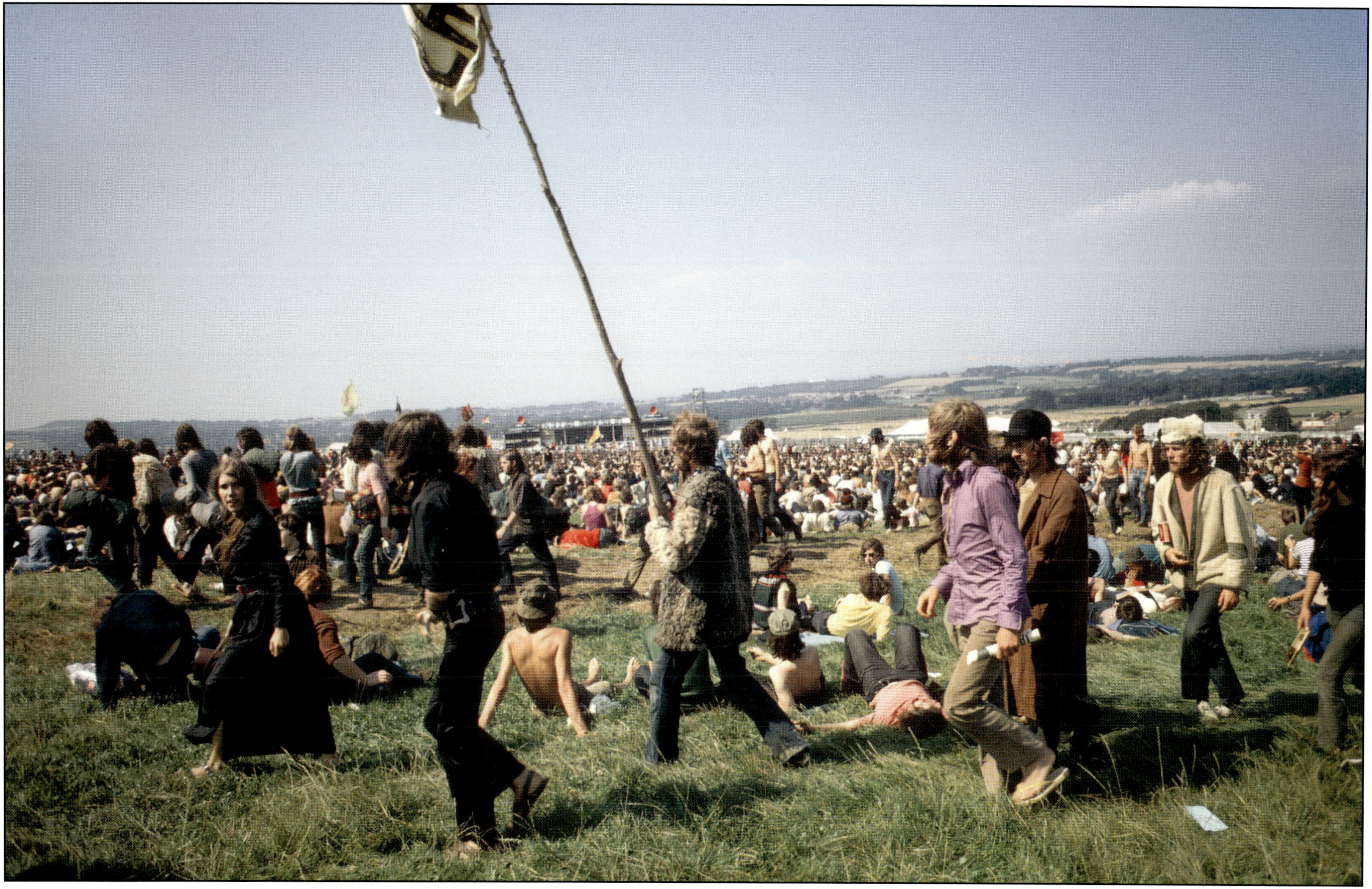

"As far as promiscuity was concerned, obviously there was more about than there is usually but if you get a couple of hundred thousand people together there are bound to be variations in behaviour – there are bound to be some bad lots amongst them. If you had a couple of hundred thousand members of the Mother's Union there'd be some awful rotters amongst them." - *Reverend Robert Bowyer, on-site minister.*

Ken Box

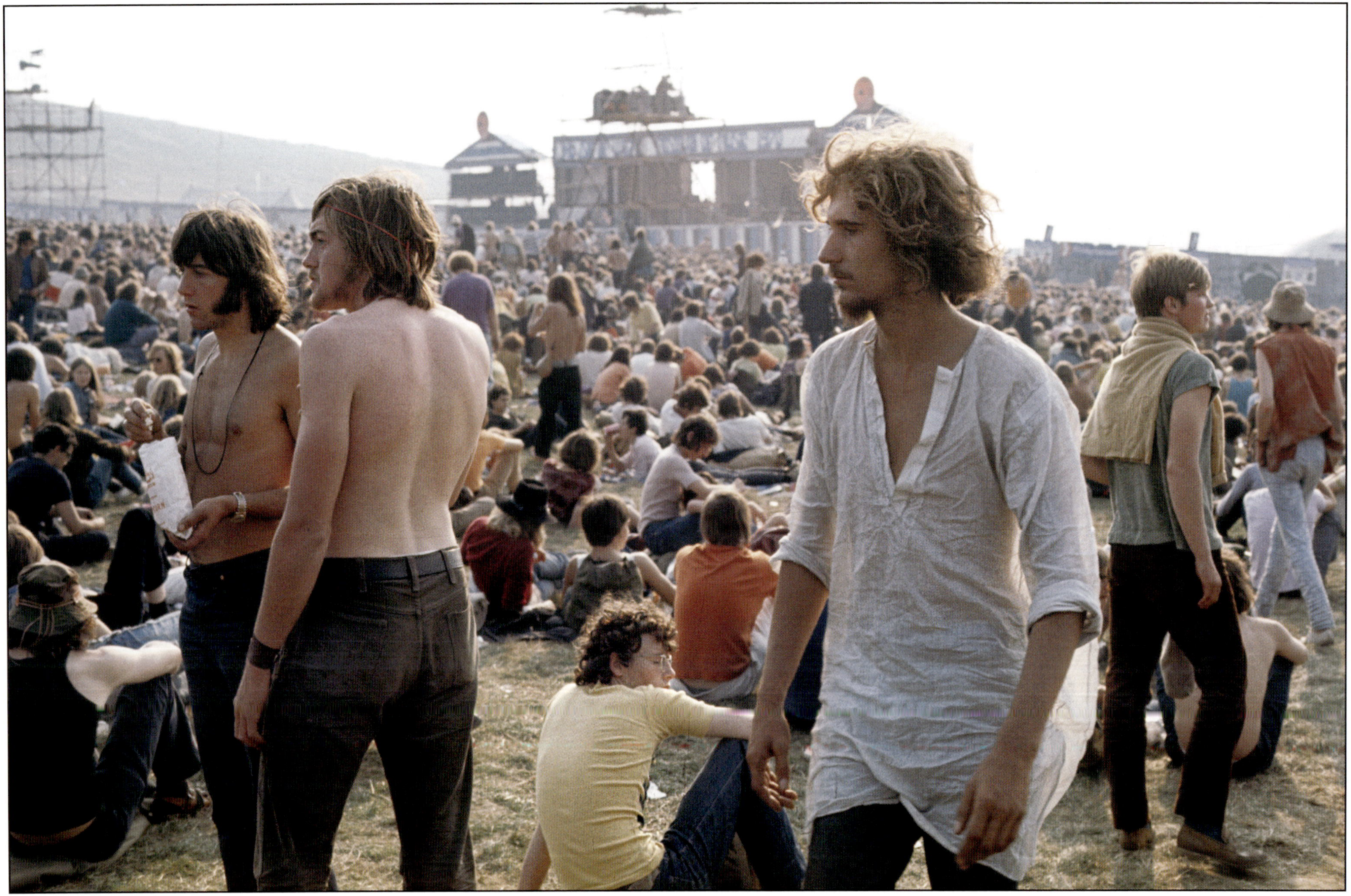

"Not all stars like playing at festivals. We offered Simon and Garfunkel £50,000 to come but they turned us down. So did Johnny Cash, for £30,000."
Ron Foulk, Daily Mirror interview, August 29, 1970.

Ken Box

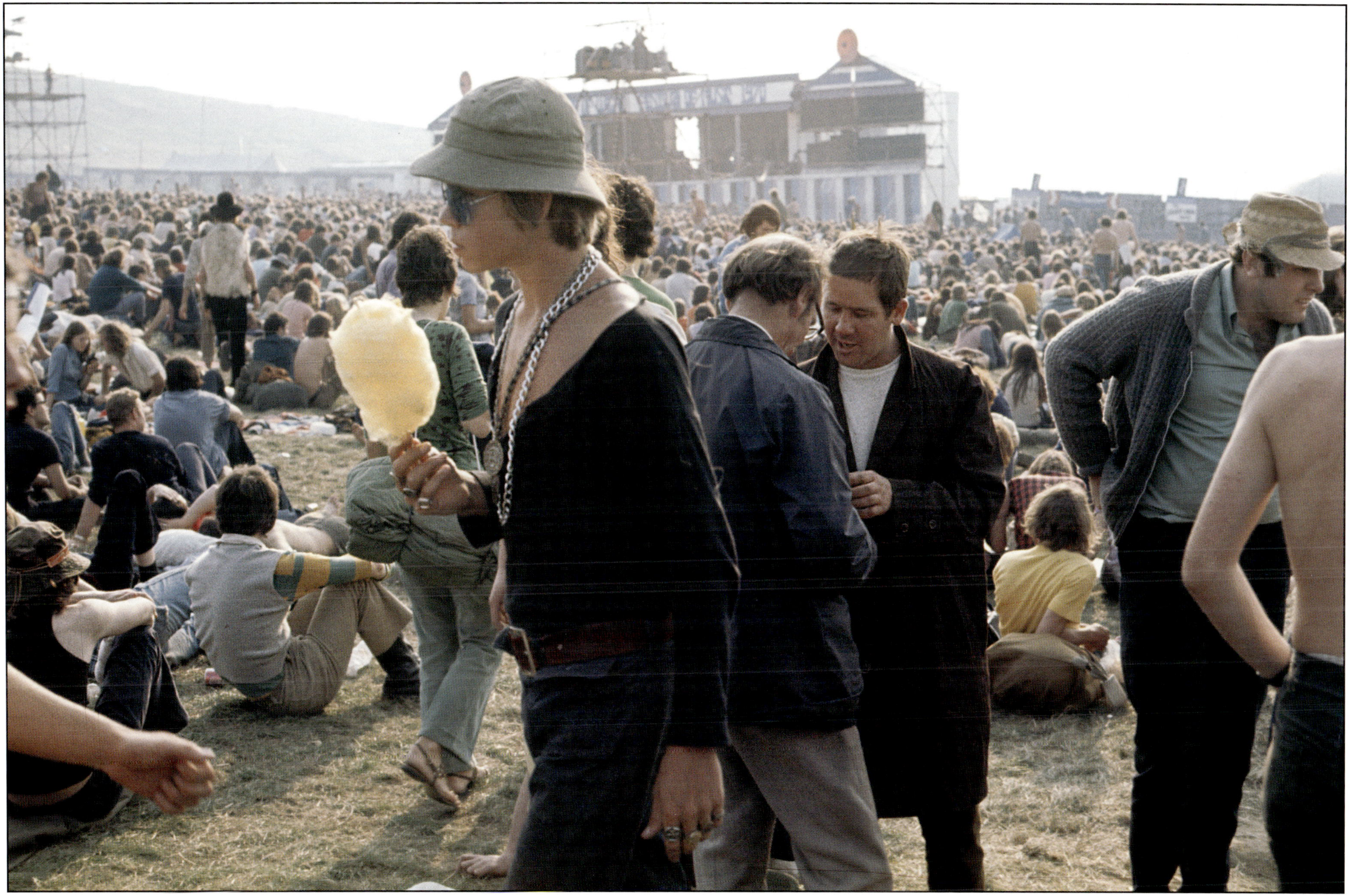

""I'm not against festivals as such but cannot see even one advantage to the Island from such happenings. The people here are not the sort that appreciate hippies and layabouts. Ninety per cent of Islanders do not want anything to do with it." - *Mark Woodnutt M.P., The Guardian, August 20, 1970.*

Ken Box

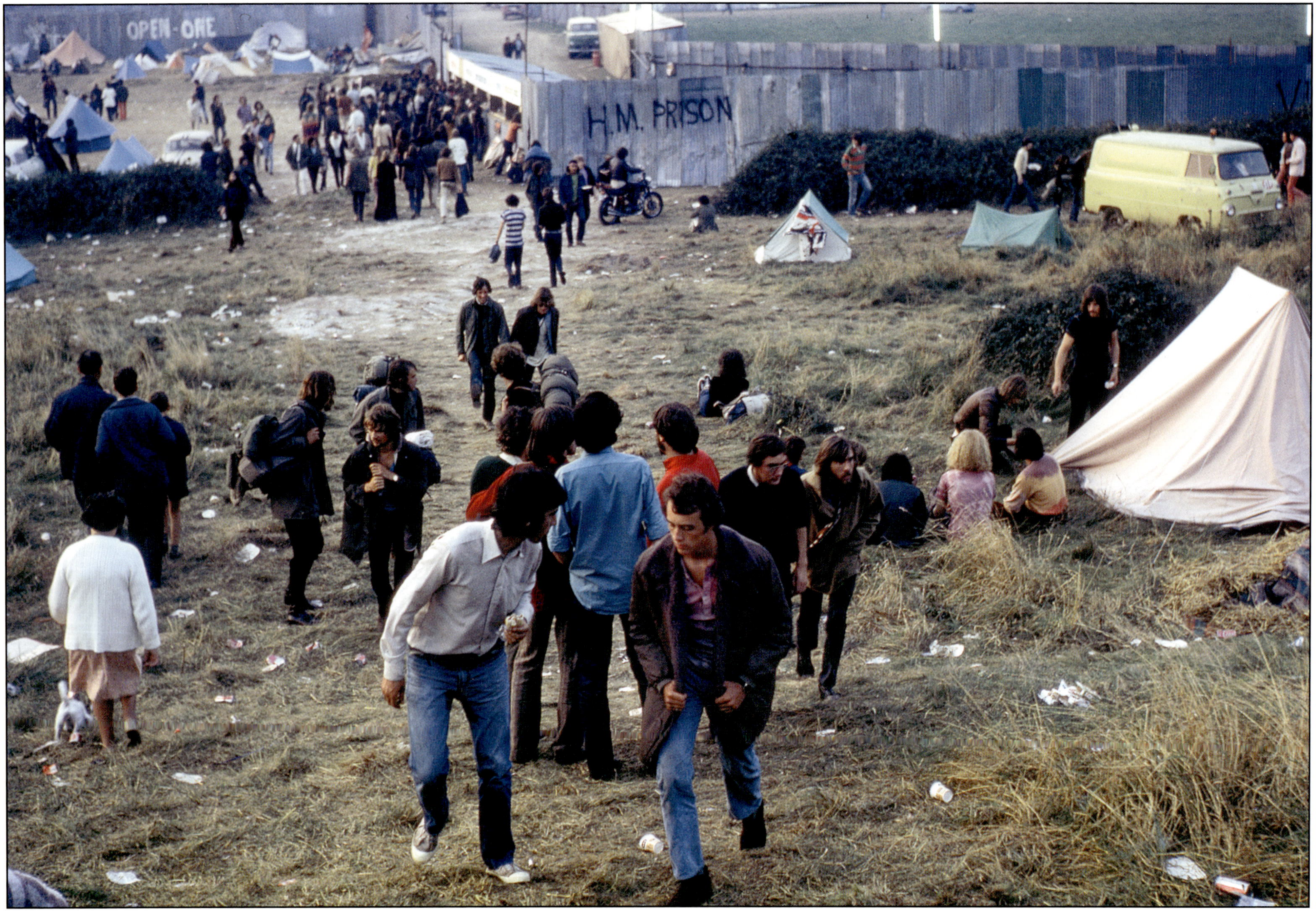
OPEN-ONE
H.M. PRISON

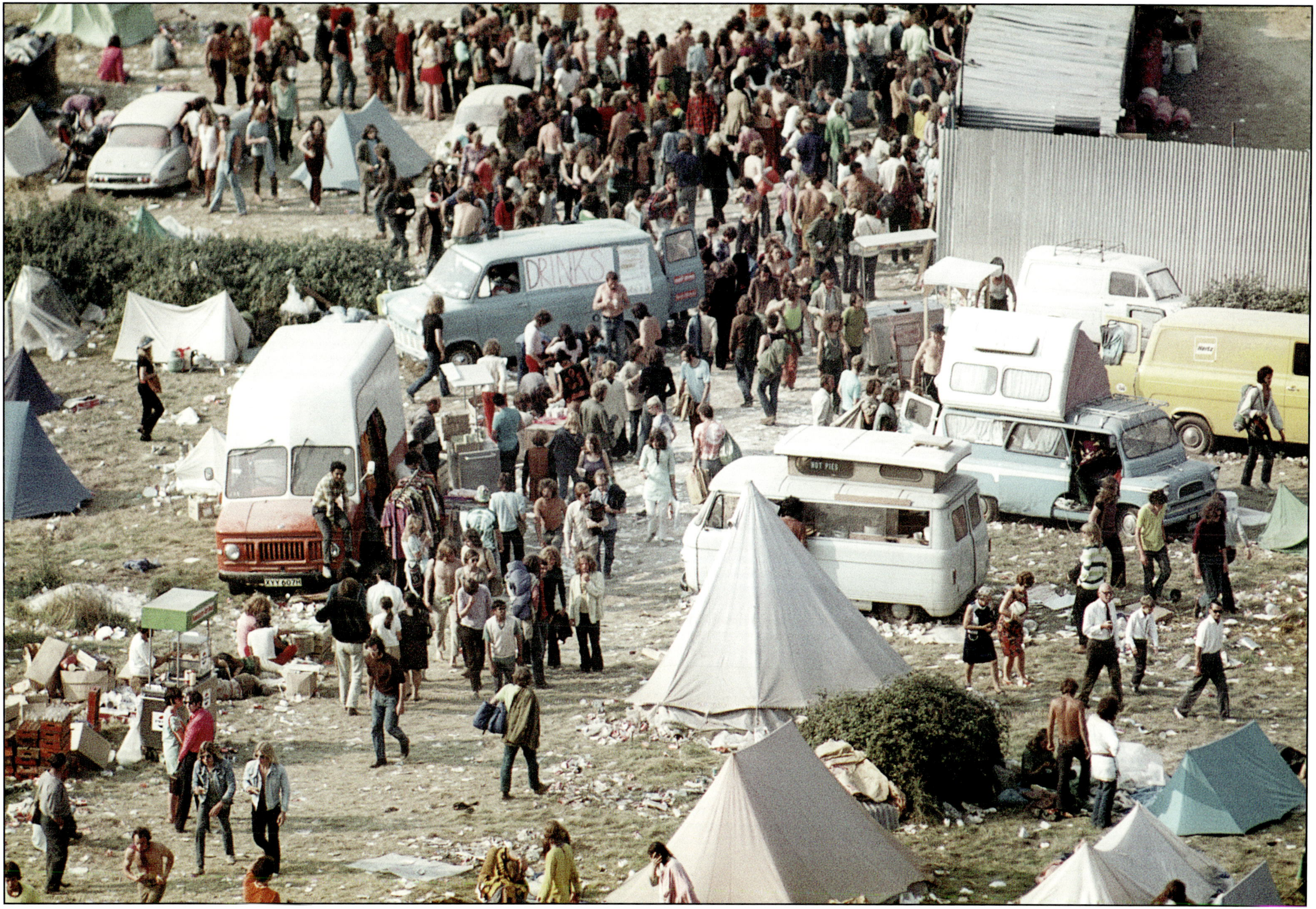

Ken Box

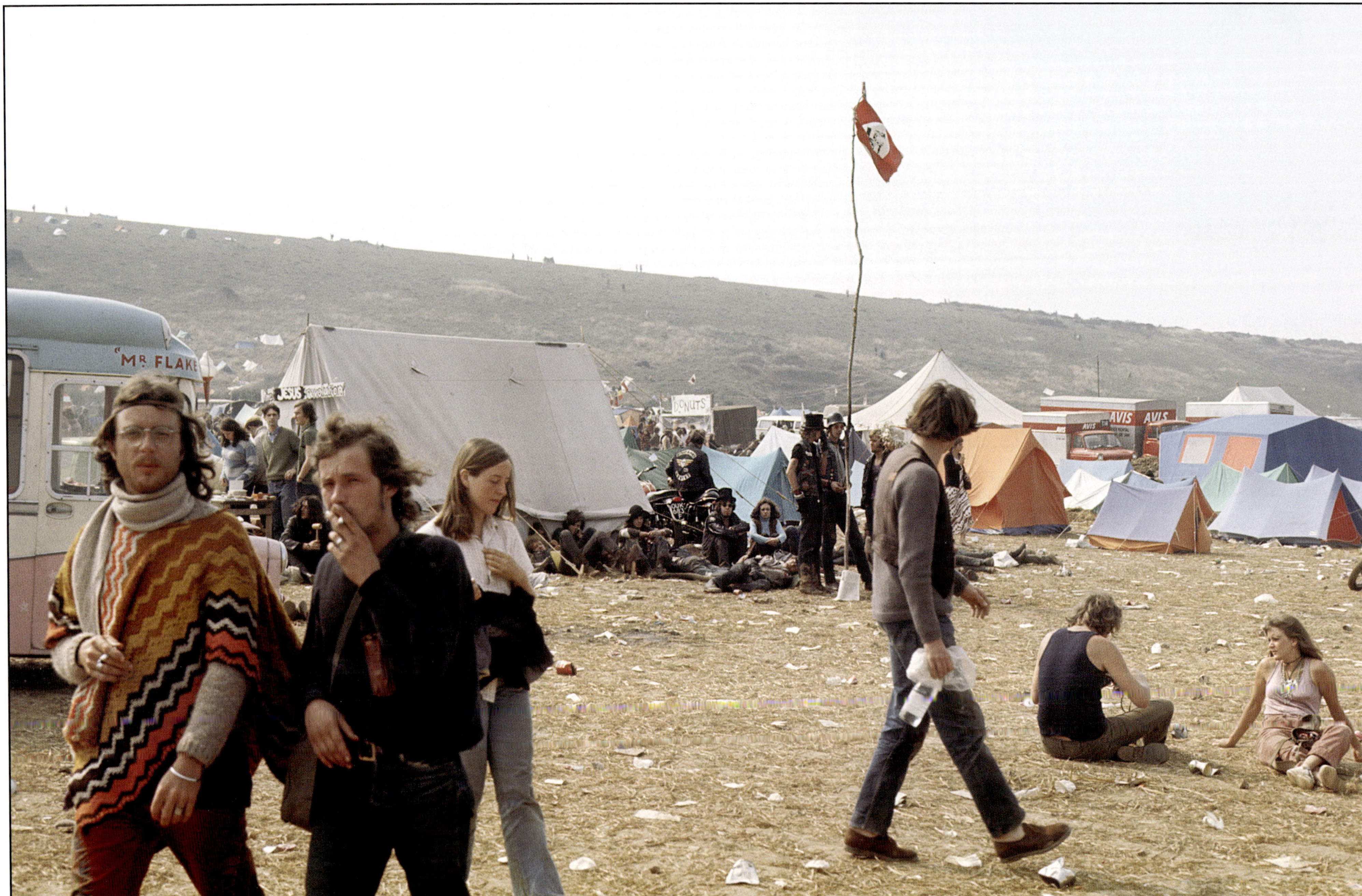

"A situation was created where it was impossible to enforce the law completely. It was a great nuisance to all the local people and it's quite out of character with the Isle of Wight. I shall do my level best to prevent another Isle of Wight festival."
Mark Woodnutt M.P., ITN news report, August 31, 1970.

Ken Box

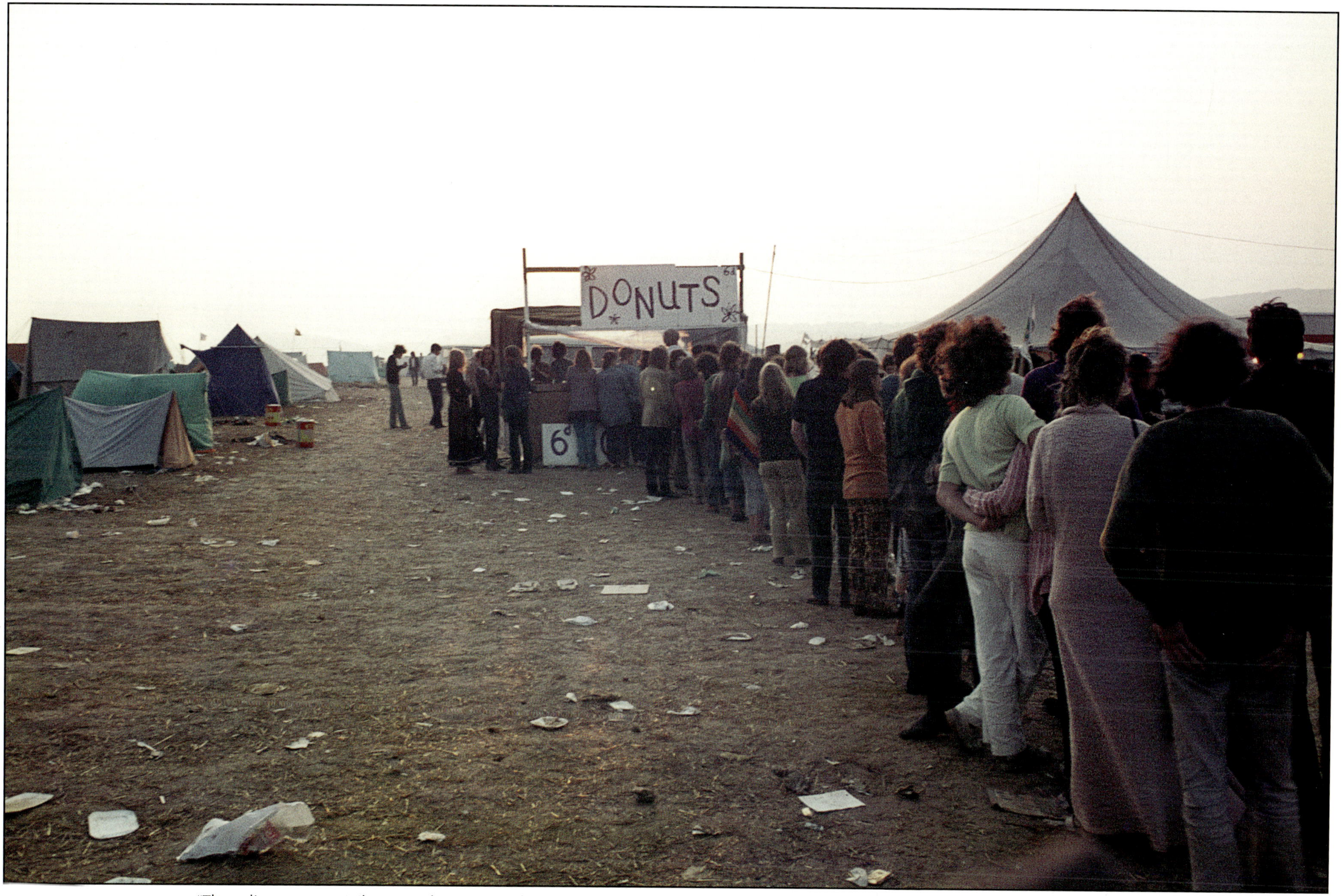

"The police were great; they were fantastic. We had nothing but good relationships with them. They didn't want to have a presence on site and we didn't particularly want them to have a presence, so they made their headquarters in a barn across the road. By and large, without the police I don't think we'd ever have got the festival on. They were very supportive." - *Ray Foulk interviewed by the authors.*

Ken Box

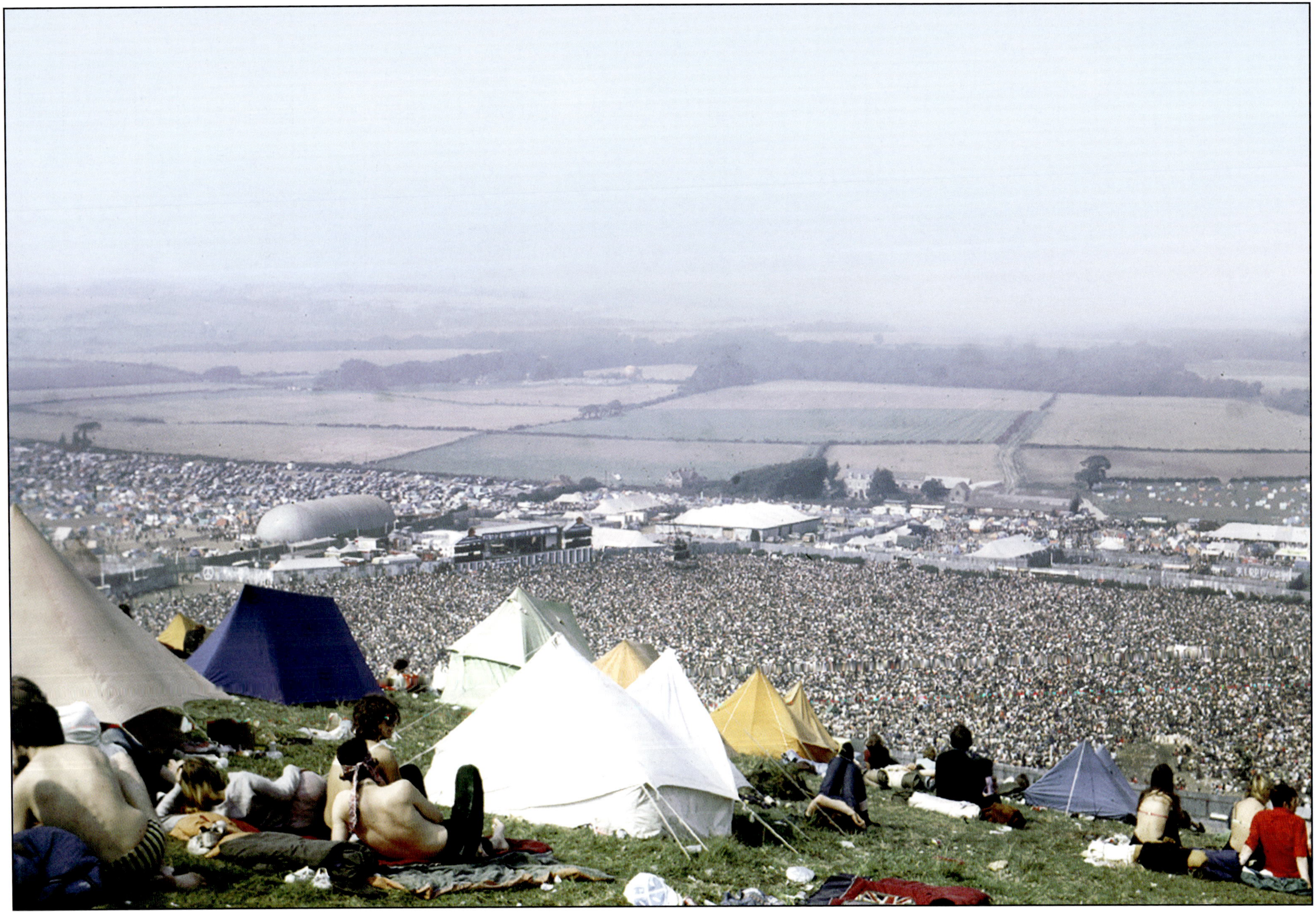

Eric Moth

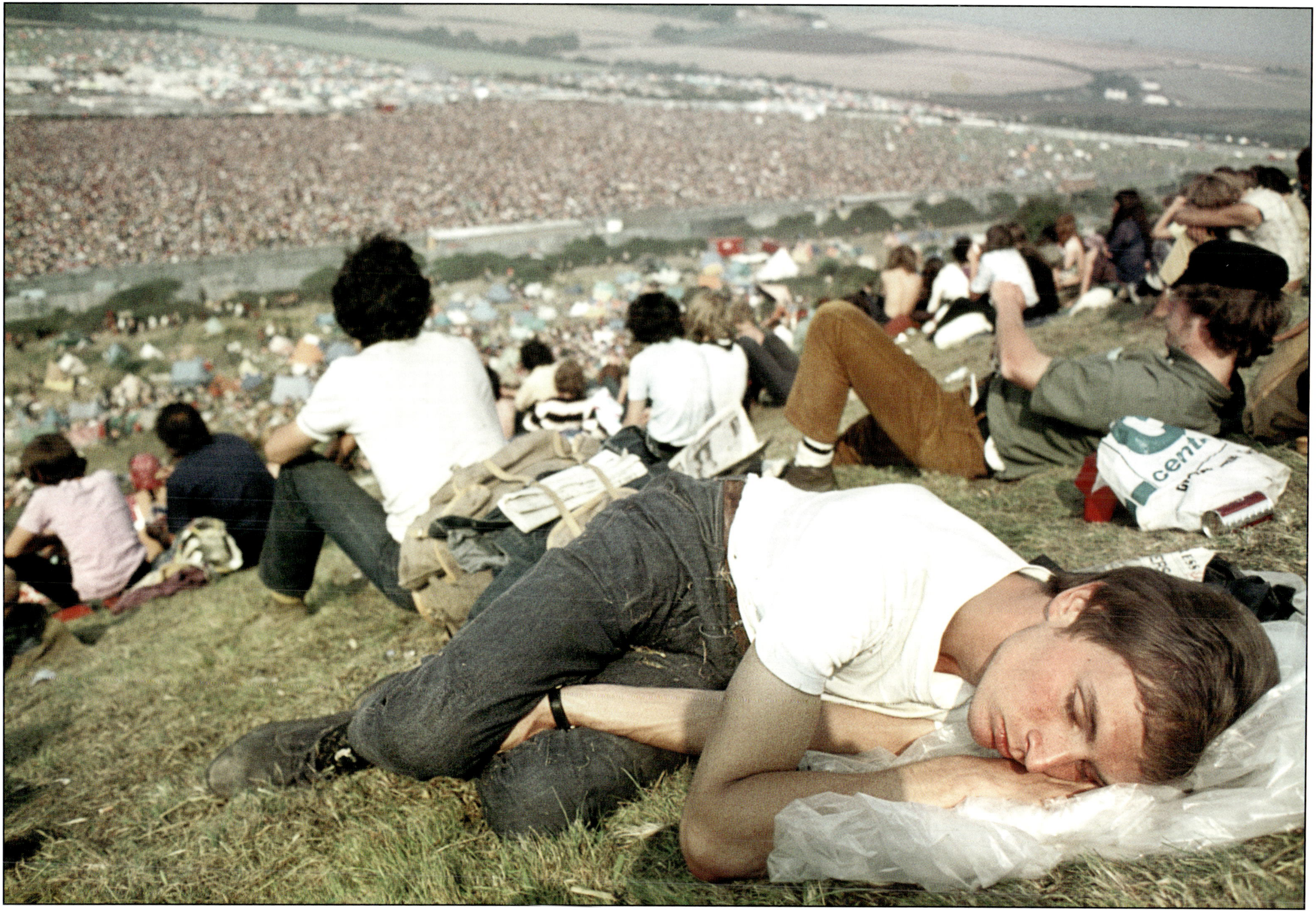

Ken Box

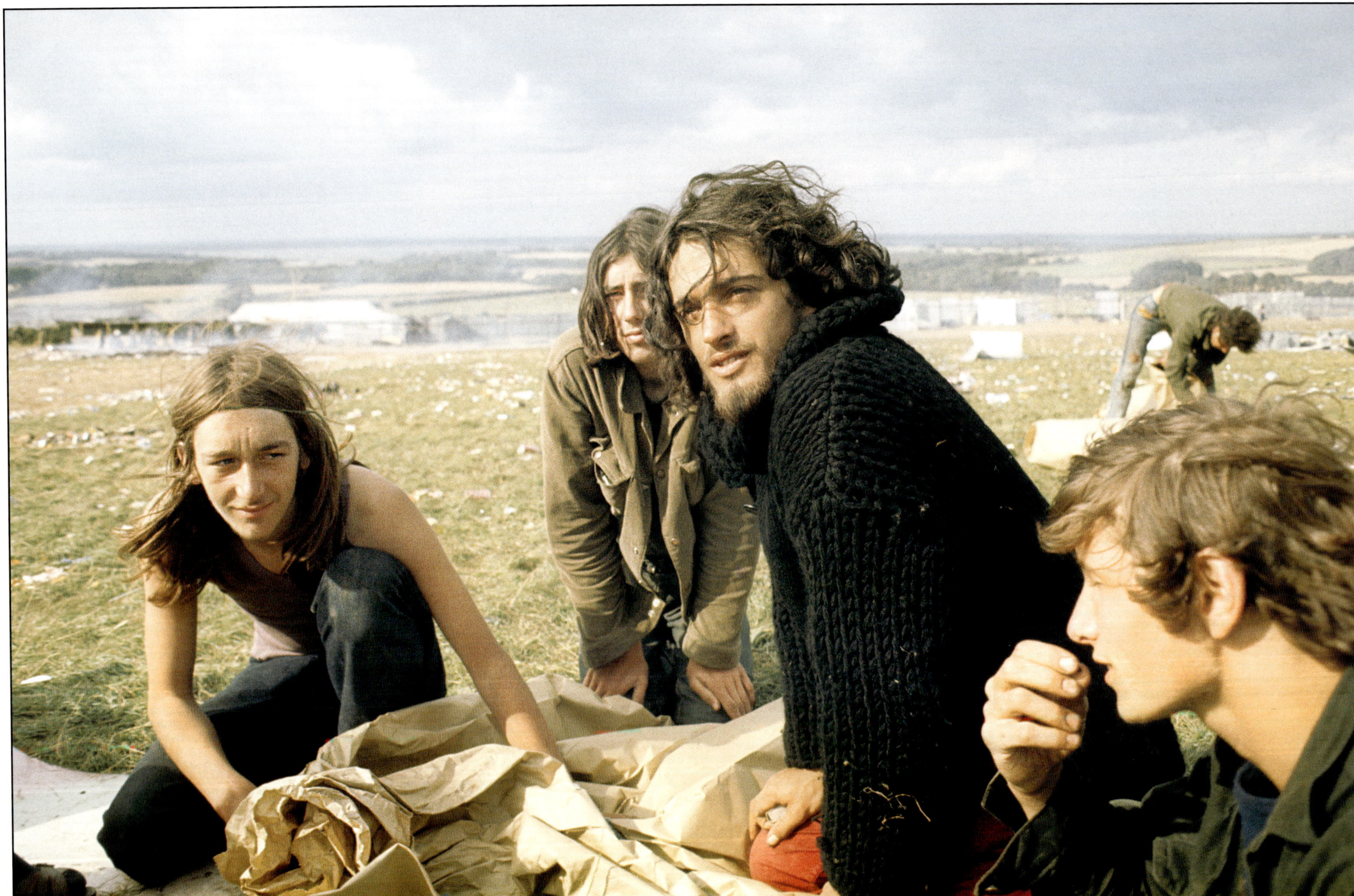

"This isn't quite paradise. But if you are young and can look after yourself and the sun stays out and the music stays loud, it doesn't matter."
Sunday Mirror, August 30, 1970.

Ken Box

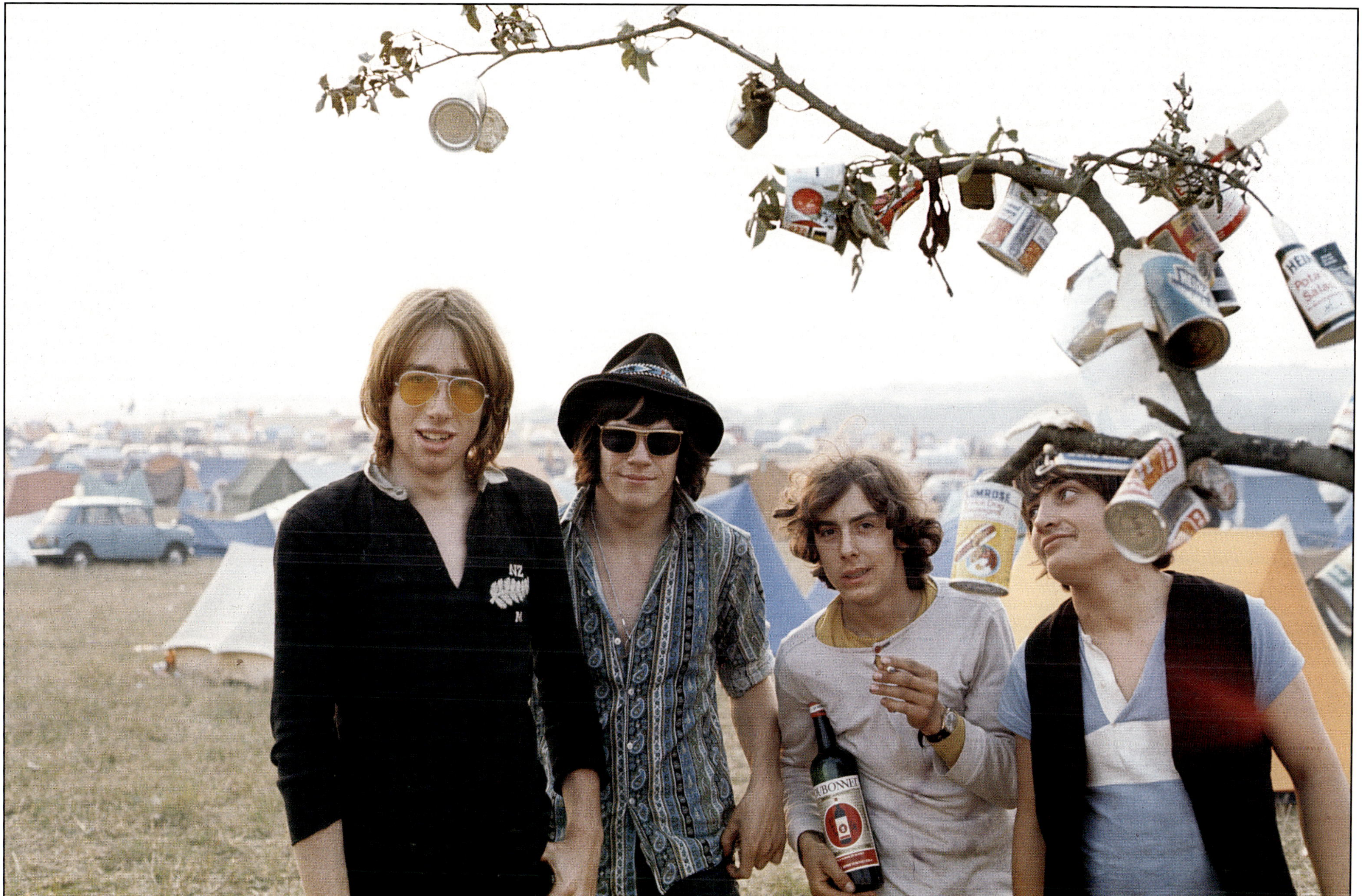

"I remember old Admiral Sir Manley Power from Yarmouth – he was going to shoot them as they stepped off the ferry and we said, 'Look, Albie you can't shoot them these days. You're not allowed to.' He said, 'I'm going to shoot them all as they step off - wretched people coming to the Isle of Wight.' "
Lionel Osman, local businessman and IW Councillor.

Ken Box

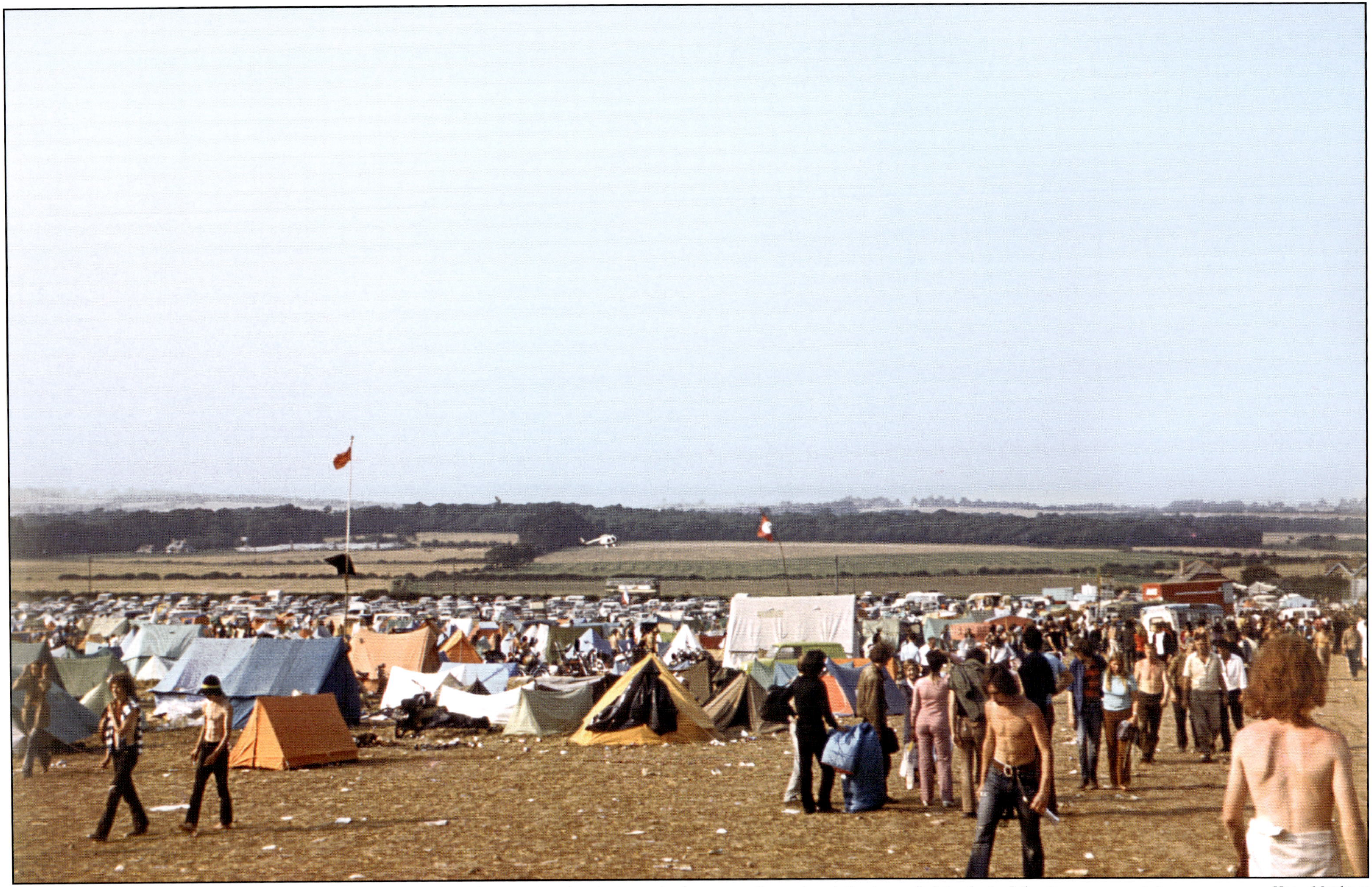

Harry Matthews

"The world's press was present and sought sensation, but in the main they were disappointed. By the end of the festival the Press representatives became almost desperate for material and they seemed disappointed that the patrons had been so well behaved. It is essential to explode the myth that all patrons of pop festivals are undesirables. The vast majority are perfectly decent, well-behaved youngsters, courteous and considerate."
Douglas Osmond, Chief Constable, 1971 Annual Report.

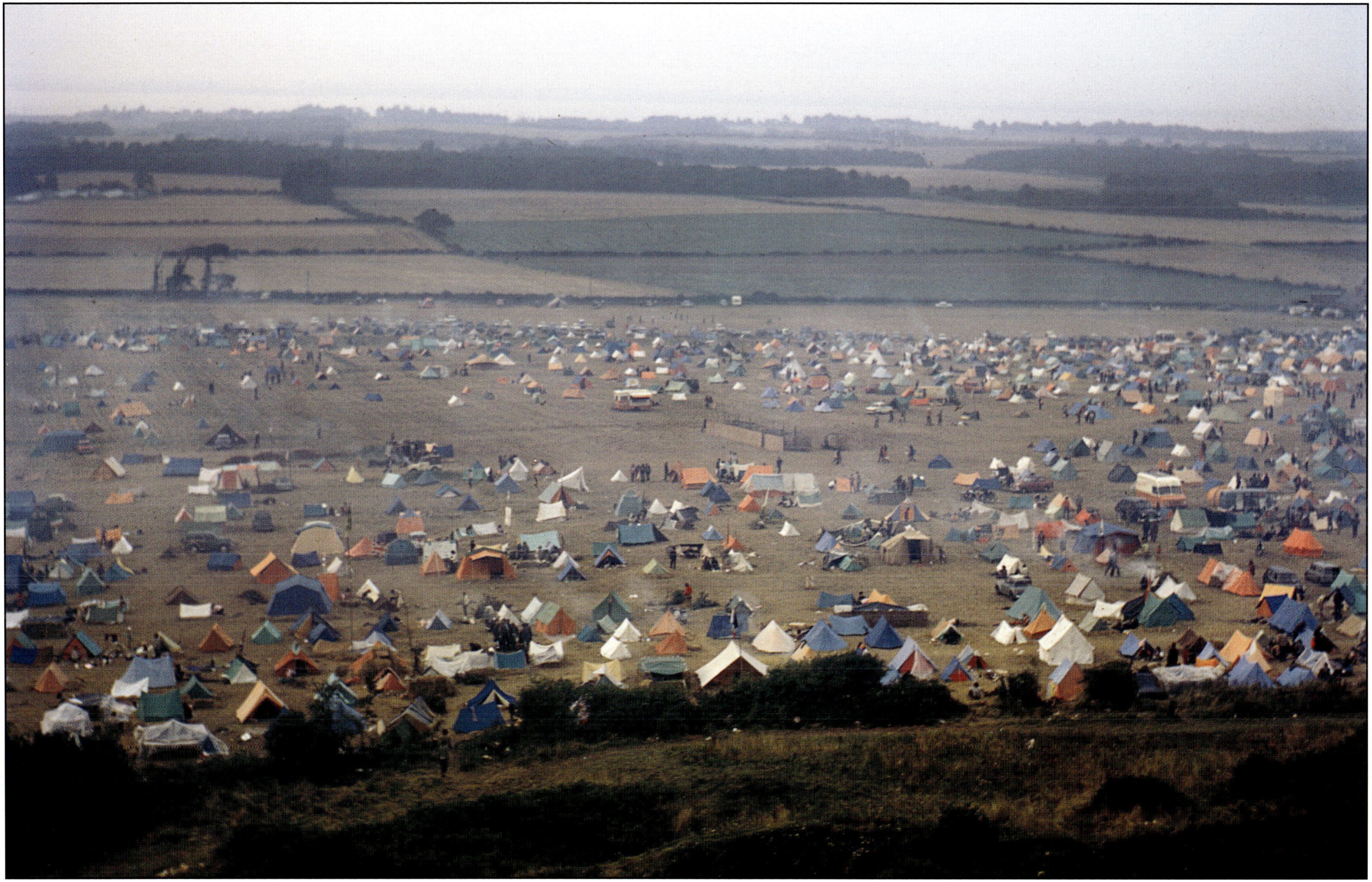

"Fiery Creations, have decided not to charge for admission on Wednesday or Thursday, which is regarded as the warming up period. This is being done as a gesture of goodwill to the 30,000 or 40,000 who have already arrived, although it could be seen as a sop to the "free music" militants. In any case it is obvious that Fiery Creations, who have committed something like £500,000 to this venture, are going to make a profit out of this weekend unless an act of God of remarkable proportions befalls them." - *David Wilsworth, The Times, August 25, 1970*

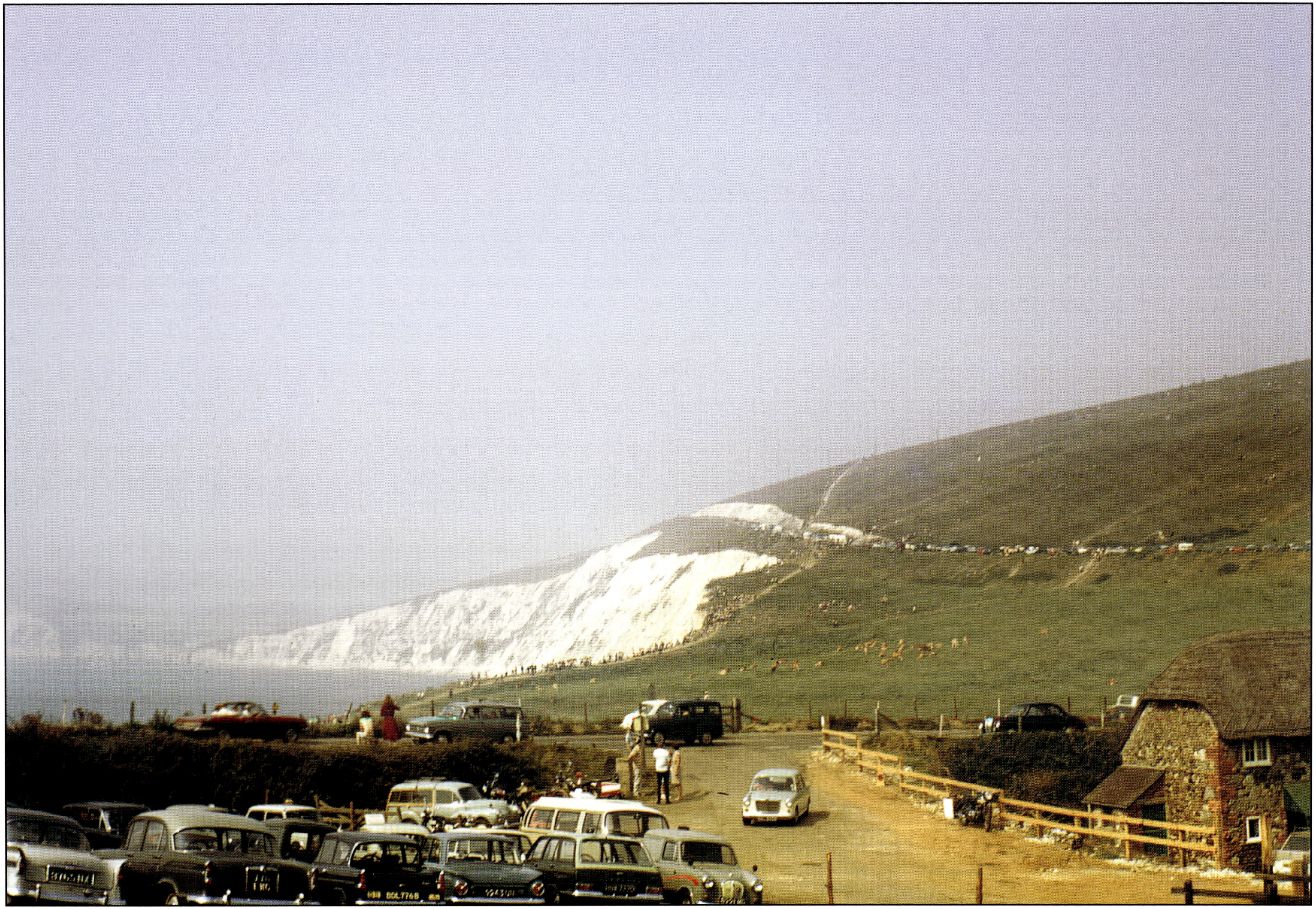

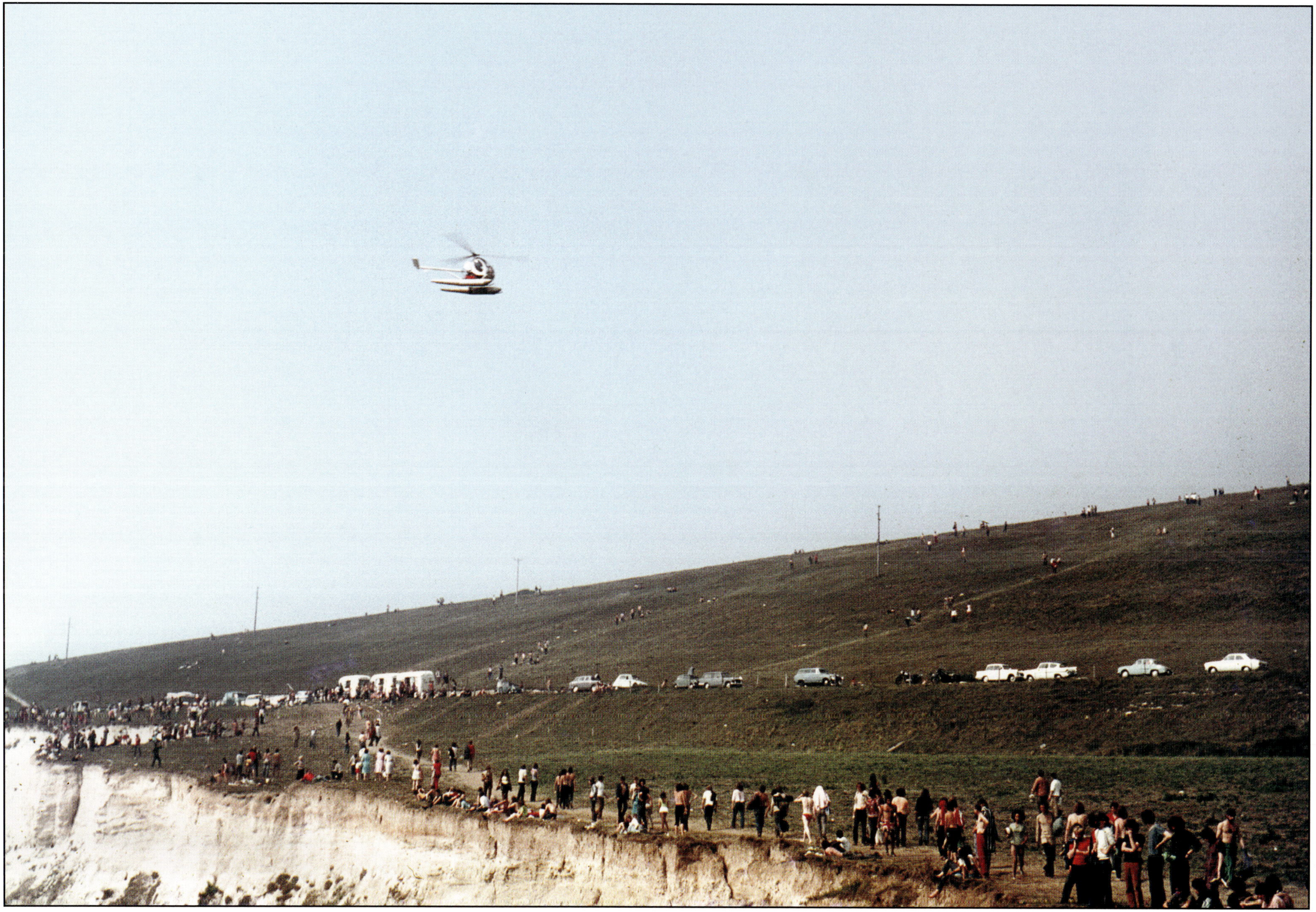

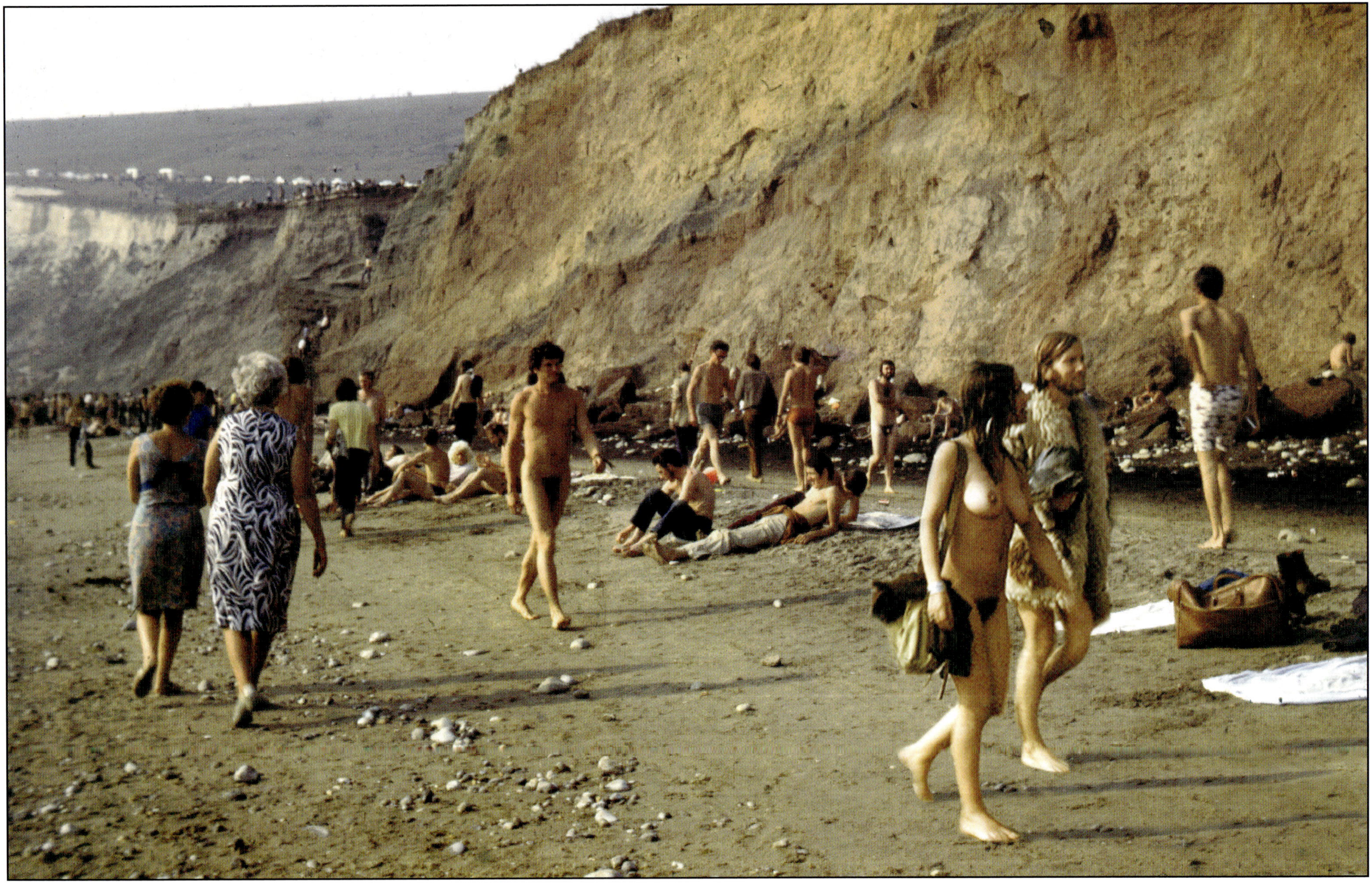

Eric Moth

"Mr Mark Woodnutt, Conservative M.P. for the Isle of Wight, said the law had been brought into contempt at the festival. 'I am not a prude and I do not mind nude bathing at the right place at the right time, but I do not like fornicating on the beach, which is what we have been seeing.'"
The Times, August 28, 1970.

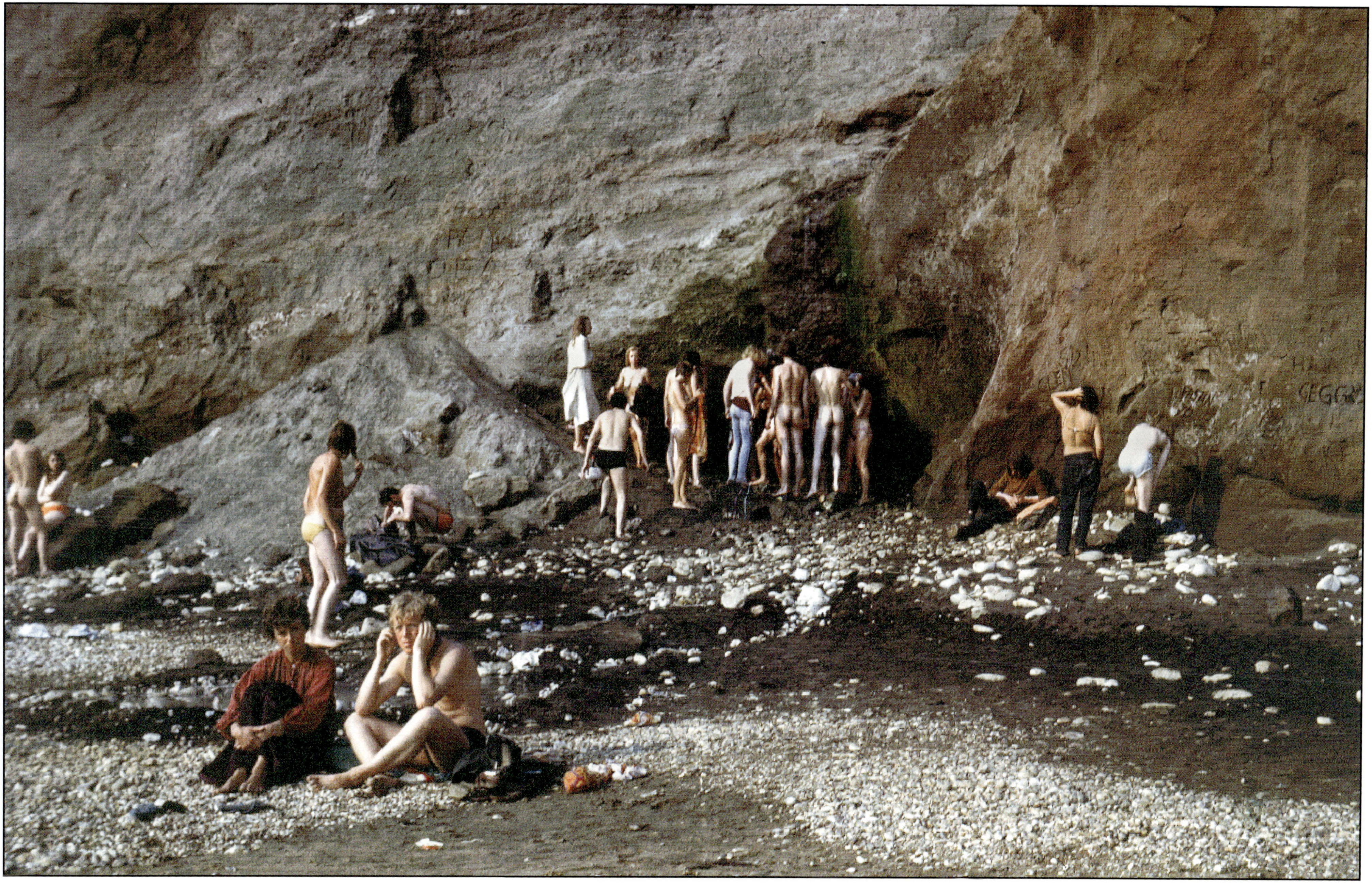

Eric Moth

"The scenes at Compton attracted crowds of onlookers and traffic was halted for about two miles as binoculars and telescopes were brought into play. By Compton Steps dozens of hippies frolicked naked beneath a miniature waterfall, making "Oh, Calcutta" look like "Alice in Wonderland."
I.W. County Press, September 5, 1970.

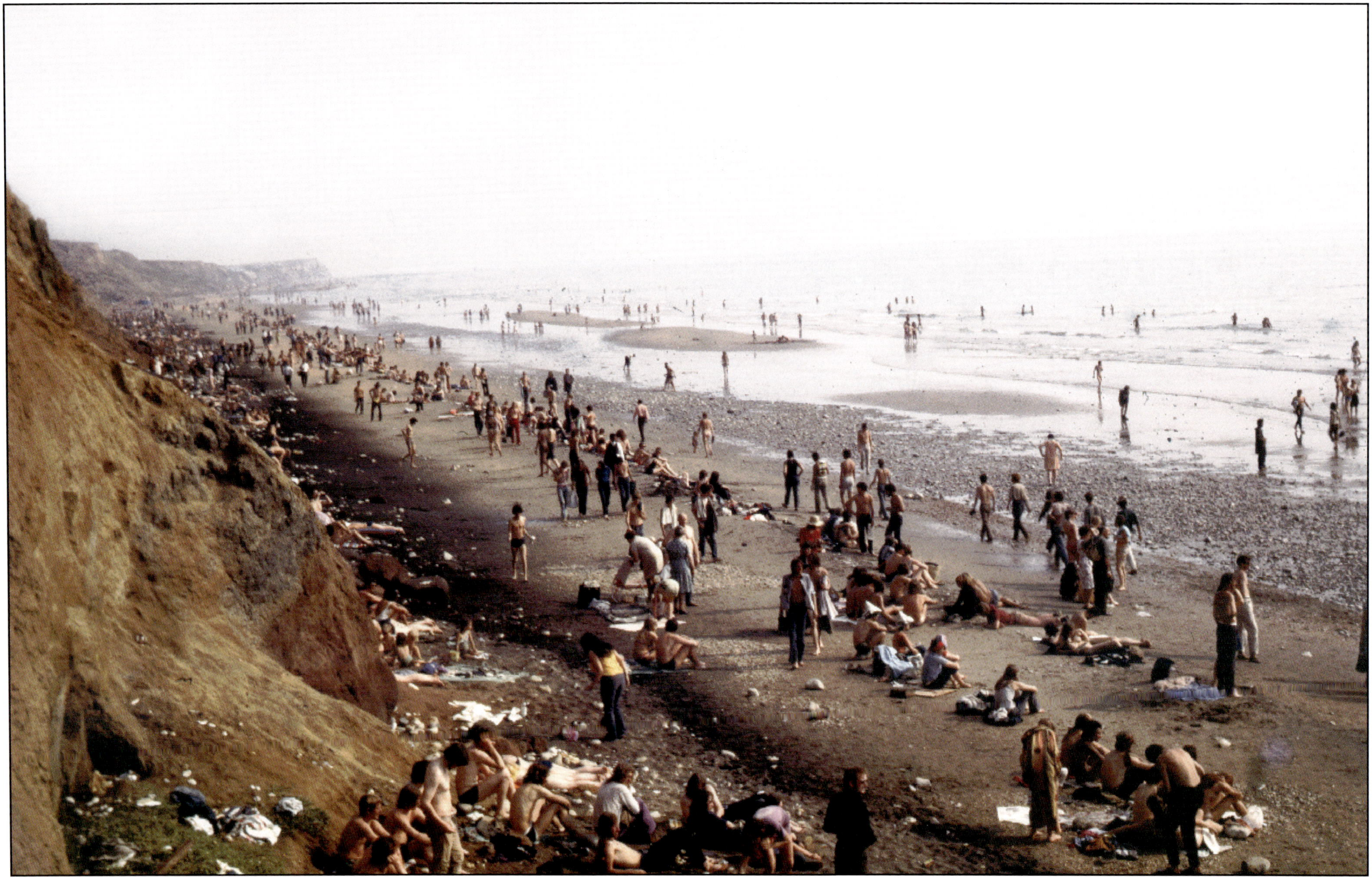

"The nude bathing on a public beach did not go down at all well with holidaymakers or local residents. On Sunday many left the area as hundreds of hippies descended on Compton, stripped and stretched on the sands; then they cavorted and bathed naked. At one stage, hippies were queuing to get down to the beach and our photographer was the only man with his trousers on." - *I.W. County Press, September 5, 1970.*

Eric Moth

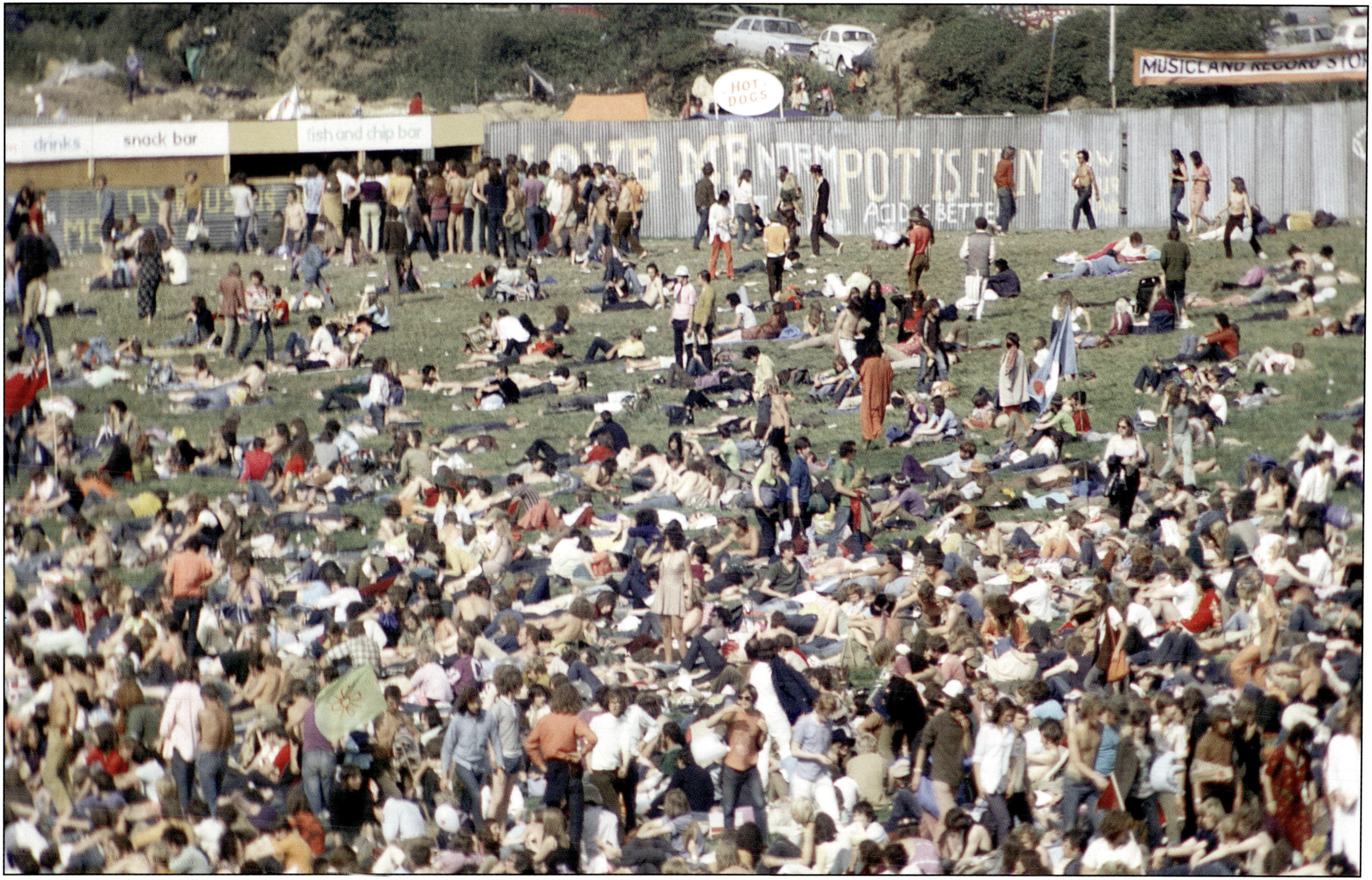

Ken Box

"A proportion of the faces were depraved almost beyond belief, and in many cases clearly drug-ridden; scores had such faces as might be seen in a criminal lunatic asylum; many seemed to be adenoidal, with mouths hanging open, slouched shoulders, and pitiful physiques."
Reader's letter, I.W. County Press, September 5, 1970.

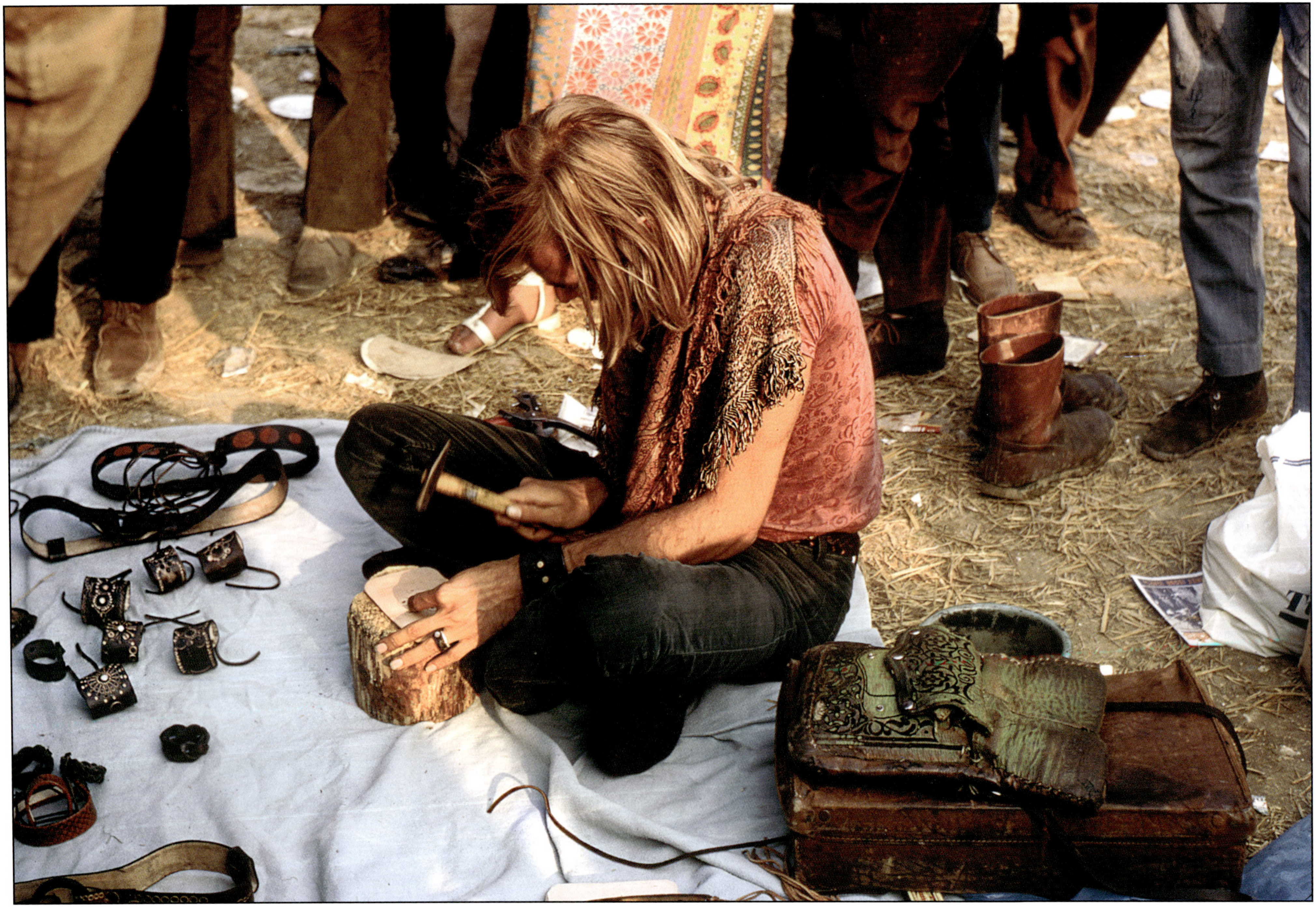

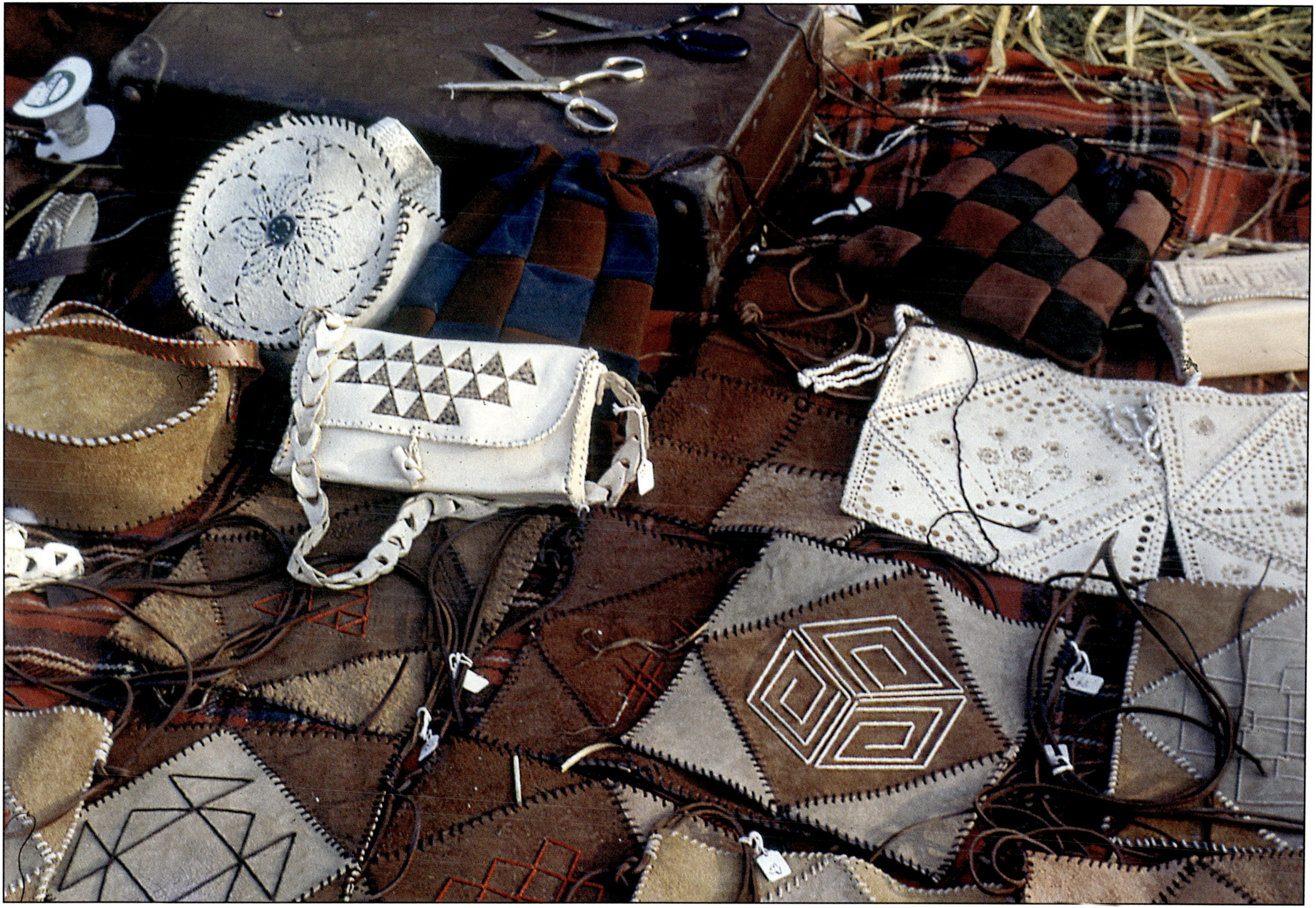

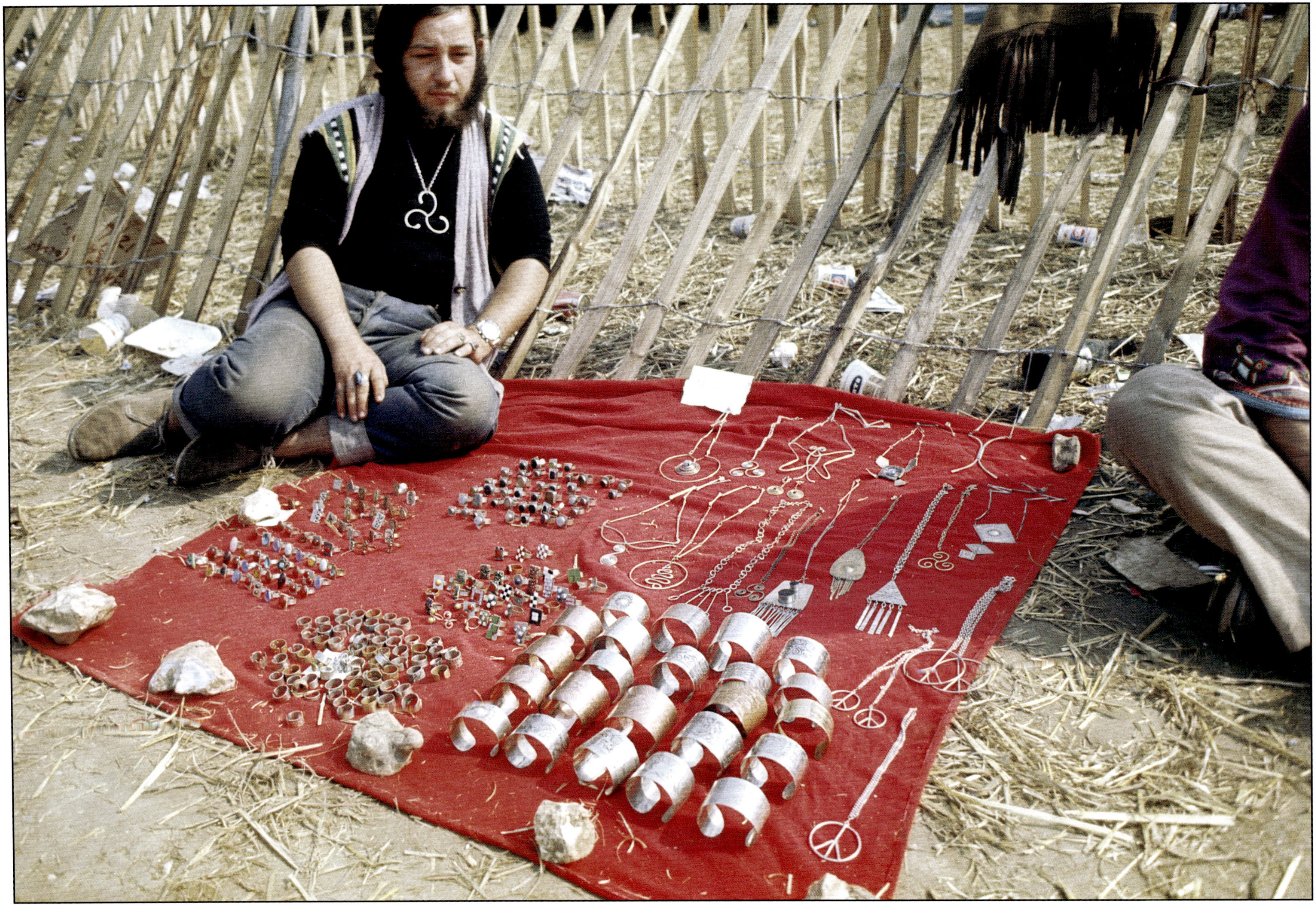

Ken Box

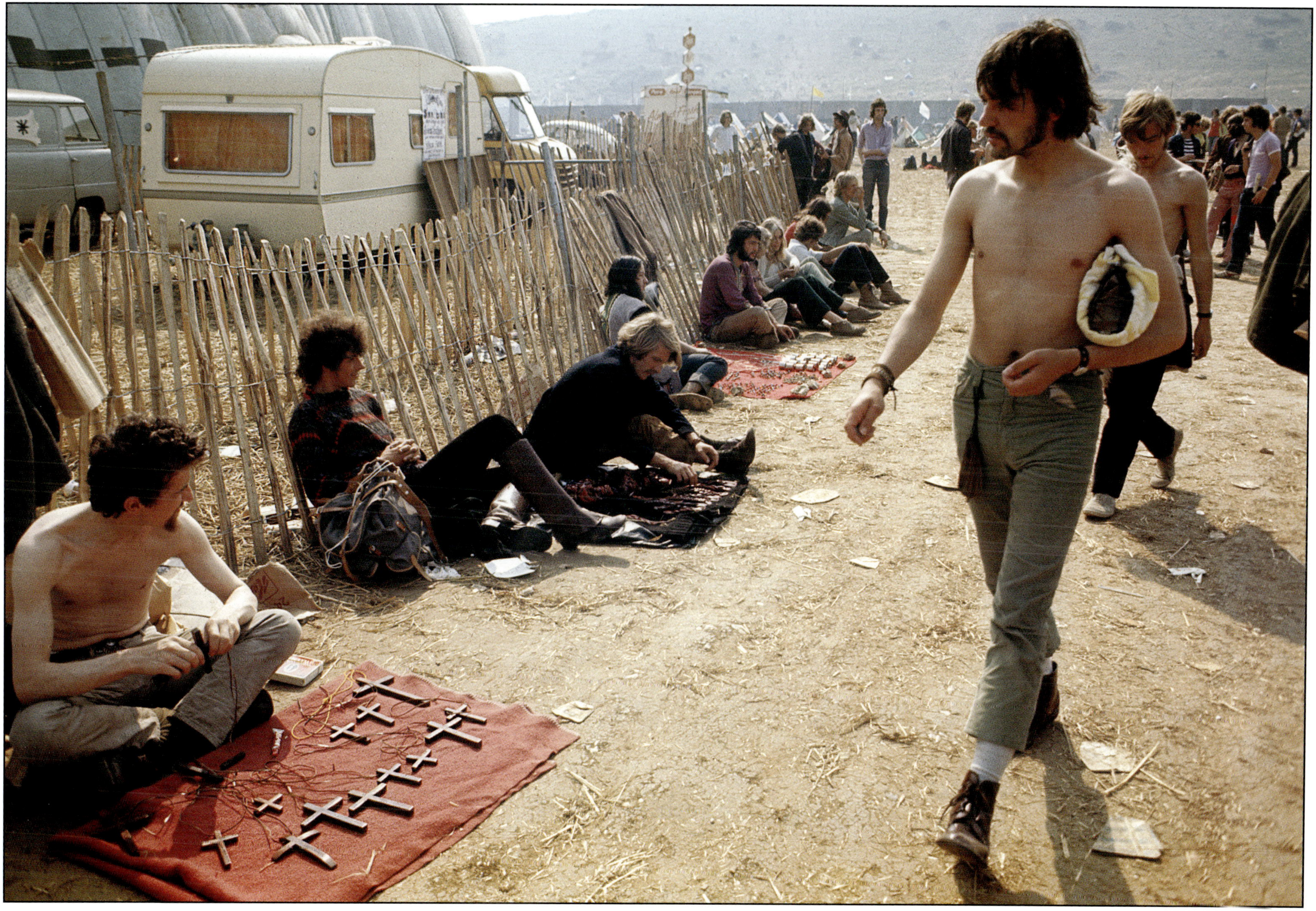

Ken Box

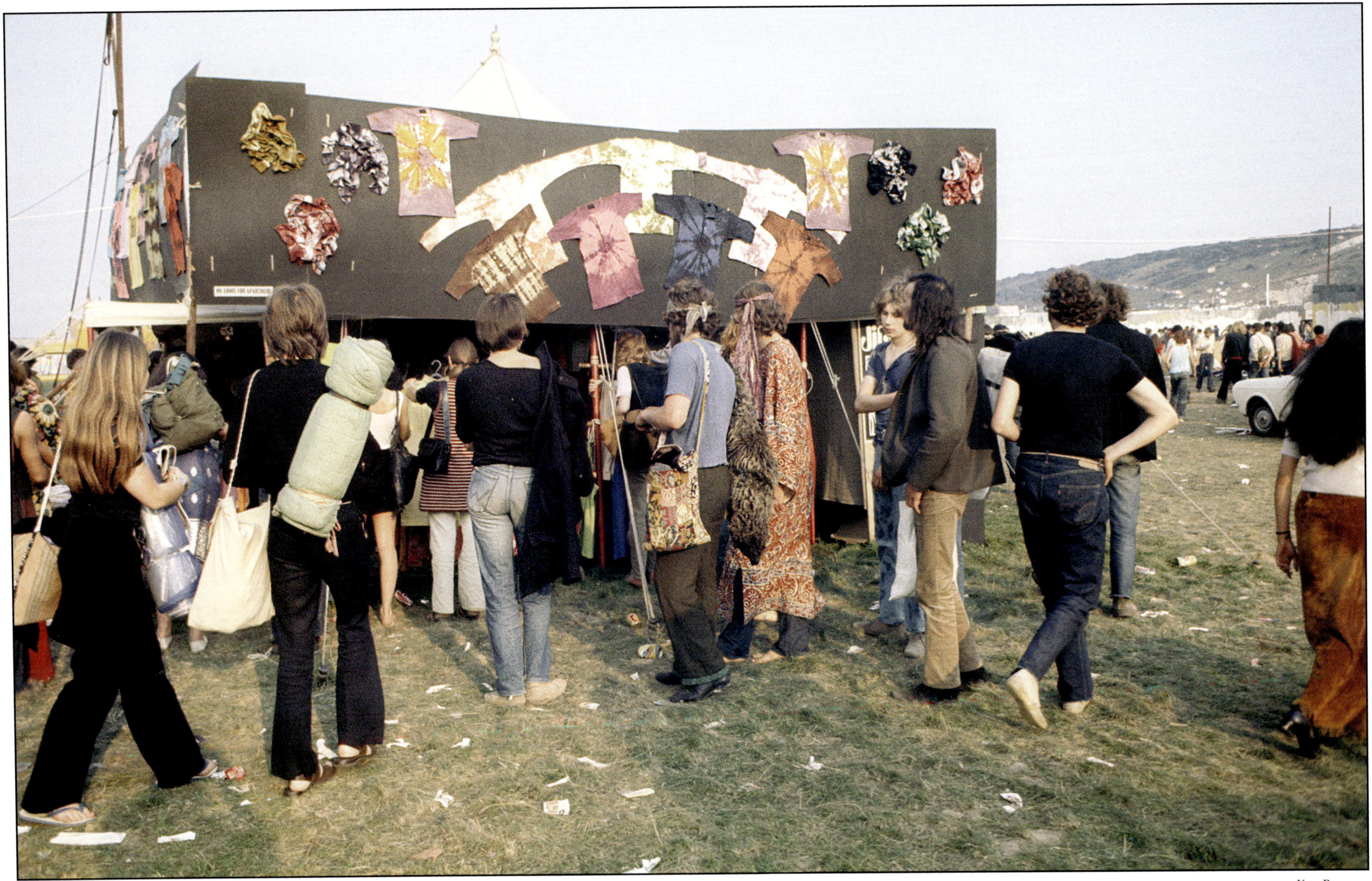

"We've got some of the world's top acts here and we've had to pay out £250,000 in artists fees alone. The site and all the equipment has cost us just as much and we've had £20,000 in legal bills. On top of this we have more than 6000 ground and admin staff to pay. We'll be counting the last pound in the end to know where it's going to go." - *Ron Foulk, Daily Mirror interview, August 29, 1970.*

Ken Box

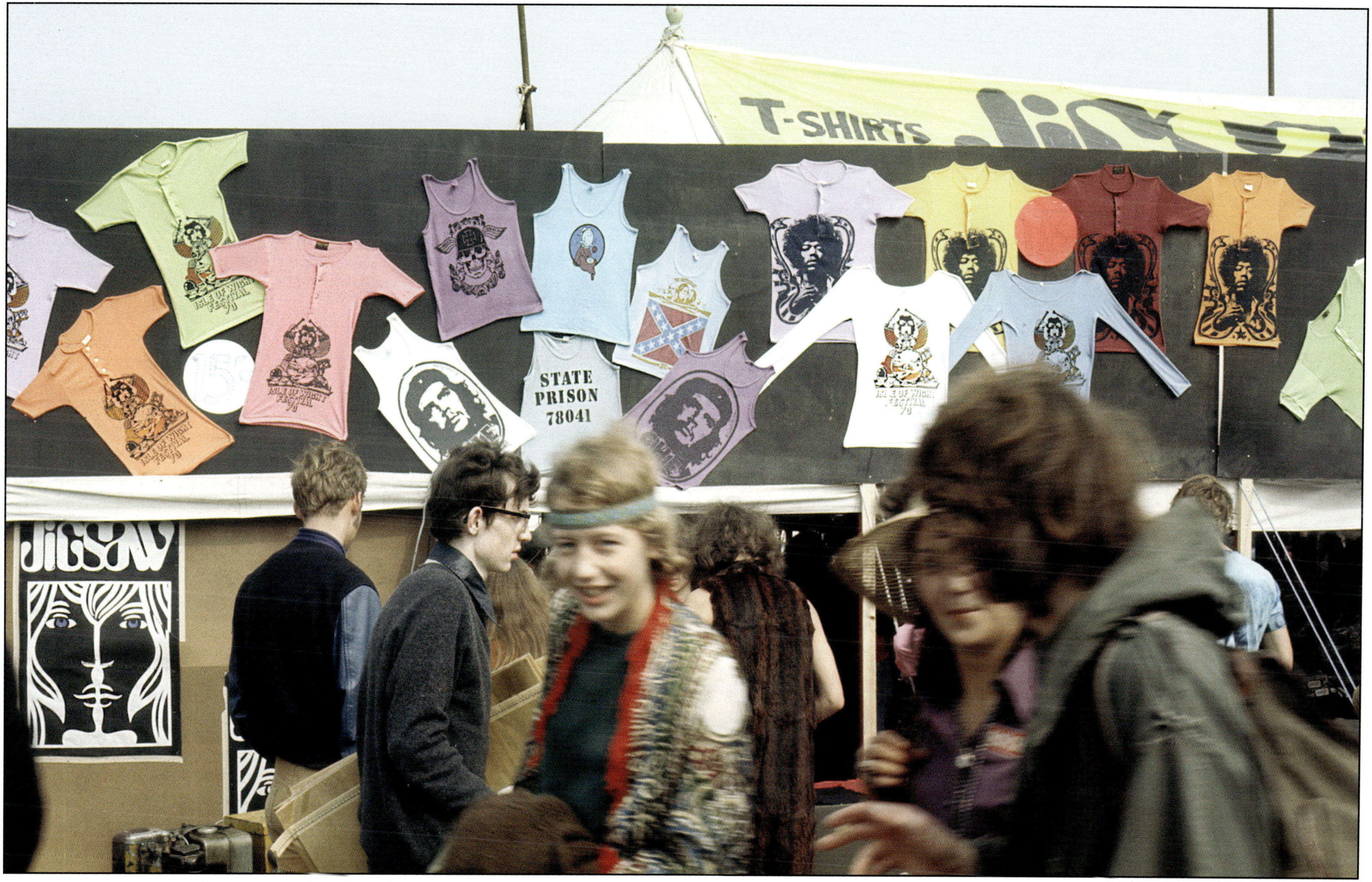

"We didn't get the ticket sales we were expecting and the budget was rocketing out of control because we kept on piling in more artists and putting in more facilities like toilets, which take up a lot of space, they're big things. We were really piling in facilities for which we were getting a lot of flak as though we were ruining the spirit of the festival by commercialising it." - *Ray Foulk, interviewed by the authors.*

Ken Box

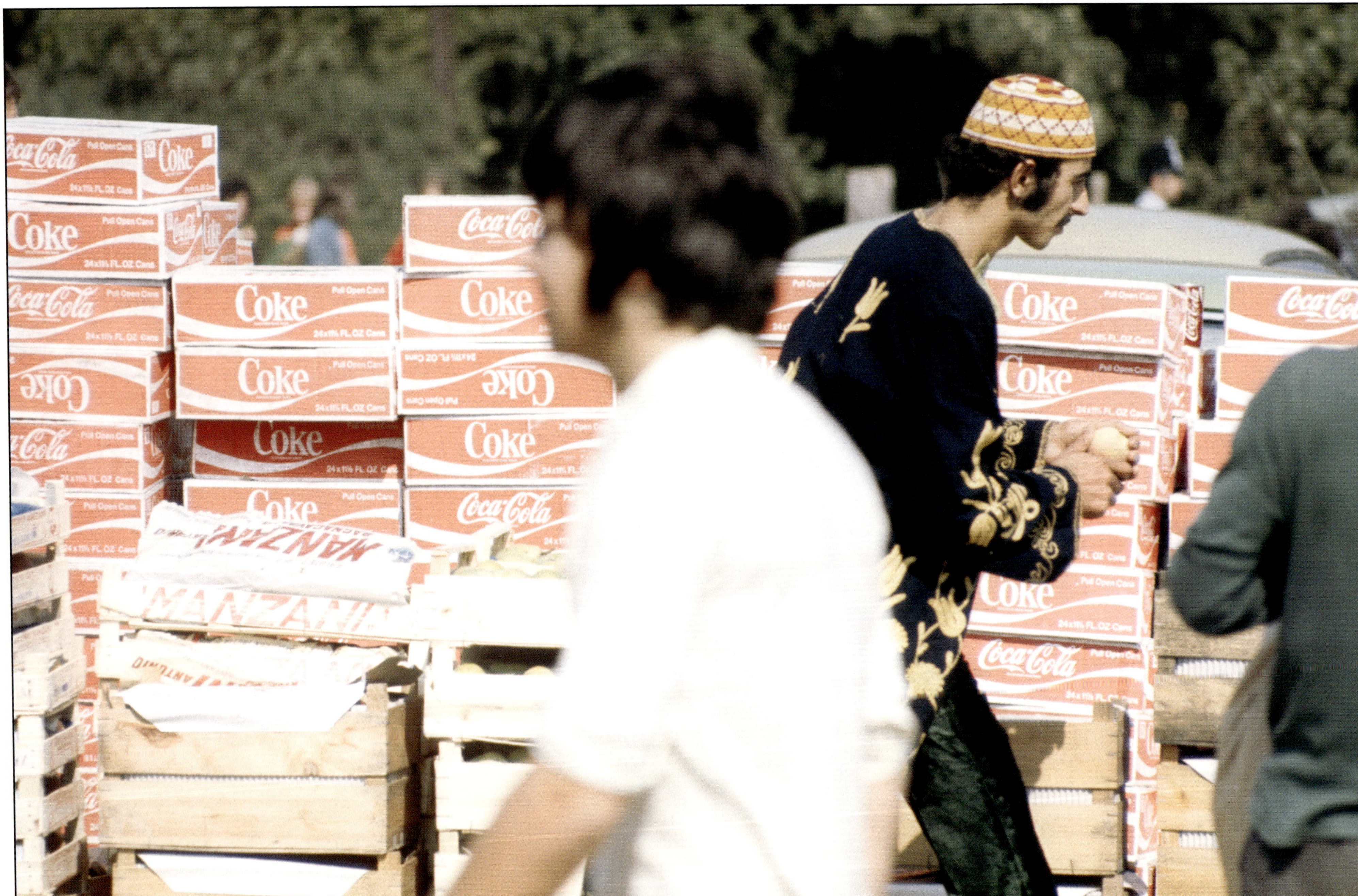

Ken Box

"IW Pop Festival. - Exhibition Caterers require a Further Few Experienced Cooks And Catering Staff. Also a number of vacancies for Cashiers which would suit responsible people on holiday and people with professional catering experience. Island residents preferred. Apply to : Exhibition Caterers Ltd, Inglefield, Madeira Road, Totland Bay. Tel : Freshwater 2162." - *Fiery Creations advertisement, I.W. County Press, August, 1970.*

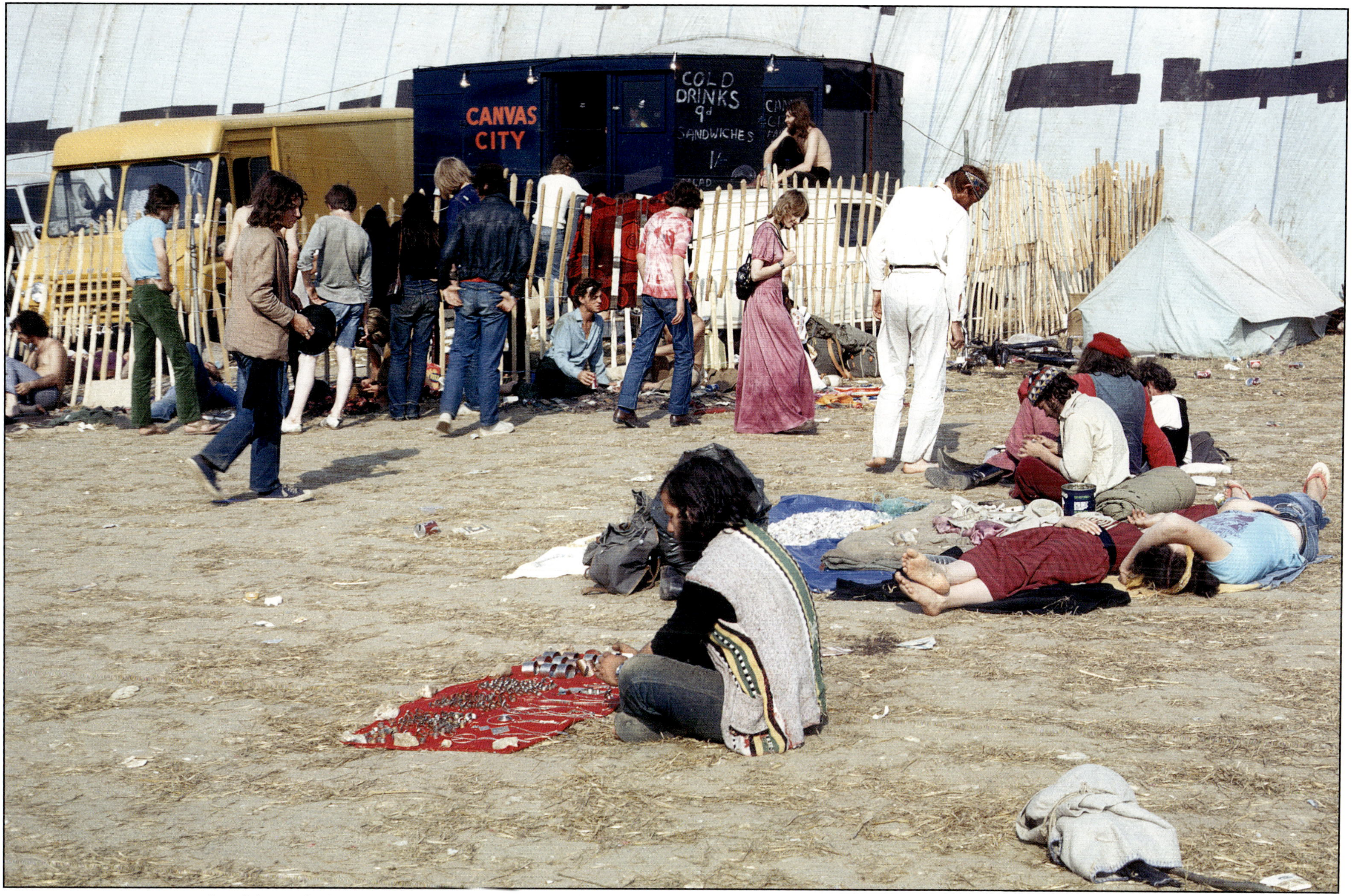

"I found the Foulks honourable, honest and they kept every promise they had made. They had taken on a stupendous production. Perhaps had they been older and wiser they would have refined it down a bit, but they didn't, and so it was a spontaneous and therefore chaotic experience. And all the better for it. There was a great deal of comradeship, of trust, and of affection. I found it an uplifting experience."
The Reverend Robert Bowyer, on-site minister.

Ken Box

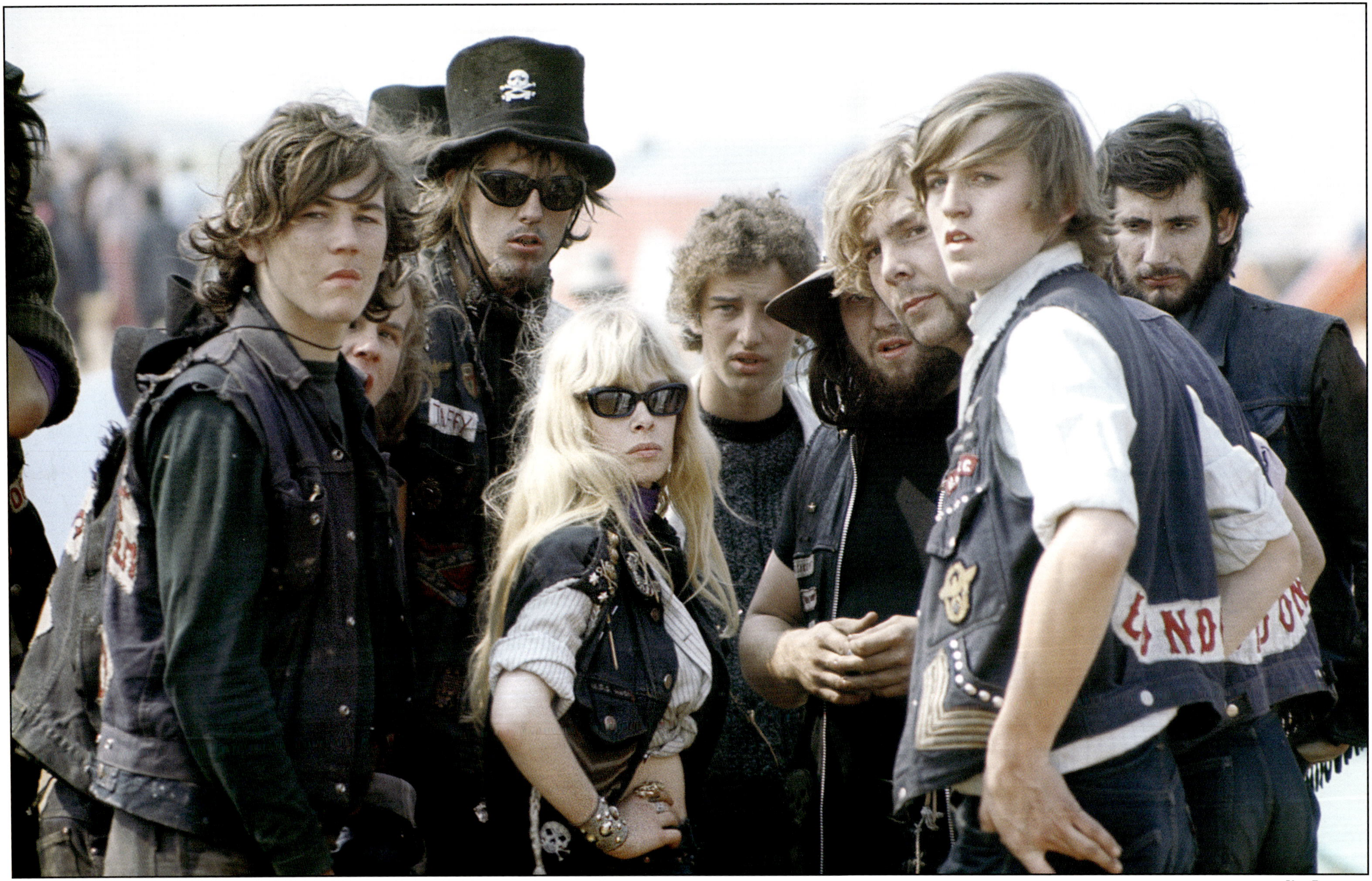

Ken Box

"I remember Dad telling me his account of photographing the Hells Angels. They spotted him, approached and surrounded him, objected to being photographed and demanded his camera. Negotiations went on for several minutes but somehow he managed to walk away with the camera and exposed film intact. I never quite understood how he managed that as he said they were quite aggressive."
Richard Box, son of Ken Box, 2020.

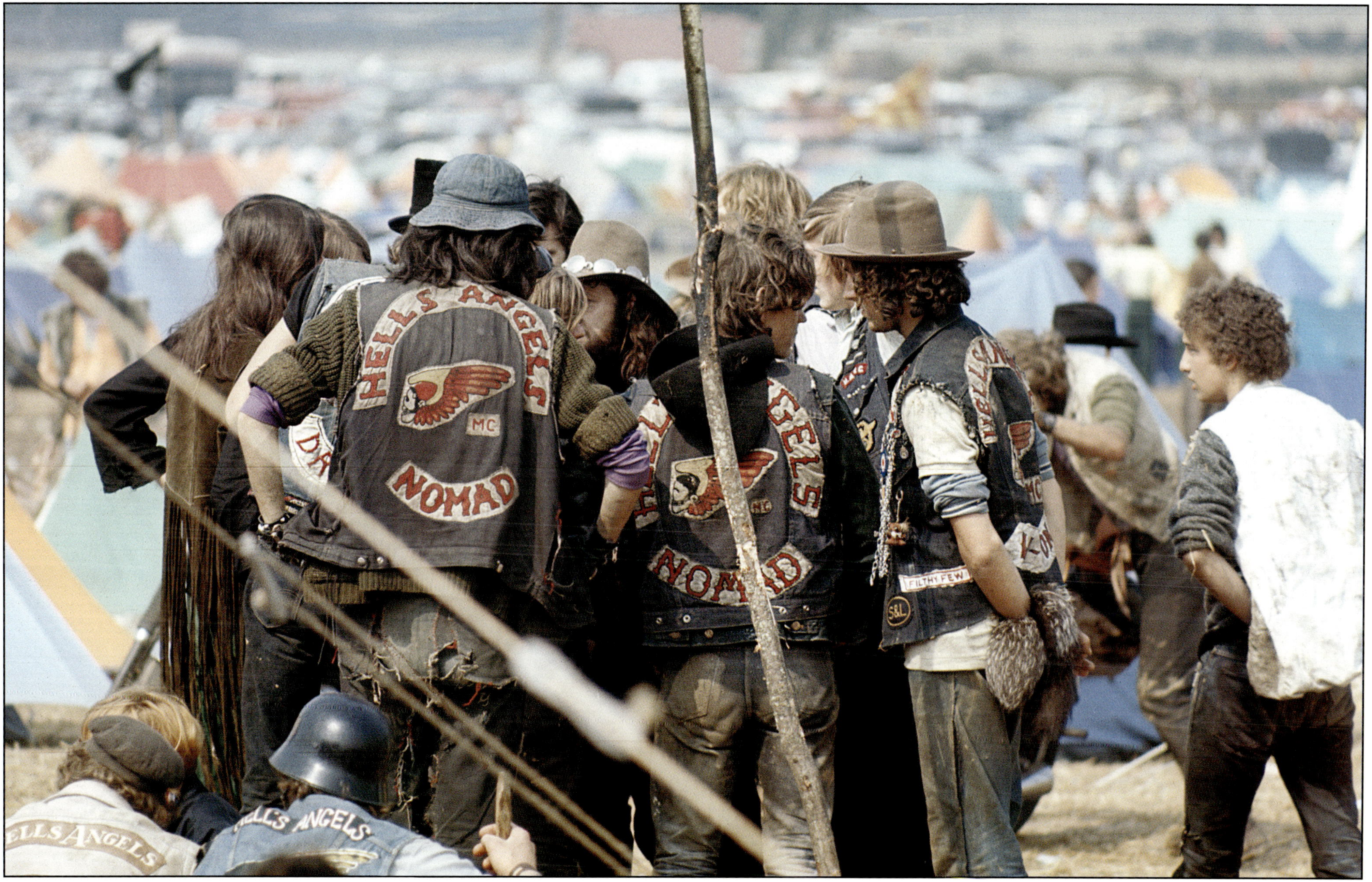

Ken Box

"An invasion by Hell's Angels was stopped at mainland ferry terminals by the police. Some of the Angels left their motorcycles on the other side and came over to the Island afoot, but weapons were confiscated beforehand. The police said they were prepared to deal with any kind of trouble from these people or any other troublemakers." - *I.W. County Press, September 5, 1970.*

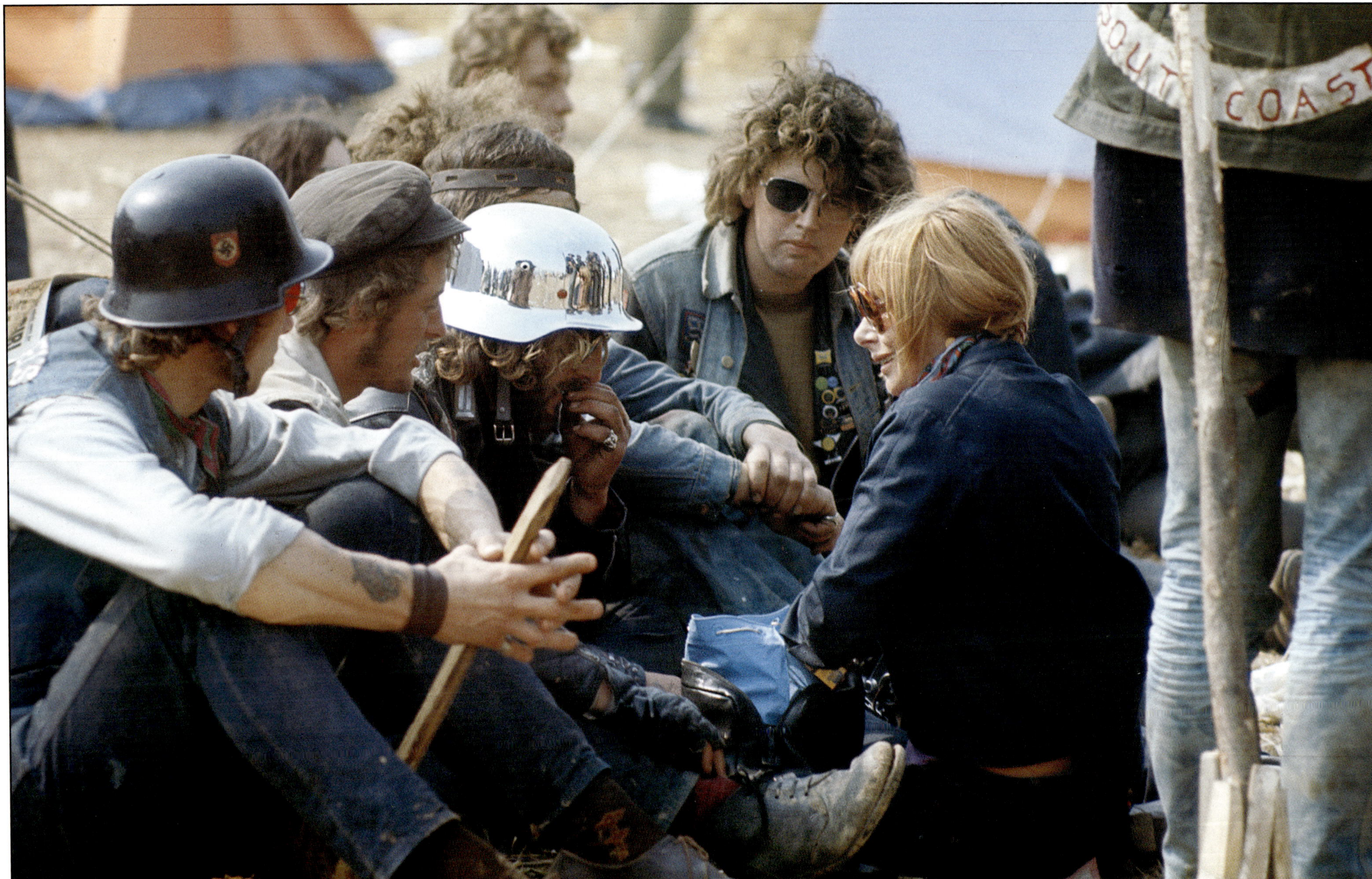

Ken Box

"Although most of the Hells Angels early arrivals were stripped of bikes, helmets and weapons before they got on the Island, by Sunday some 40 of them built up their corporate image sufficiently to terrorize a few kids and concessionaires. This, of course was reported as a looting rampage; in fact, it was quelled in short order by the police." - *Rolling Stone Magazine, October 1970.*

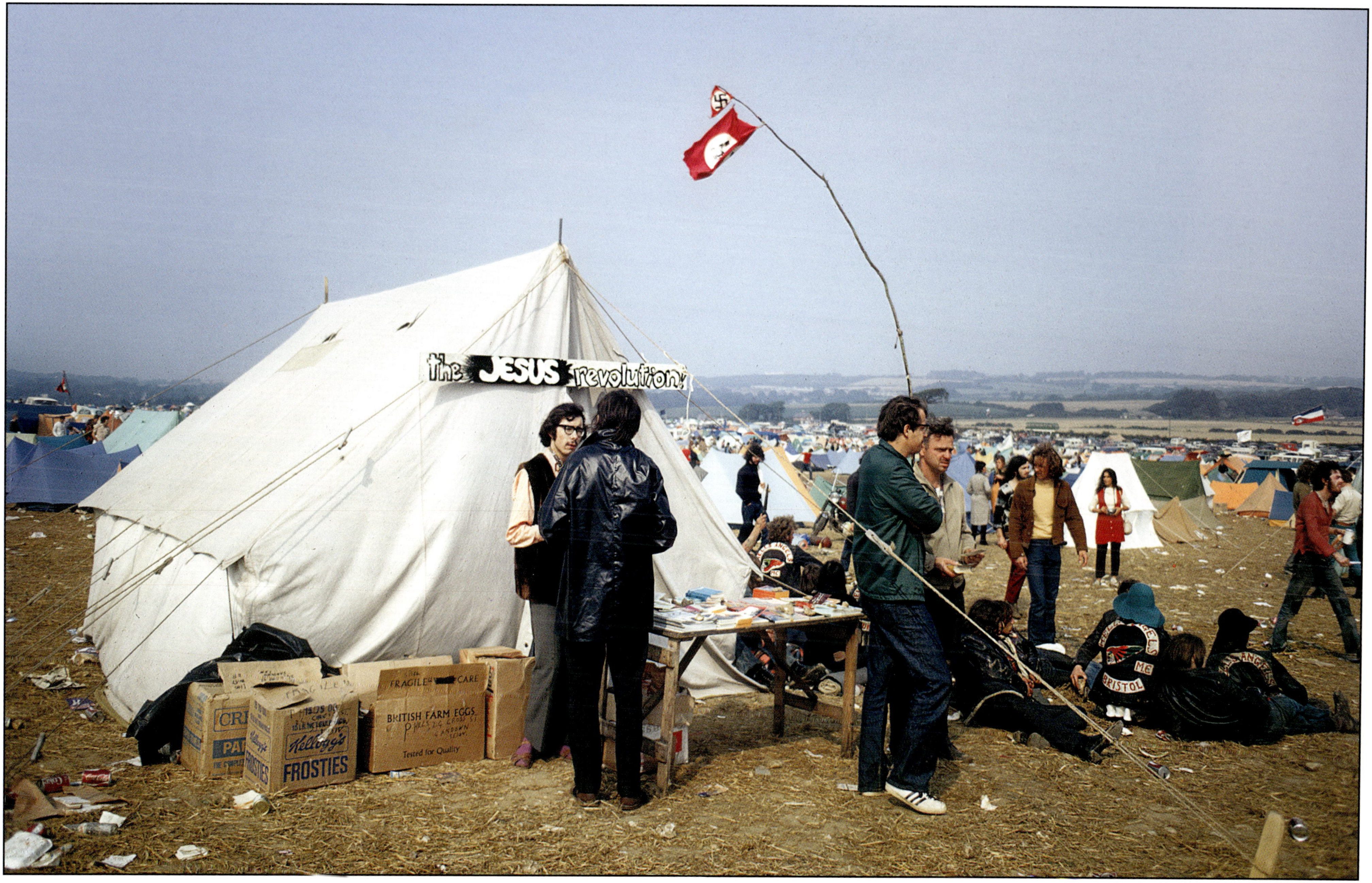

Ken Box

"Marching behind a Nazi style swastika banner, Hell's Angels, together with the anarchists from Devastation Hill, made a foray against catering stalls and fences surrounding the arena. They caused much damage and for a time terrorised the more passive element. 'It was a frightening experience for those of us who simply came to hear the music,' said one young girl." - *I.W. County Press, September 5, 1970.*

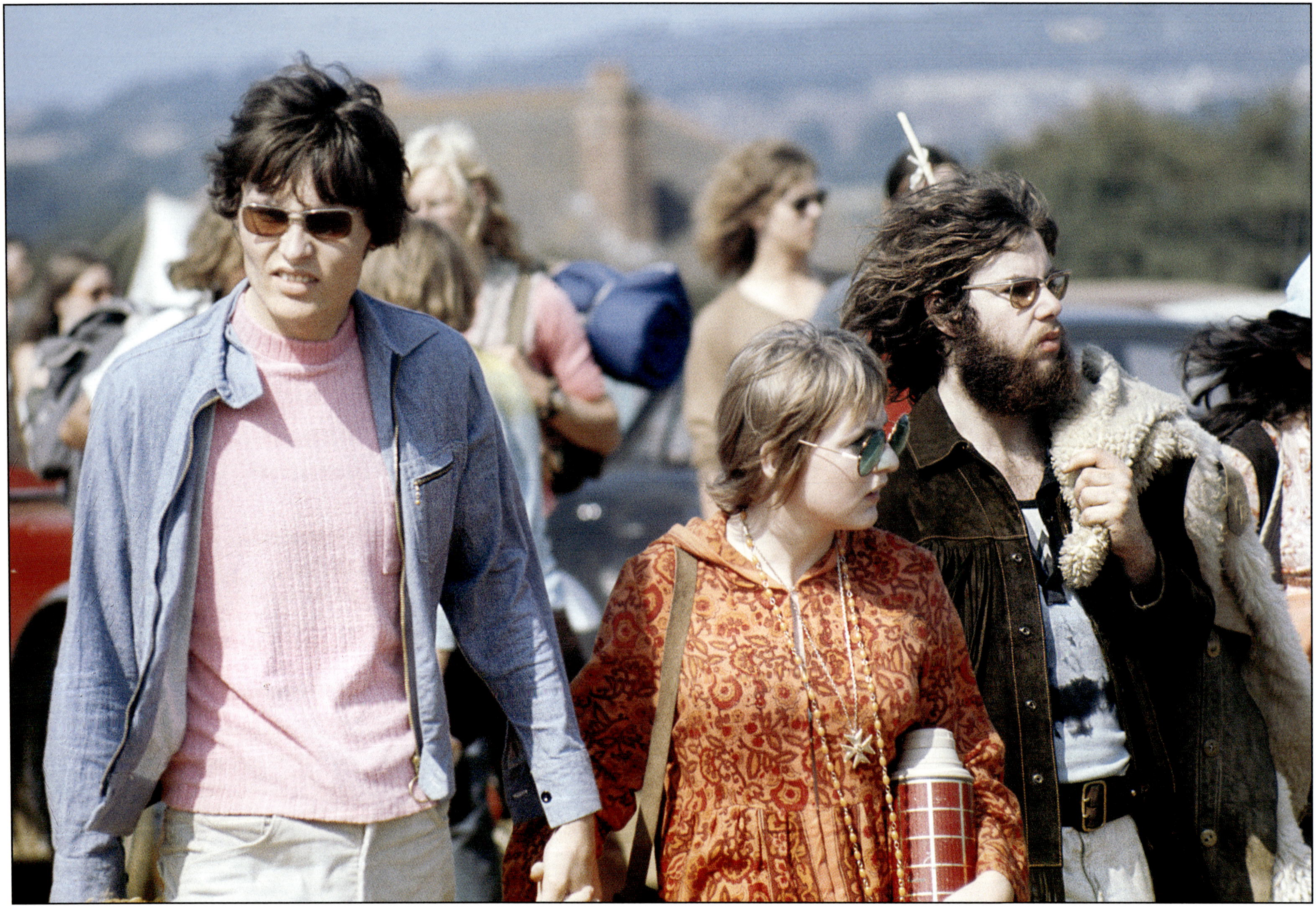

Ken Box

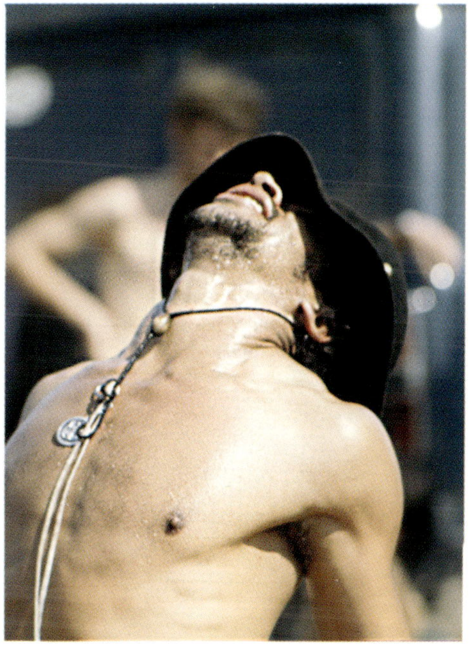
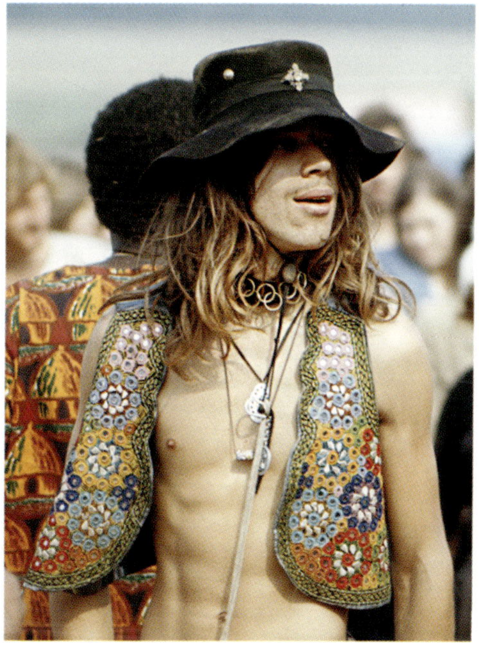
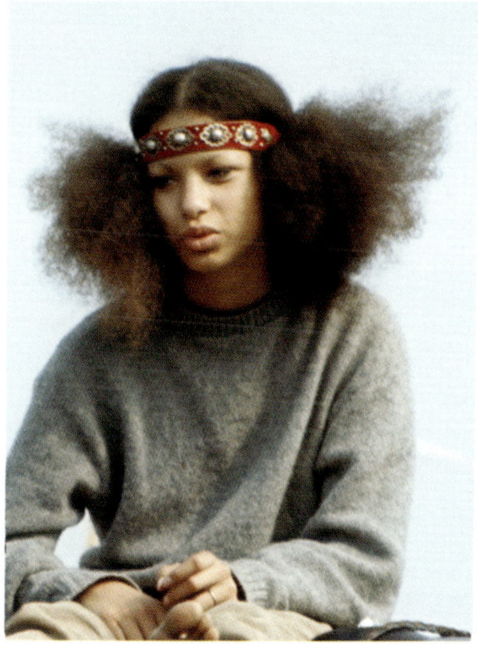
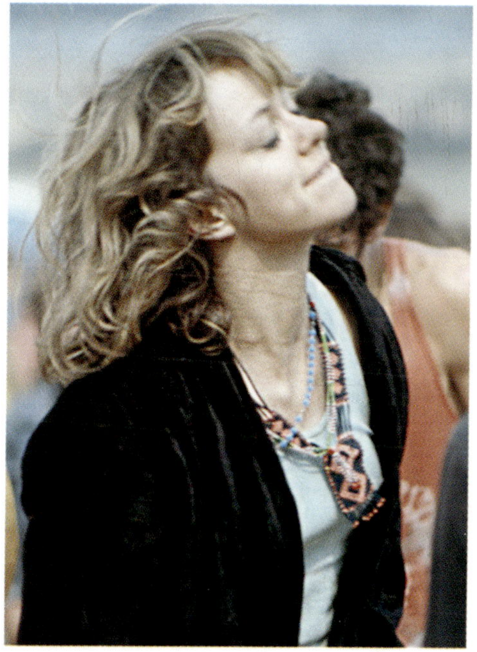
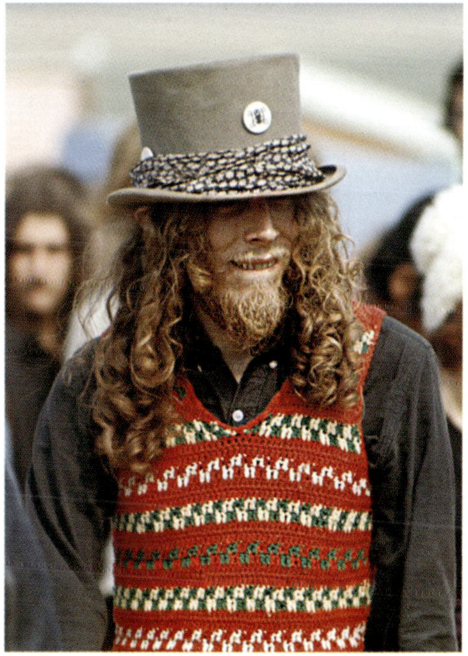
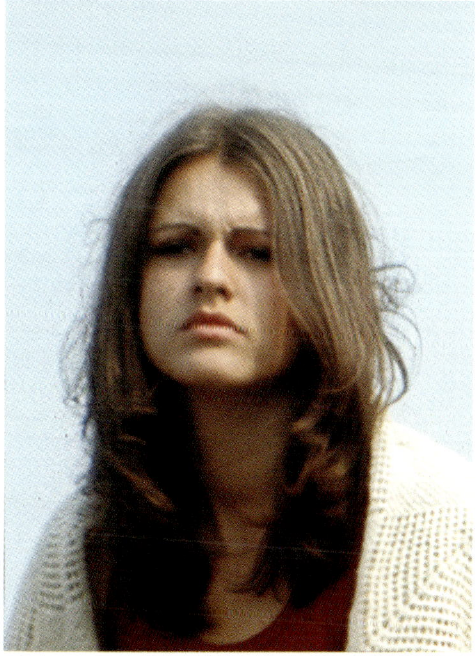
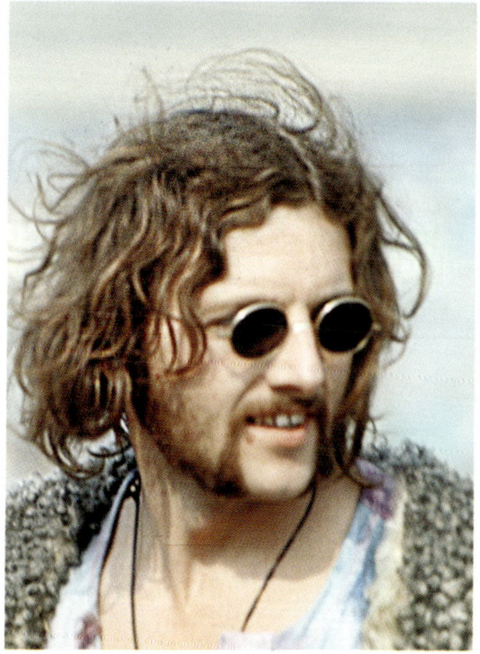
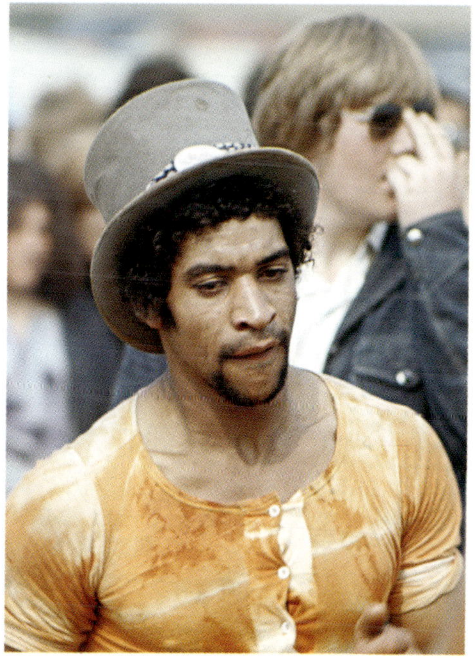

Ken Box

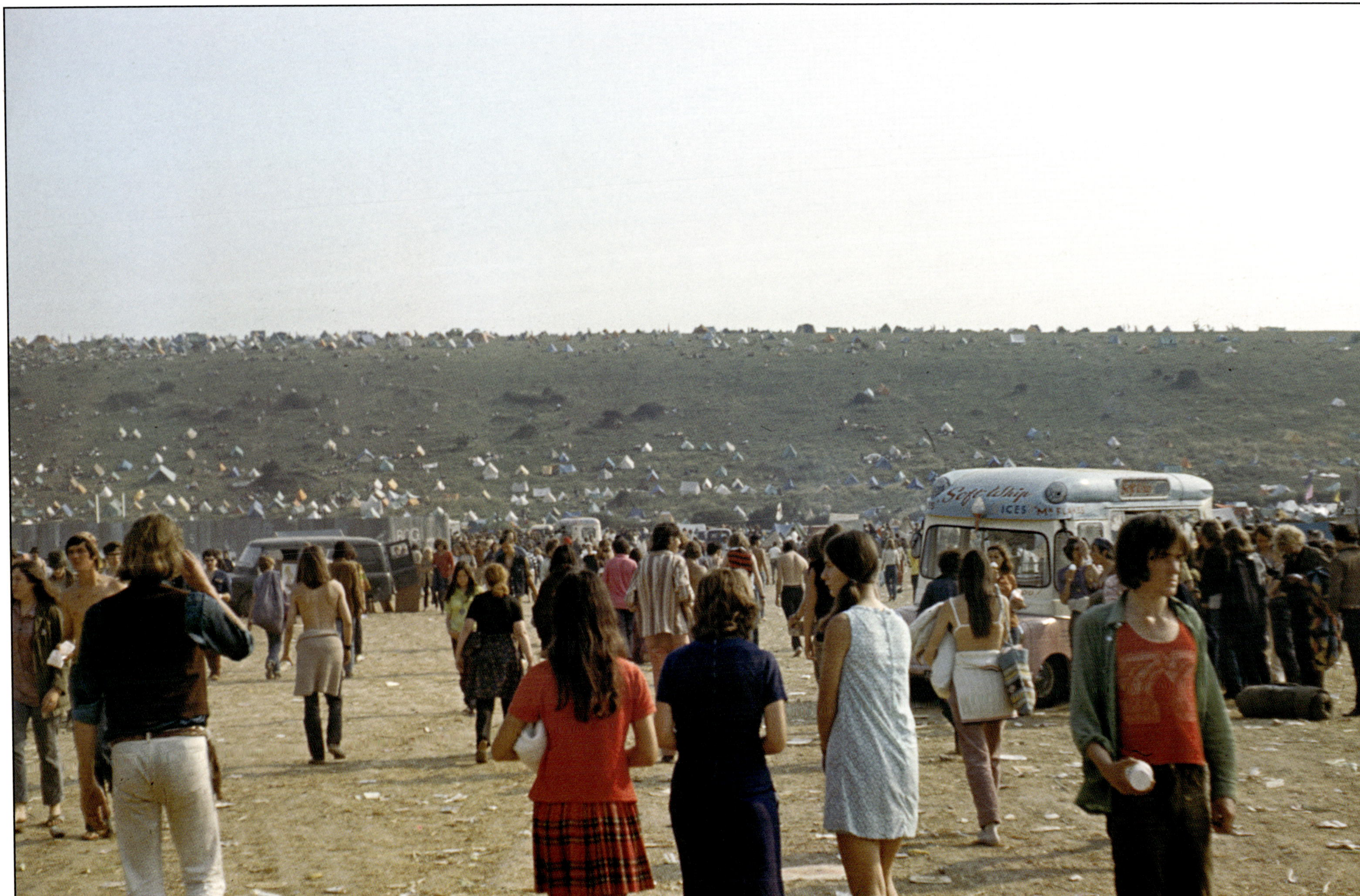

Harry Matthews

"The throng of young people visiting the Isle of Wight for the start of the pop music festival today found that they had themselves become a minor tourist attraction. Family men driving past the festival site in family cars were stopping to let the children 'see the hippies'. Anybody with a rucksack and long hair is a hippy in their view." - *David Wilsworth, The Times, August 26, 1970.*

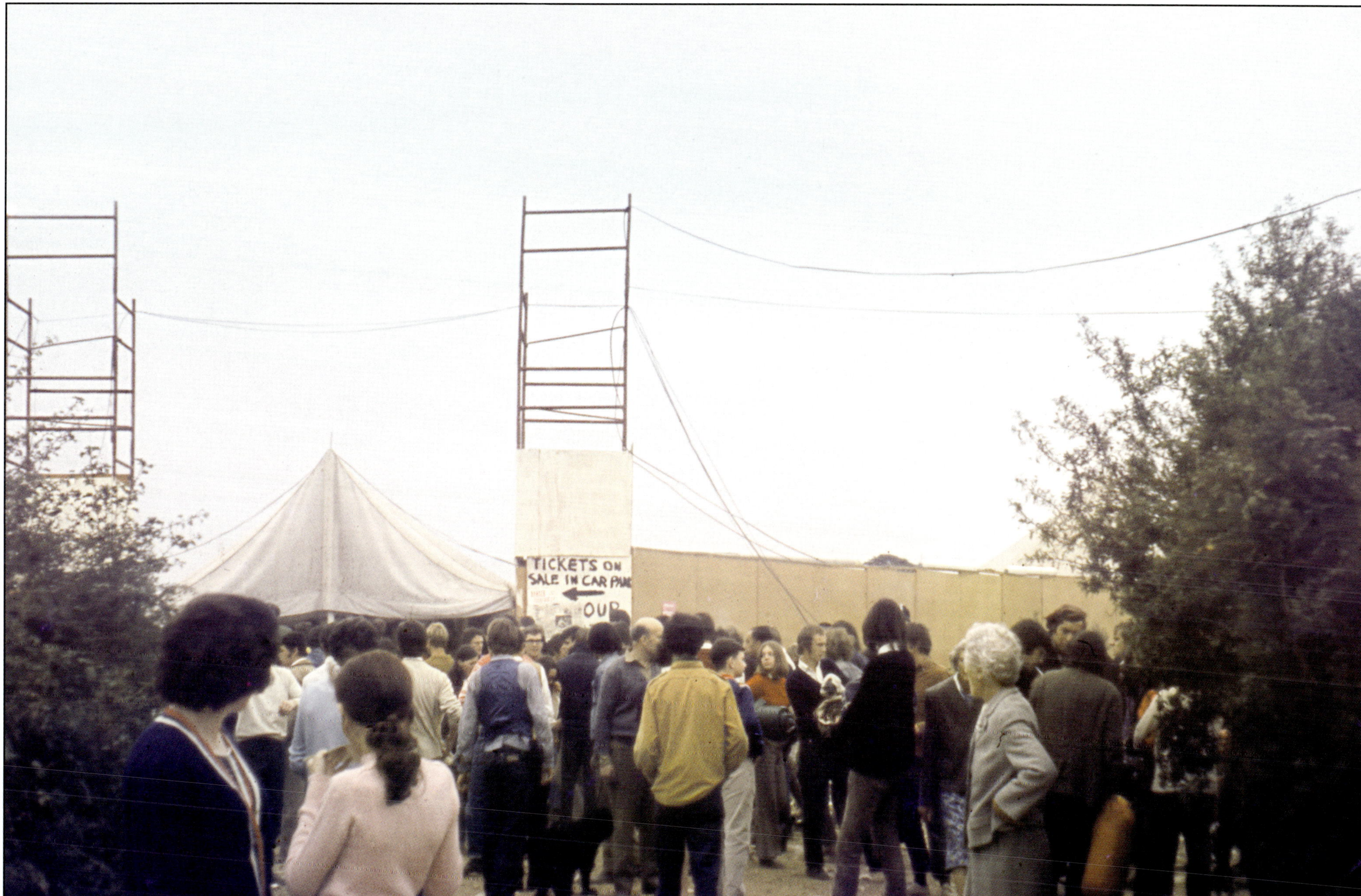

Harry Matthews

"The festival ticket price was almost the same price as a double album in those days. Three pounds was pretty cheap really, for a weekend's entertainment. It's a pound a day but some people will find anything expensive while other people will find that remarkably cheap. It depends on your point of view doesn't it?" - *Ray Foulk interviewed by the authors.*

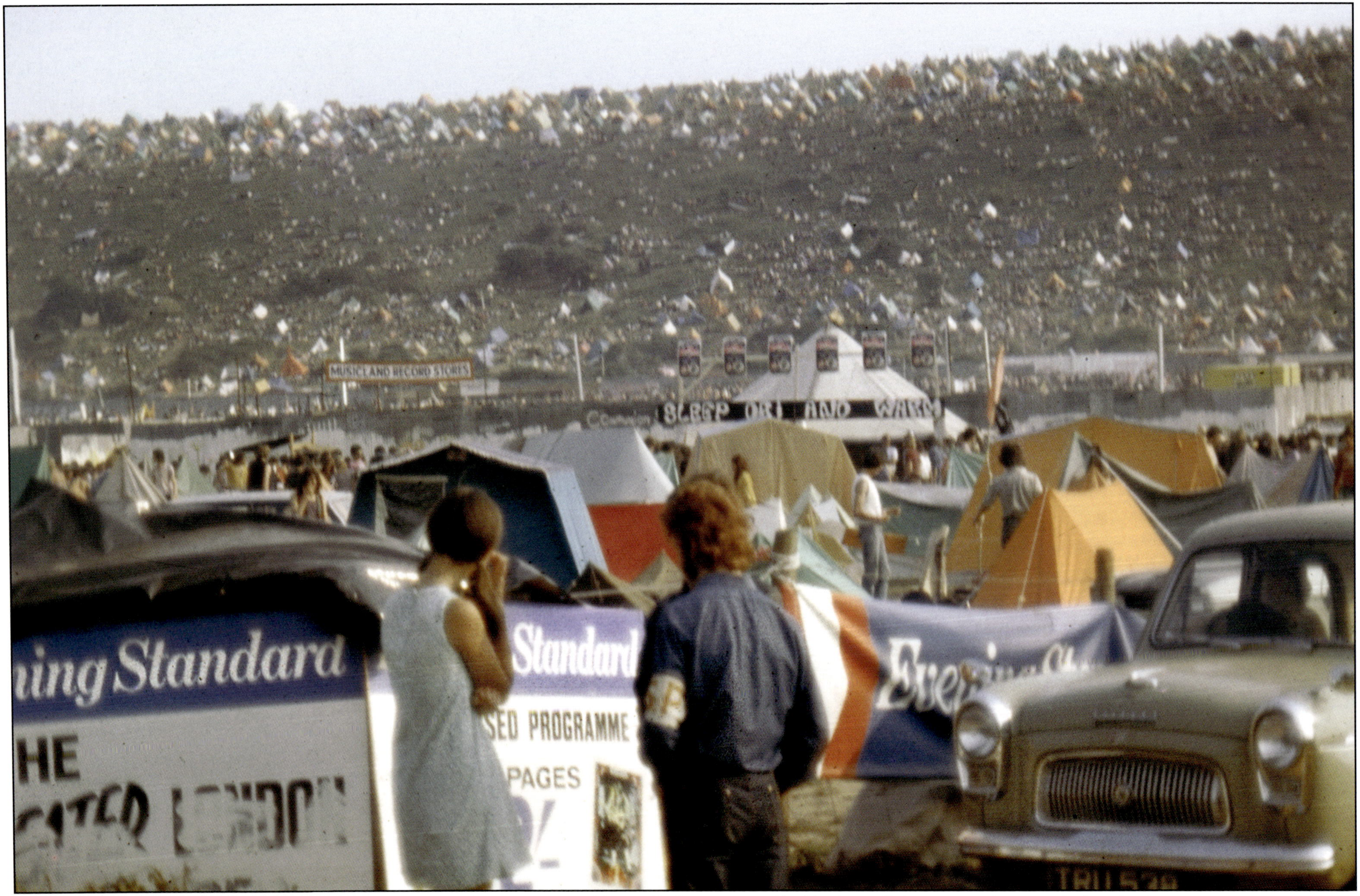

"We had a contract with the National Trust to say we'd fence off Afton Down and build a fence all the way round it. With the benefit of hindsight it was a very ill-conceived scheme. It was an impossibility to wall that down off. As fast as we could build the wall, people were taking it down at night." - *Ray Foulk interviewed by the authors.*

Harry Matthews

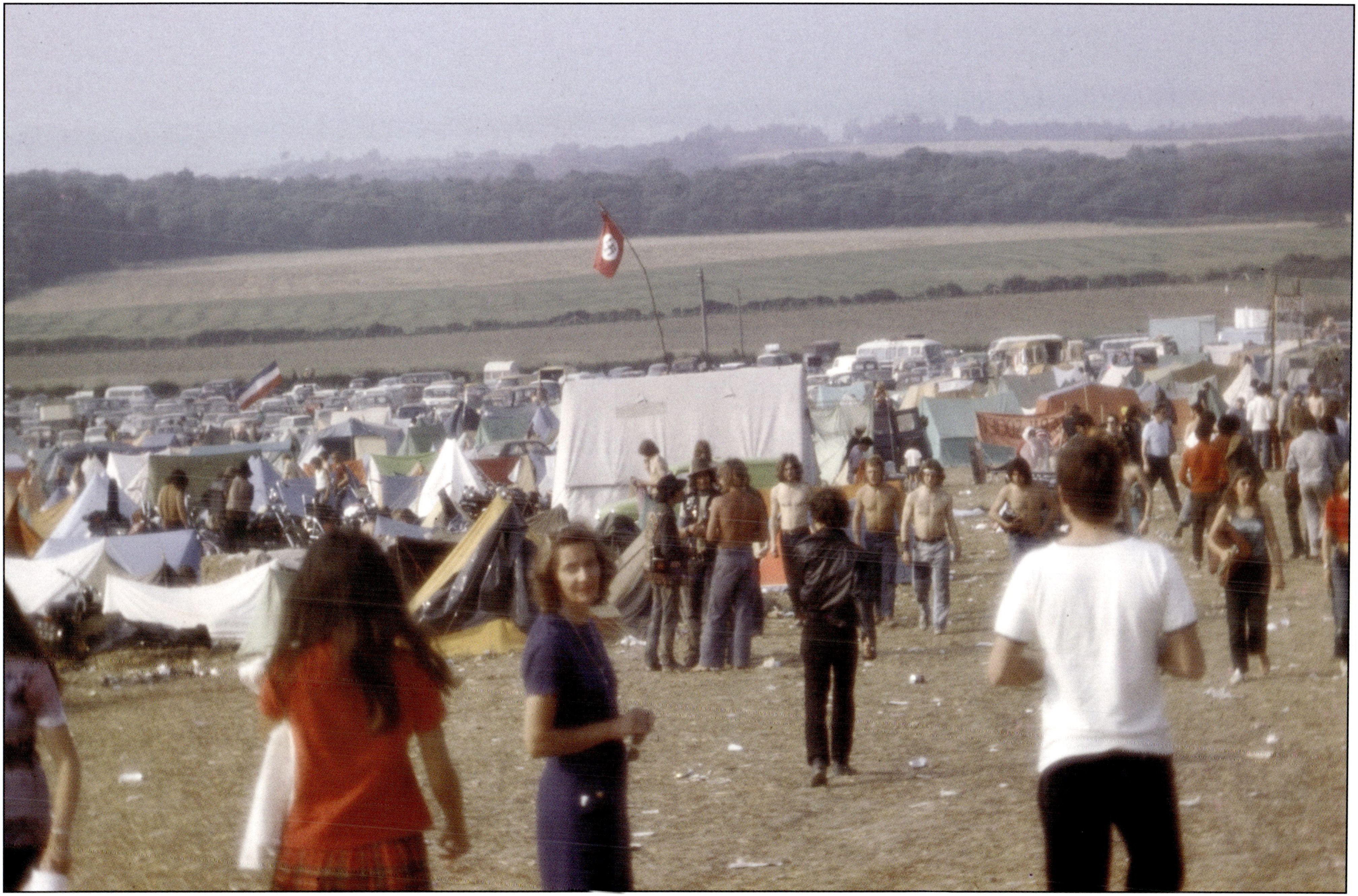

"I had really the only place in the West Wight upon which the pop festival could be held. One day a bewhiskered gentleman confronted me in a certain place and said, "If you have the festival, of course you will no longer be any part of the Isle of Wight establishment and you may indeed be sent to Coventry. Certainly you will not go to any cocktail parties on the Island that are worth going to." - *David Clarke, festival site owner.*

Harry Matthews

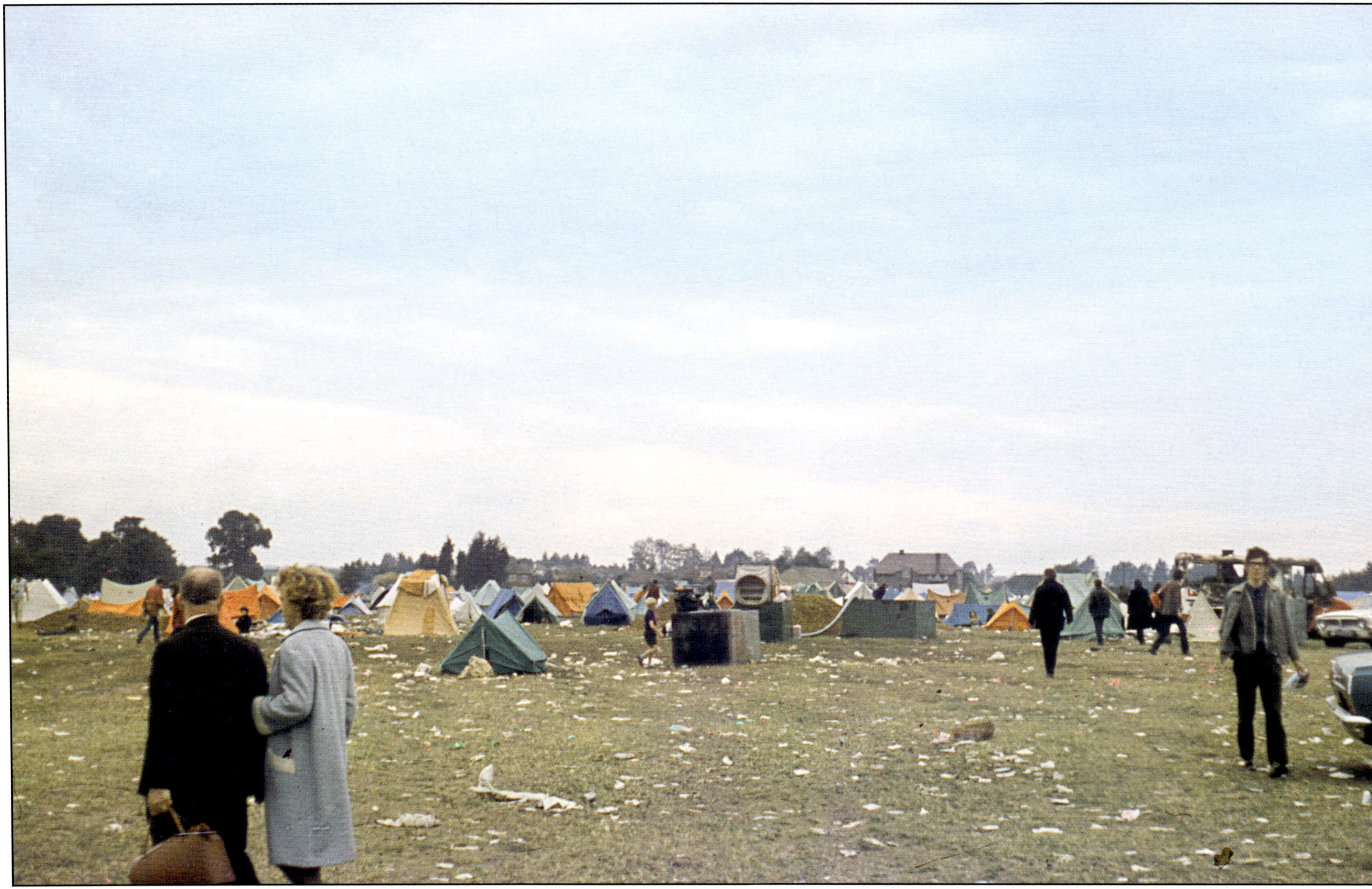

"Finally you get the go-ahead to proceed and in three weeks you've put up a new site. Then the dream you've worked on for a whole year becomes a nightmare. There are a number of people who are out to cause trouble. We gave into them by opening the gates for the first two days without charge. But they weren't satisfied, they're chanting that they want the whole festival to be free. I don't know how they think we could manage that." - *Ron Foulk, Daily Mirror interview, August 29, 1970.*

Harry Matthews

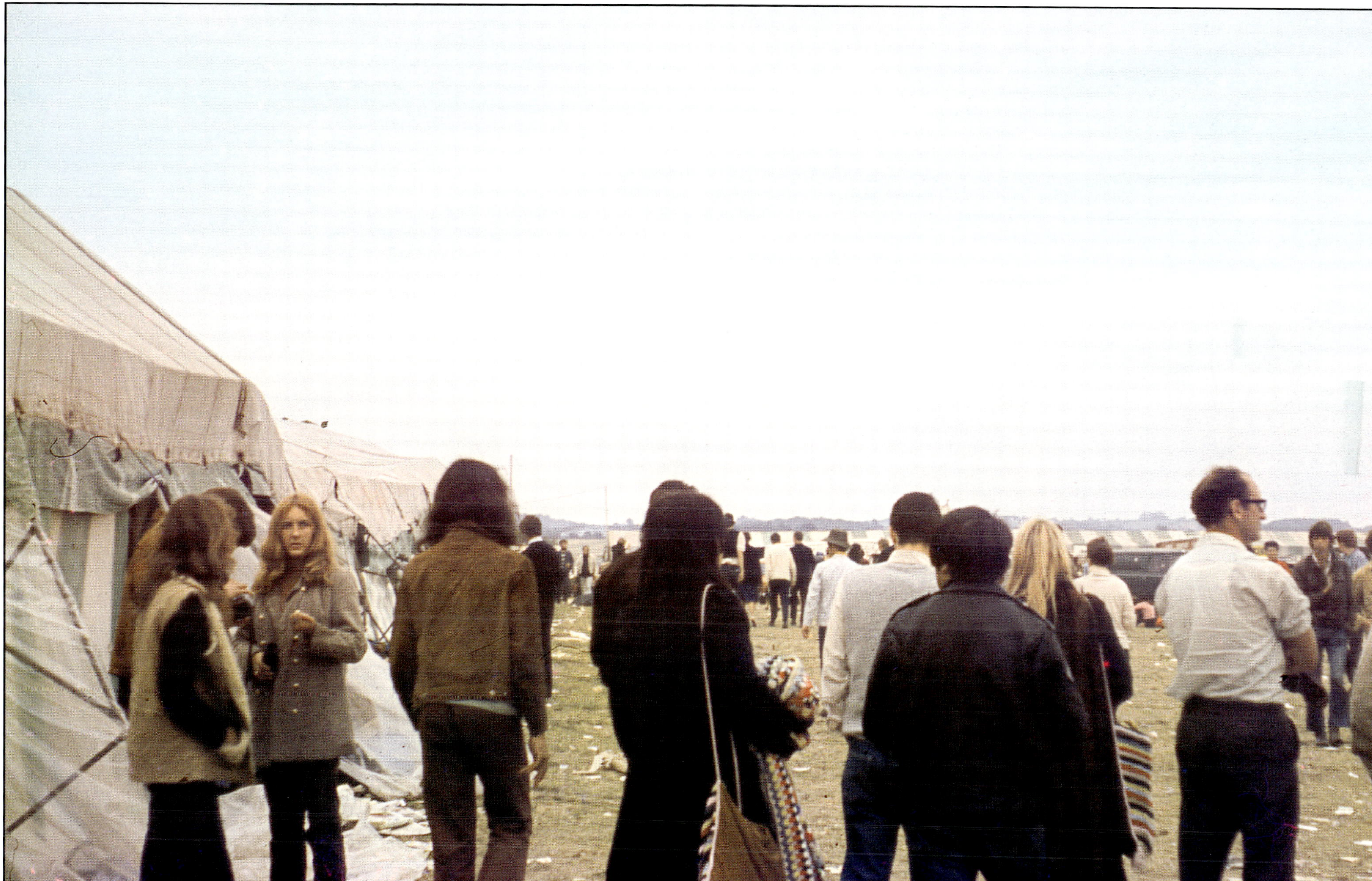

"Millionaire? I'll be lucky if we break even. This is the last festival. Enough is enough. It began as a beautiful dream but it has got out of control and become a monster. All I'll get is a million pounds headache. I don't know what I will do. I haven't had time to think. All I want to do is go home and catch up with some sleep if I can." - *Ron Foulk, Daily Mirror interview, August 29, 1970.*

Harry Matthews

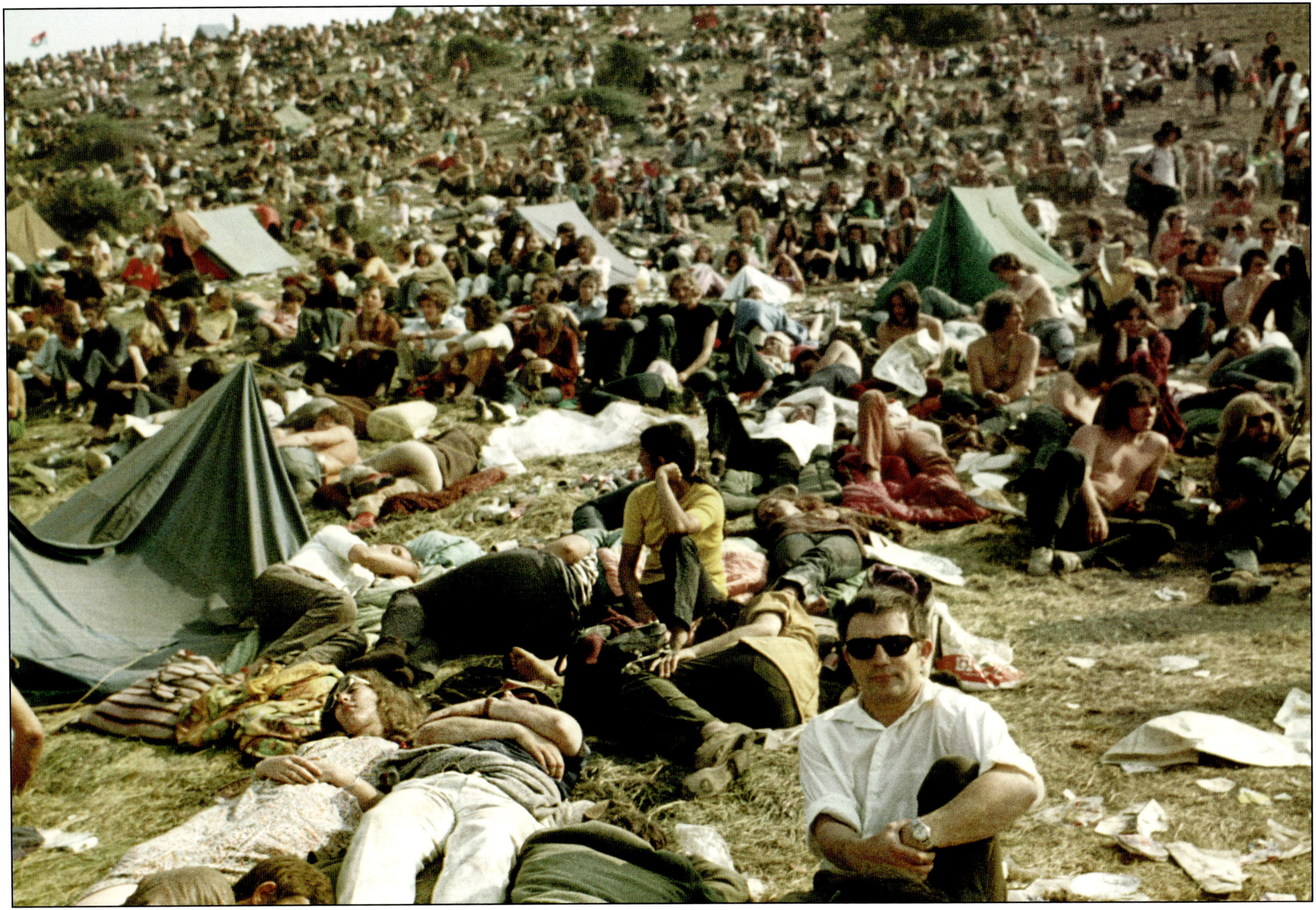

Ken Box

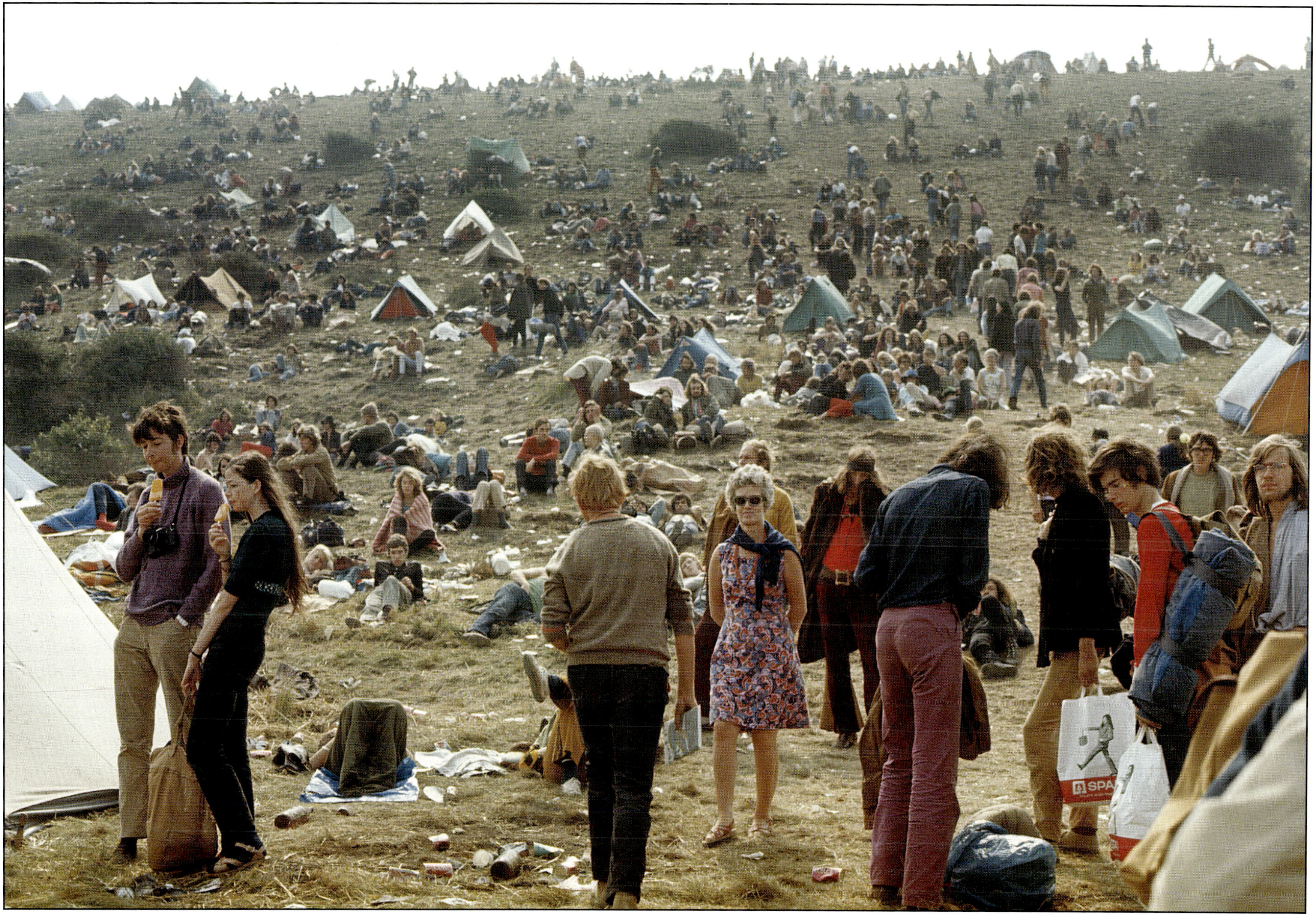

Ken Box

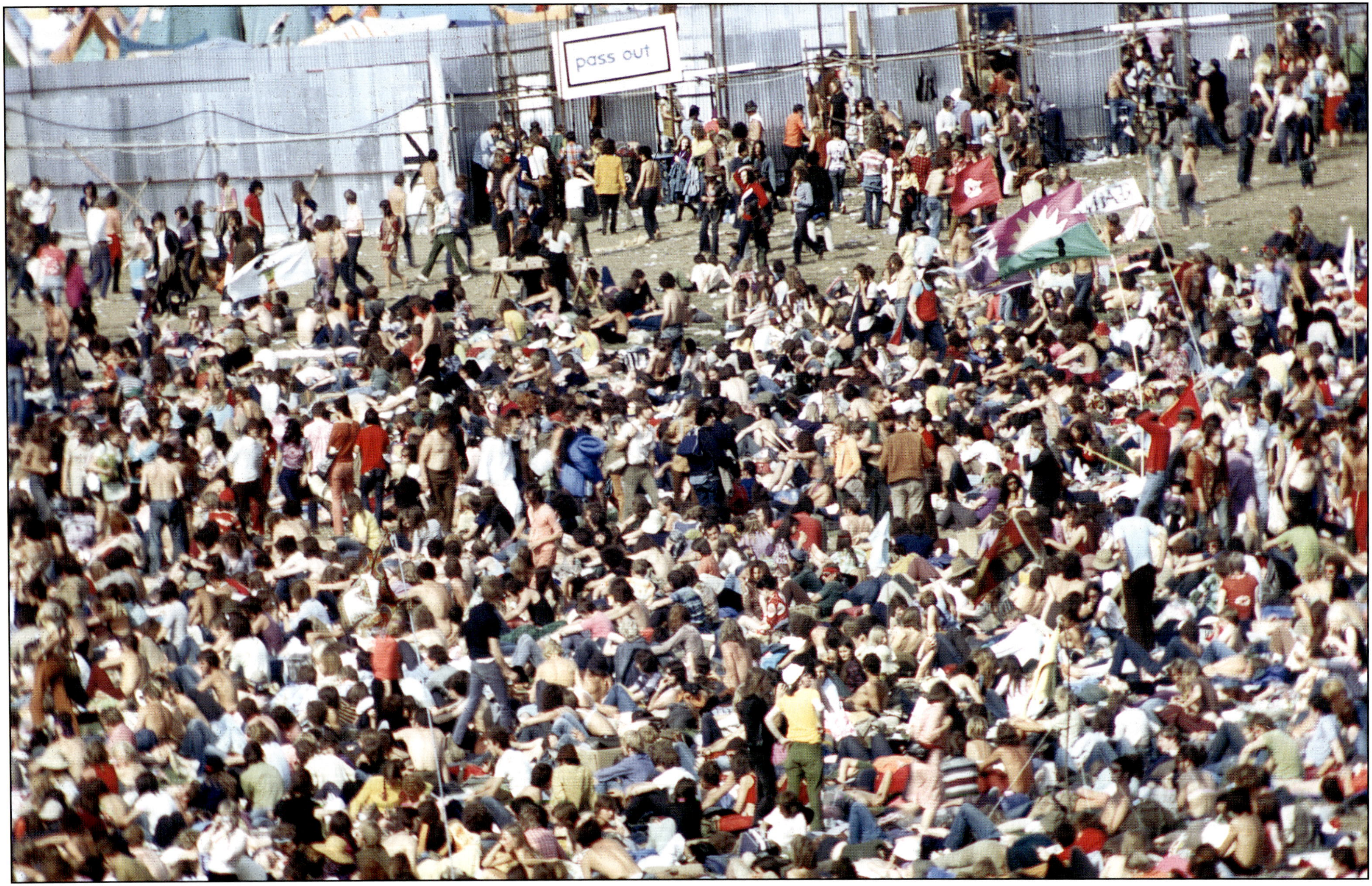

Ken Box

"Pop Festival Disorganises Island - The organisers of the pop festival at East Afton, Freshwater, stated at the weekend that it would be the last such event they would hold on the Island. Estimates of the attendance varied from 150,000 to 400,000. The presence of so large a gathering disorganised life in the Island, particularly in the West Wight, where many people are angry at the intrusion of such a horde of unwelcome guests, against their expressed wishes." - *I.W. County Press, September 5, 1970.*

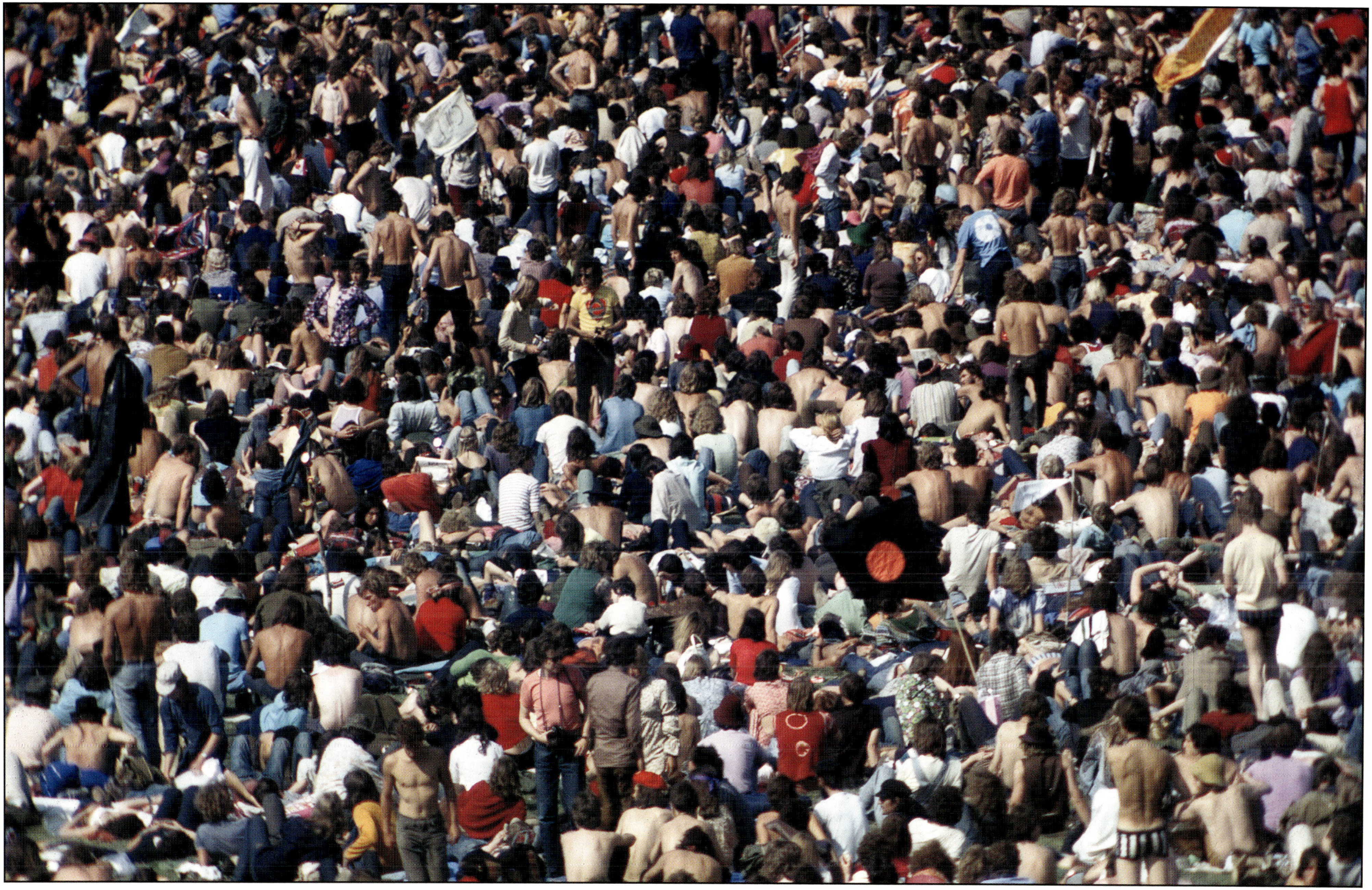

Ken Box

"A few days before the event, Fiery released their pre-festival estimated expenditure : Artists' Fees – £250,000; Site construction, fencing, water supply etc – £100,000; Staff wages – £40,000; Office and admin – £30,000. Total : £420,000. Total audience required at £3 per ticket to break even was 140,000." - *Friends Magazine, October 15, 1970.*

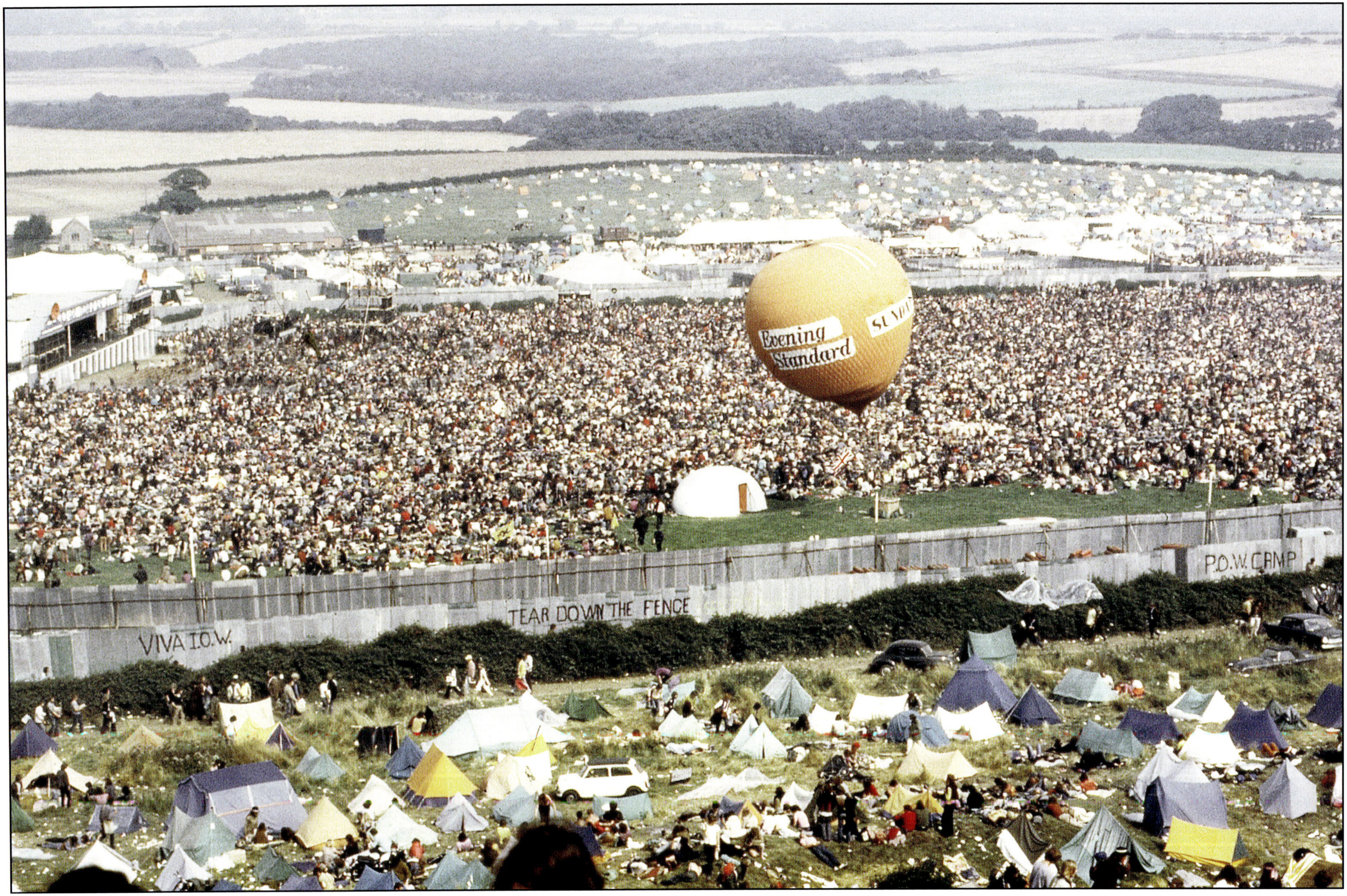

Ken Box

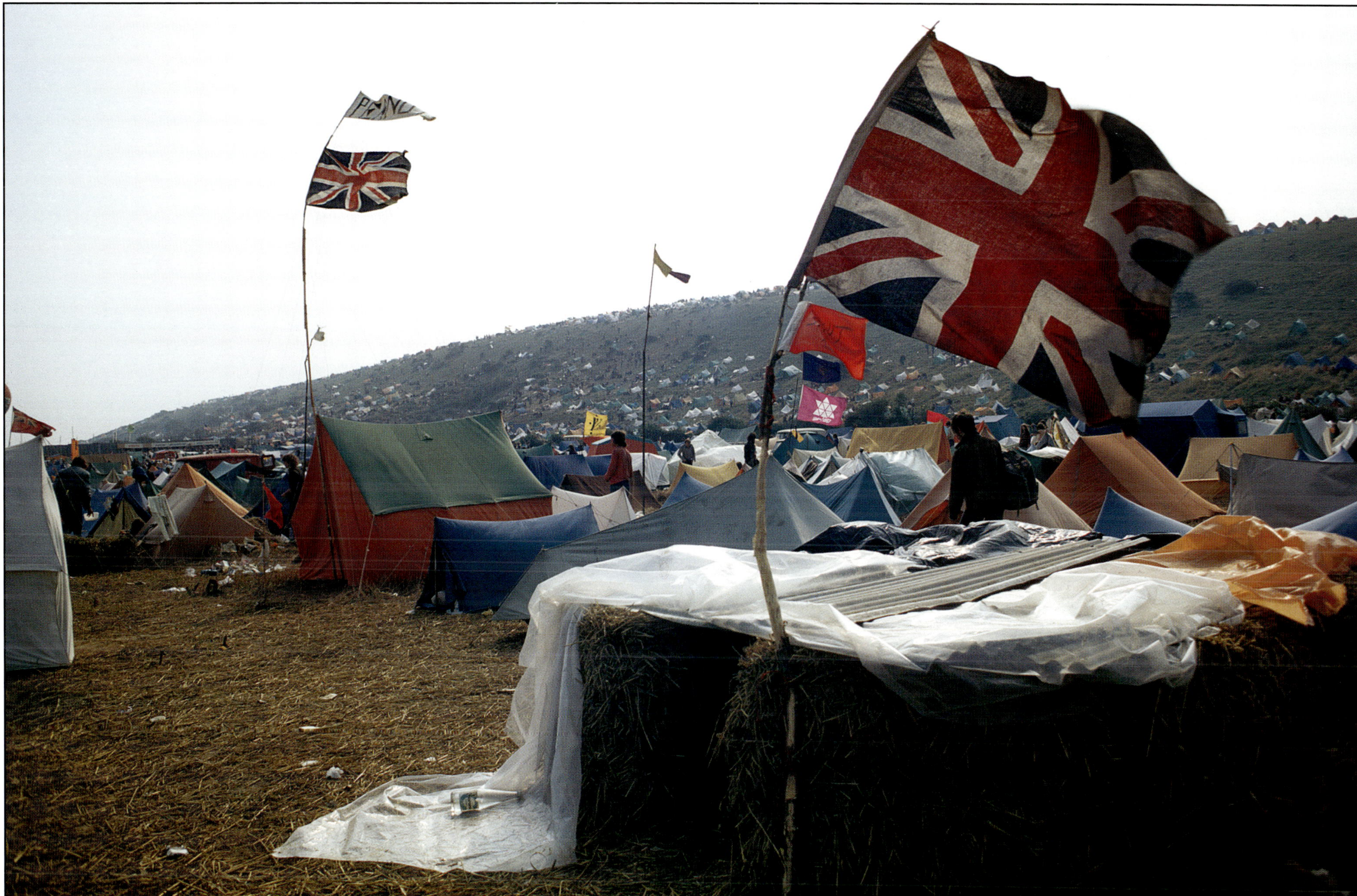

Ken Box

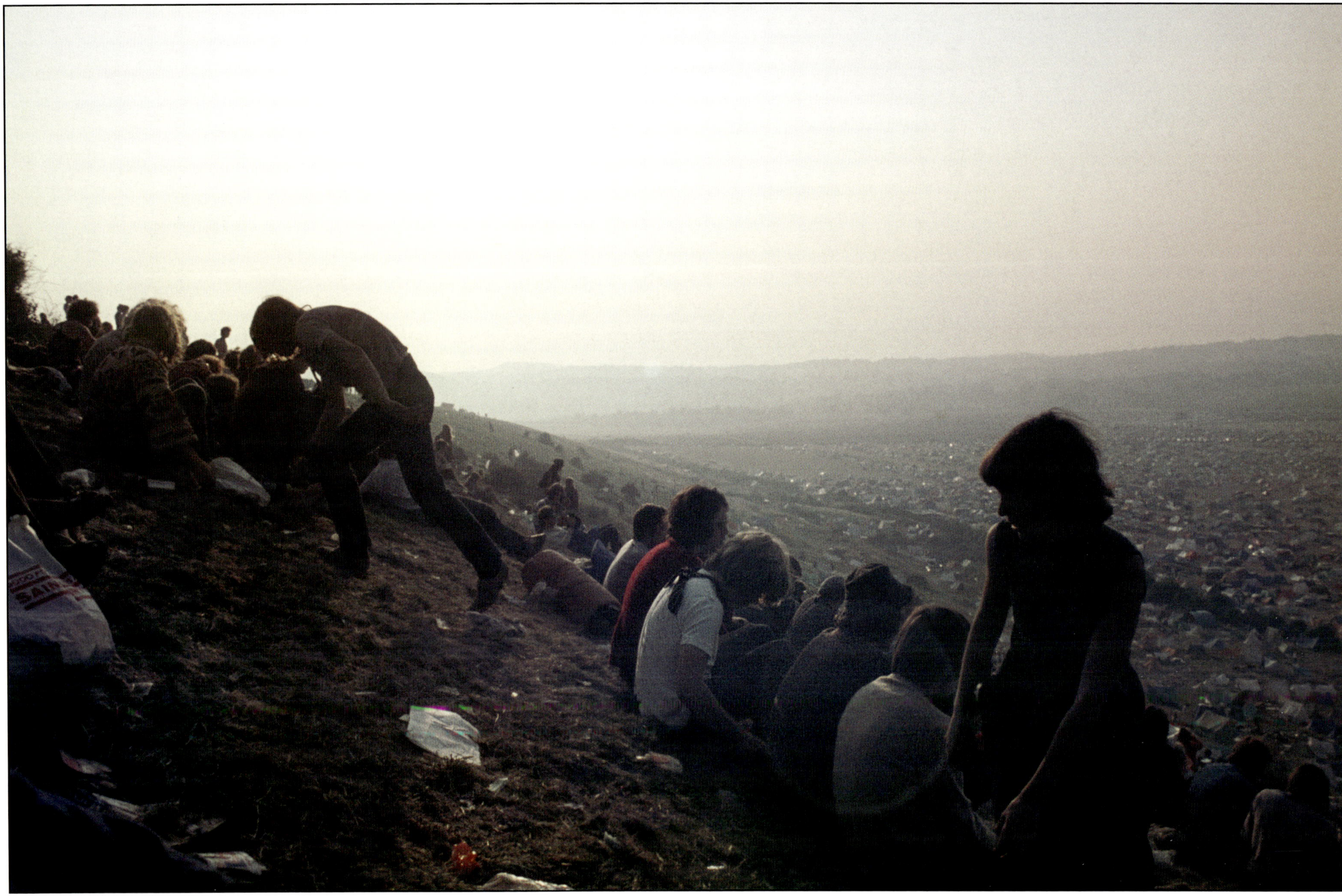

"We weren't in the greed business at all. It just wasn't like that because if anything our downfall was being too generous and trying to do too much for our public. We were putting on the best show we could, with the best facilities, and spending too much money." - *Ray Foulk, interviewed by the authors.* *Ken Box*

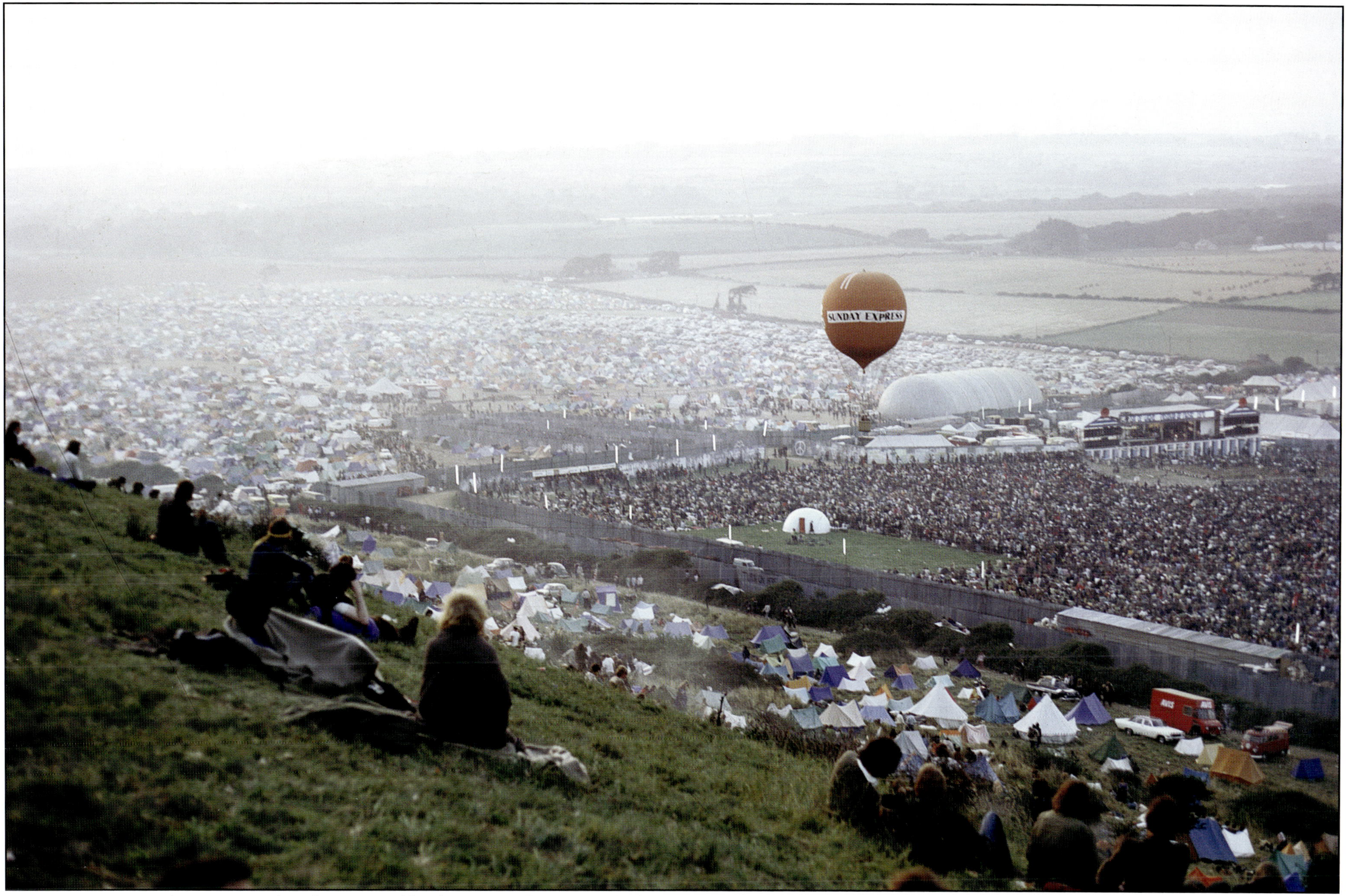

"When one remembers the amount of local opposition there was to the festival and the local prophets' warning of certain violence, it is extraordinary that the vast majority of the people who came here did nothing more destructive than sit on the grass and listen to the music."
Michael Nicholson, ITN news report, August 31, 1970.

Ken Box

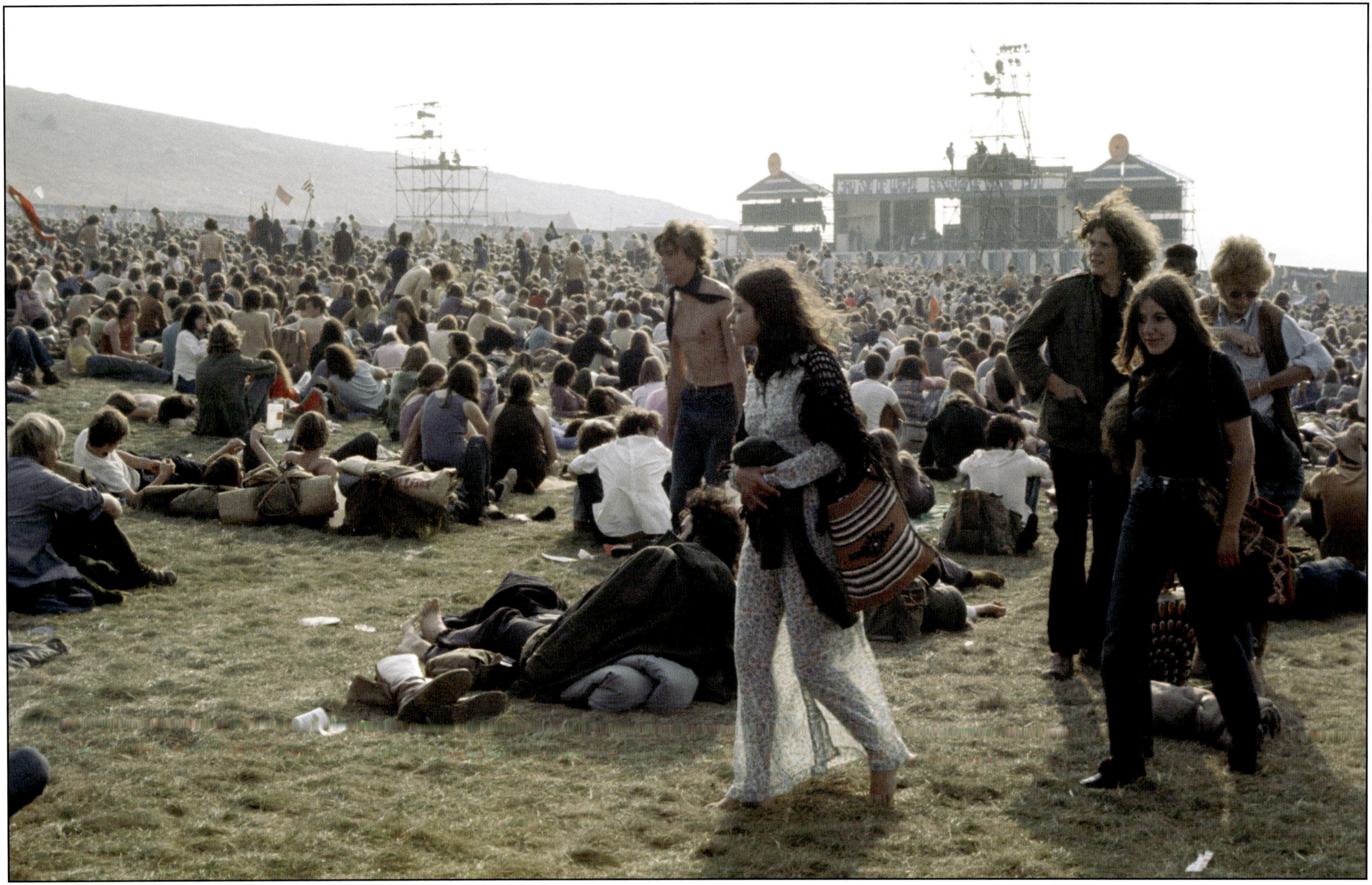

Ken Box

"I spent two days at this festival incognito in my hippie outfit — [Interruption.] — and the scene both during and after the festival was one of indescribable squalor and filth. The people who organise events of this kind are not people who appreciate the needs of the young but are promoters who seek maximum profit out of what they do. [Hon. Members: "That is Tory philosophy."] I very much doubt, judging from the young gentlemen I know, that they were Tories." - *Mark Woodnutt MP during second reading of the IOW Bill, Hansard, March 18, 1971.*

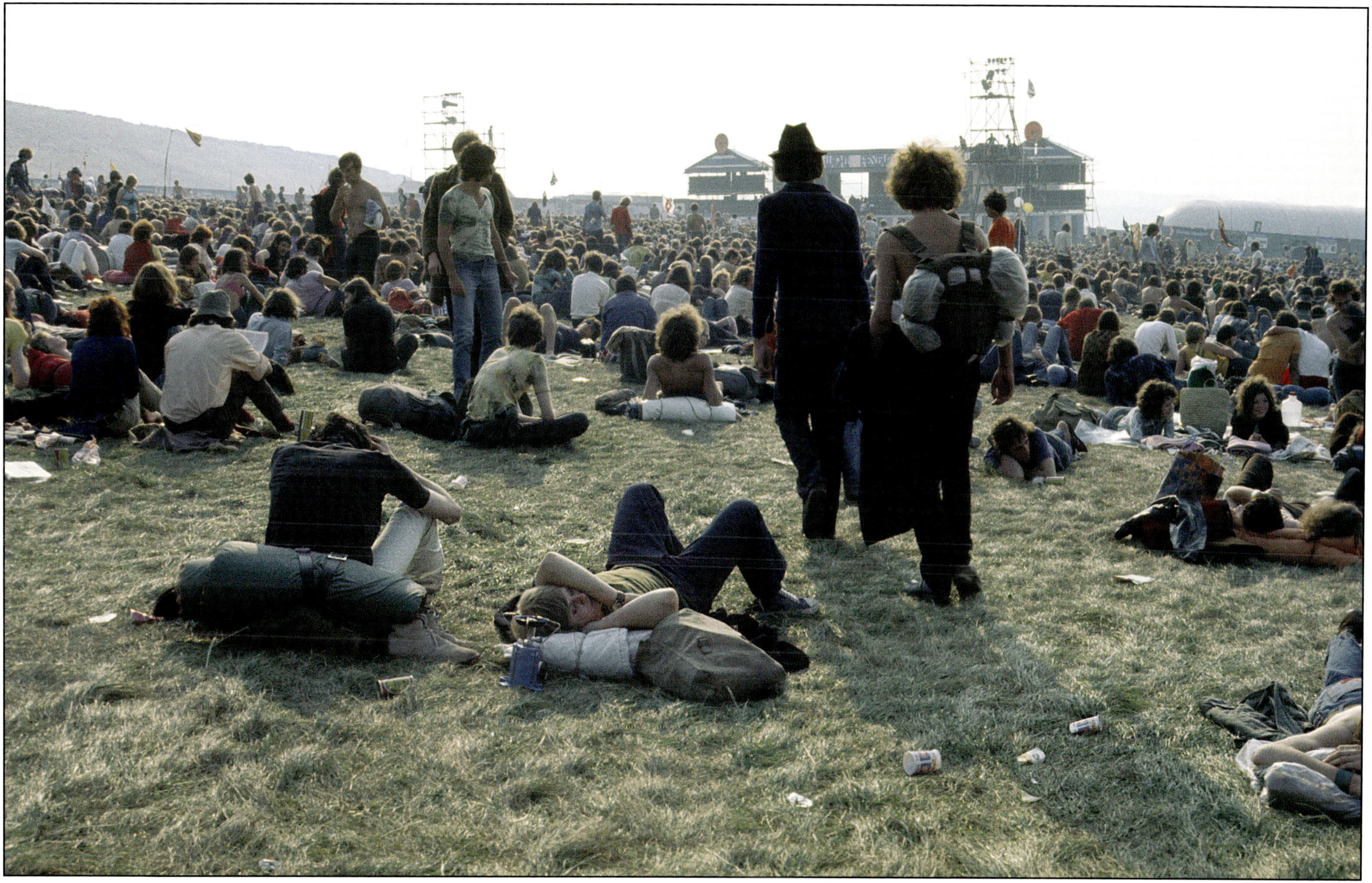

"We got some marvellous material for our programme *Southern Scene,* which gives an objective impression of what the festival was really like. The vast majority of the youngsters there were normal, average, intelligent people in 9-to-5 jobs who were just enjoying themselves on a long holiday weekend that was slightly different. It was like a trip to another world. We have tried to put the troublemakers, who were a very small minority, in perspective - an aspect which I don't think has been shown properly before." - *Christopher Peacock, Southern Television reporter, September 16, 1970.*

Ken Box

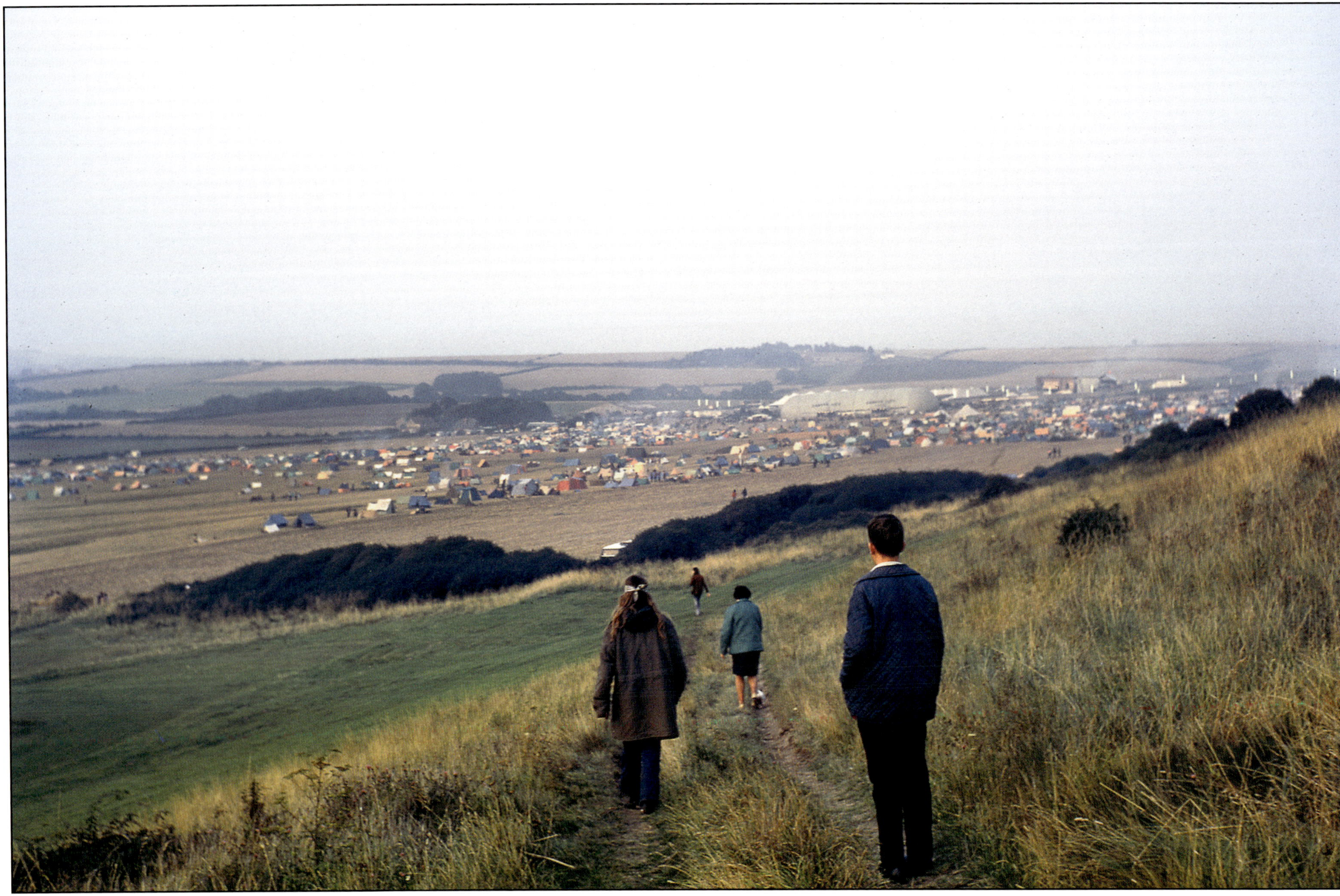

"After an initial cold shoulder from the festivalgoers, as the festival progressed they saw that some of our colleagues were enjoying it probably as much as they were and we felt we could get in amongst them and talk to them. A good repartee was built up and I think that went a long, long way to allaying any serious sort of trouble on the site. The amount of trouble we experienced was very minimal. Yes, I enjoyed it." - *P.C Pointer, Local policeman.*

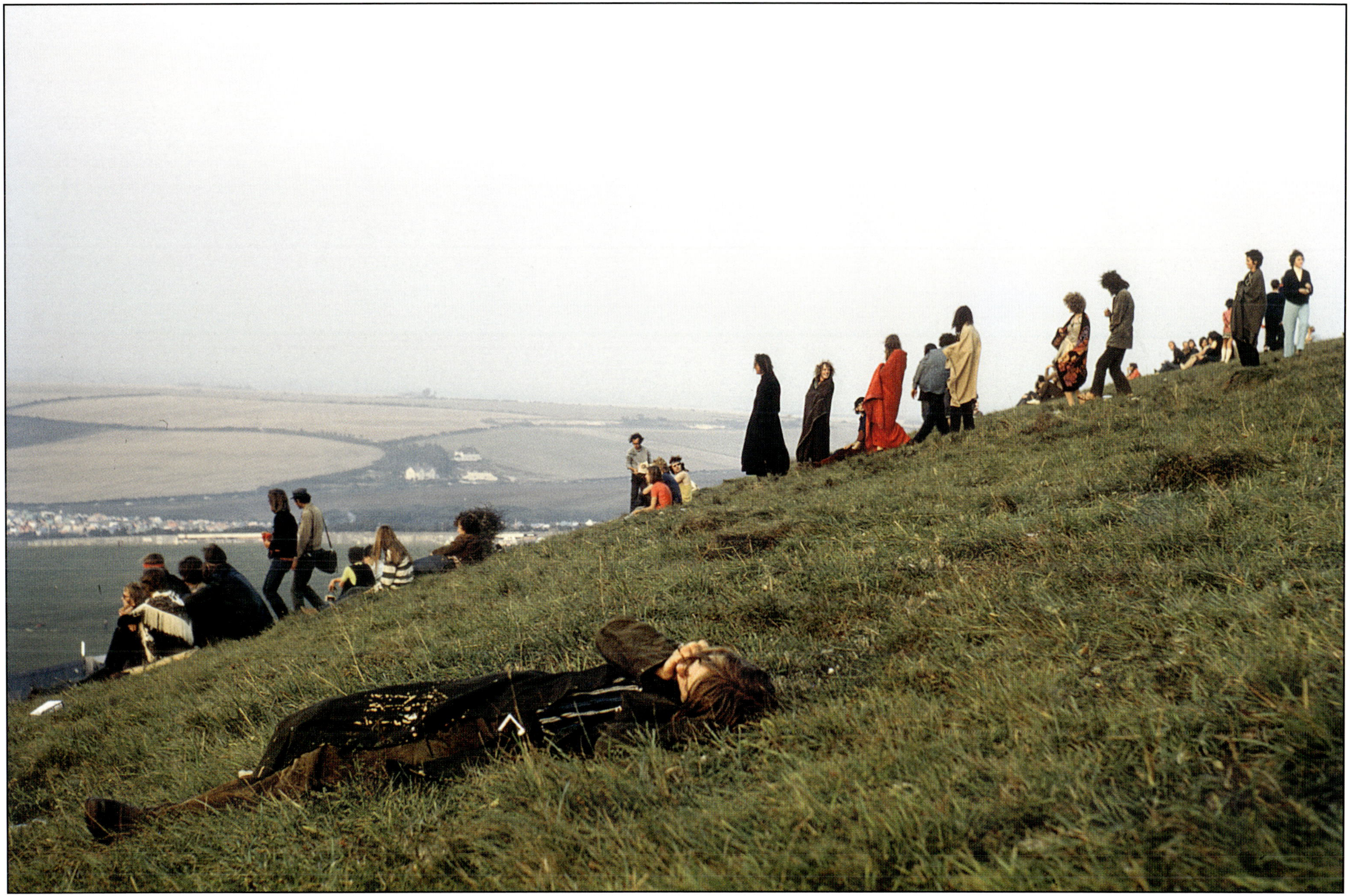

"As the tatterdemalion army of youngsters streams away from the Isle of Wight, let's hope they enjoyed themselves. But it will do no harm if they have learned a basic lesson : That most things in this world have to be paid for, even pop festivals." - *Daily Sketch editorial, August 31, 1970.*

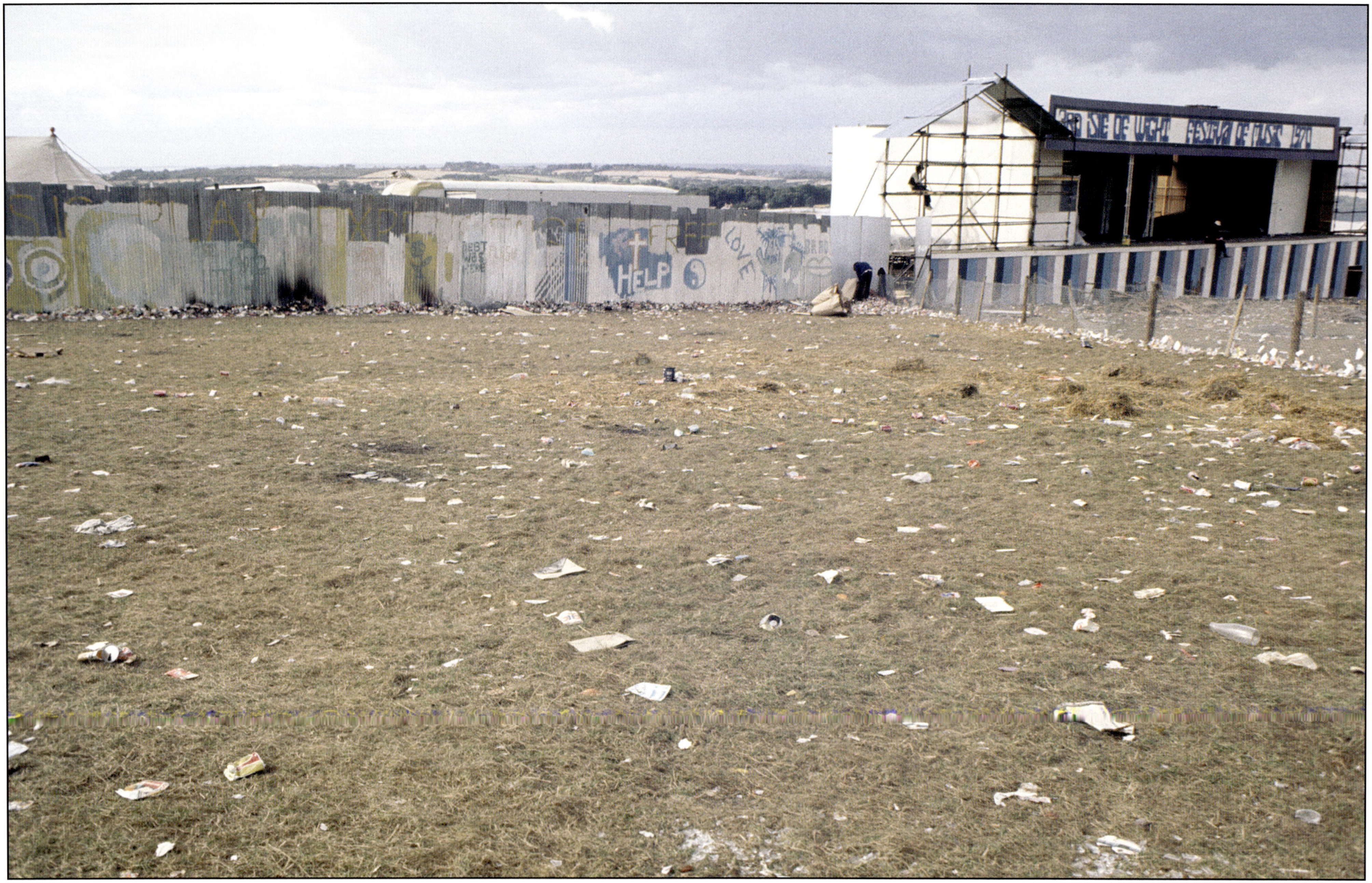

"I should like to make clear to the general public the position of my company in connection with the monumental transport exercise we were compelled to mount during the past week. I should like to settle some anxieties which exist in the minds of people, particularly mothers, by stating that we have commenced disinfecting and spraying all our vehicles as a precautionary measure. I leave it to the imagination of your readers to understand what the alternative would have been had we not taken the decision which we made." - *Mr. H. Harding, General Manager, Southern Vectis, September 5, 1970.*

Ken Box

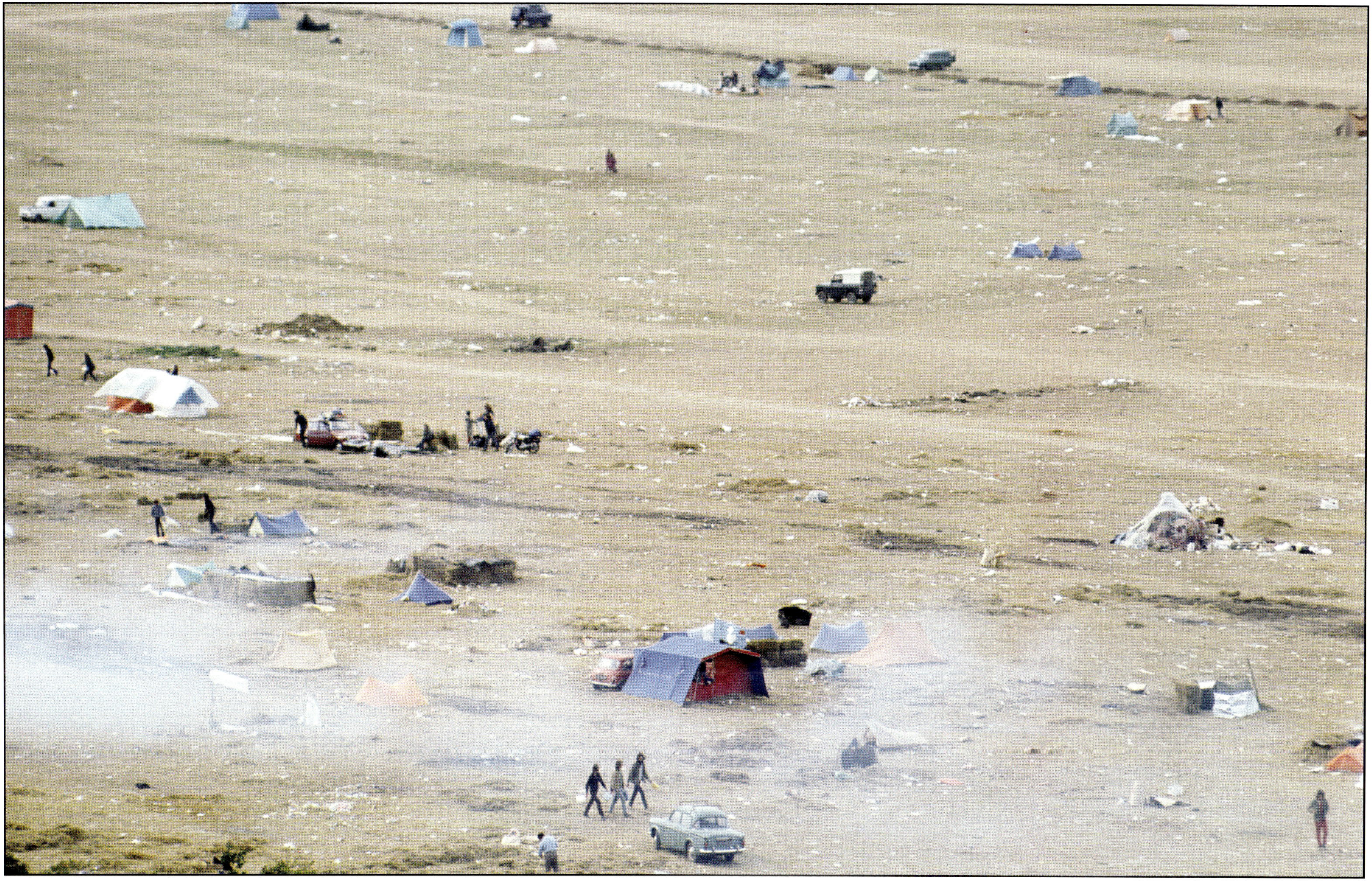

Ken Box

"Councillor Quick said the festival was now a memory, to some a bad dream, an experience that would probably never be seen again in the Island. Good, bad or indifferent, it was the greatest advertisement for the Island for all time. Many people in Freshwater had never seen the outside world, so the world came to Freshwater and Freshwater was amazed. It was an experience never to be forgotten, with conventions flung to the winds on winds of change that stirred the imagination. Totland was not affected because they had their usual aloofness of the vulgar scene! When Mr. Quick sat down he was congratulated by Mr. Hollis on his 'poetic effusion.' "
IW County Press, October 3, 1970.

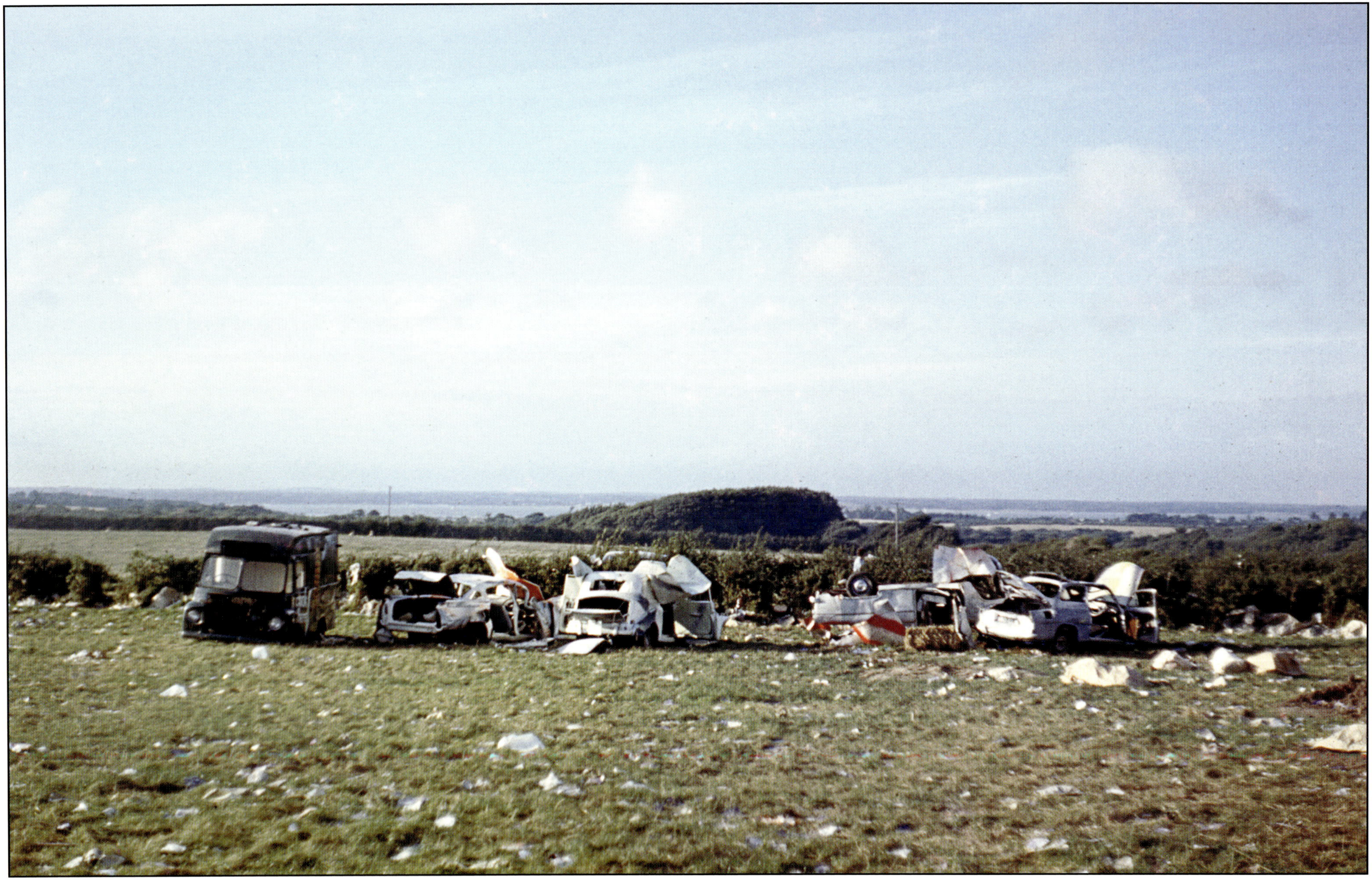

"At the festival site hundreds are still camping amid acres of litter. Dr. Douglas Quantrill, the island's medical officer of health, said today that he was satisfied with the general standard of hygiene during the festival and the litter was not a public health hazard. The promoters have two weeks in which to clear up the site or lose the money they deposited with Hampshire County Council as a guarantee. The queue for buses leaving the site stretched almost a mile today." - *David Wilsworth, The Times, August 31, 1970.*

Harry Matthews

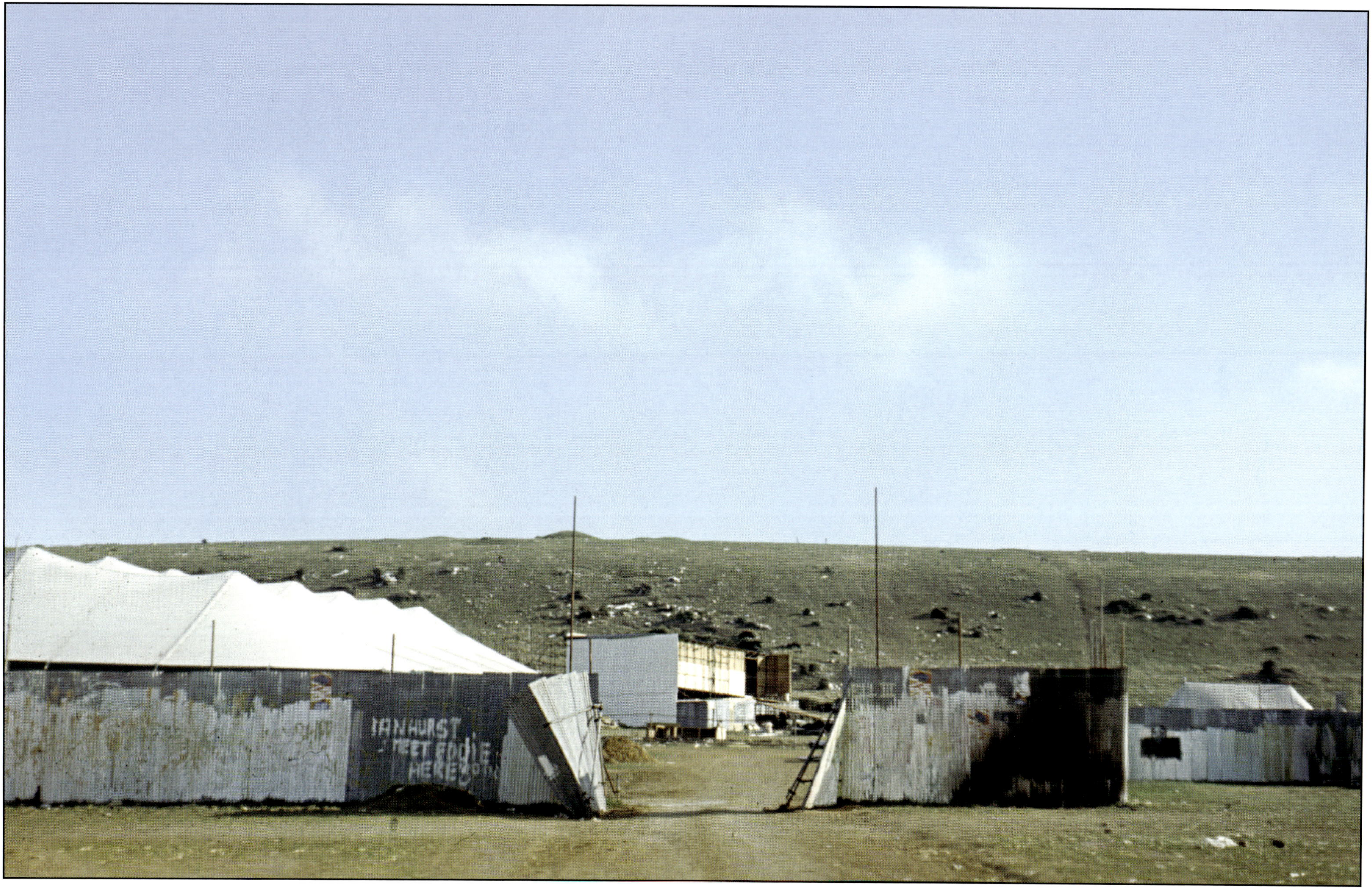

"As the light came into the sky, and the music ended, the weather changed with symbolic abruptness. The sun which had beaten down for three days vanished, replaced by a biting wind and a cold intermittent drizzle, to make the business of going home that much more unpleasant. What could have been a pilgrimage ended with shivers and sneezes, but much good humour remained to console the returning fans."
Melody Maker, September 5, 1970.

Harry Matthews

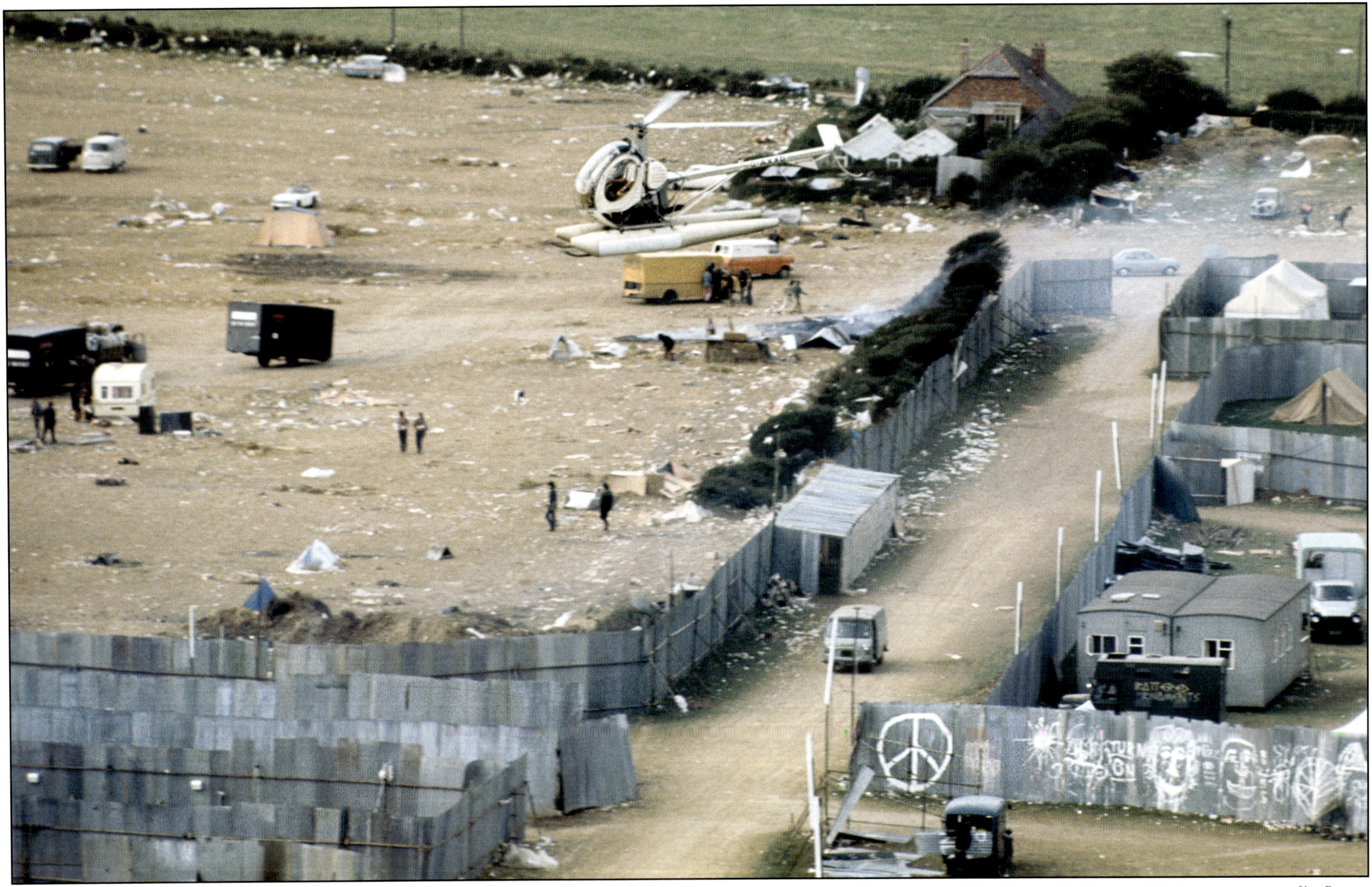

Ken Box

"This is definitely the last Isle of Wight Festival, according to Fiery Creations publicity director, Peter Harrigan. 'The kids may win, but we certainly lose. The kids have destroyed the festival.' There are lots of problems but the basic one seems to be that to break even they need £500,000 gate money. By 4 pm today there were 100,000 people inside, meaning a revenue of £300,000. 'If any White Panther cares to take the show over and spend nine months next year to fight to put the festival on against local opposition, they are welcome to,' said Harrigan." - *Freek Press, on-site daily news sheet.*

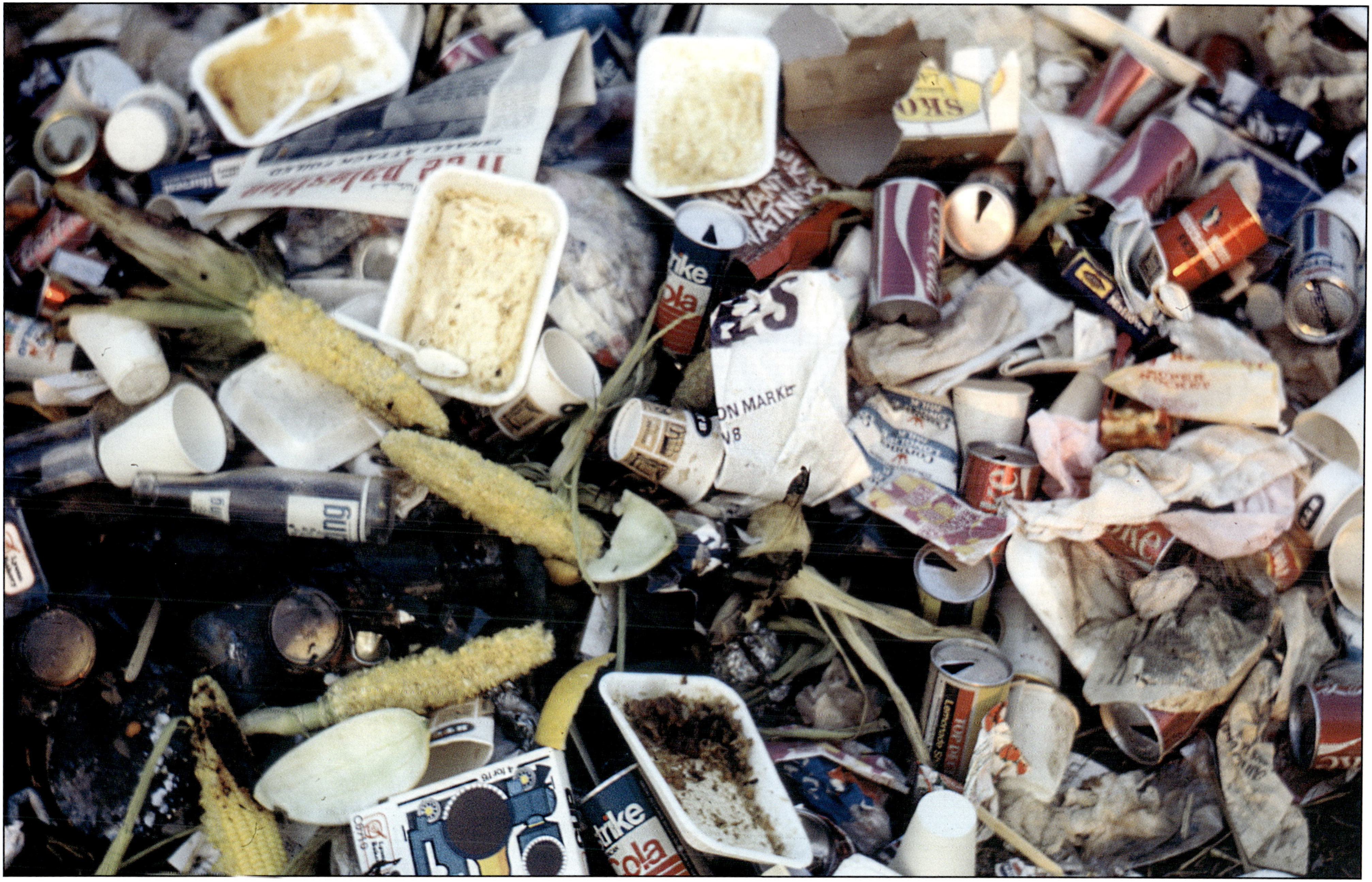

"We set up our own catering company, 'Exhibition Caterers,' an army-style catering unit in a massive kitchen marquee. We had shops all the way around the site within the double wall system and the food was transported from these kitchens to the shop units and that worked rather well. The food prices were okay as well. The food tariffs were printed out, pasted up everywhere, so there couldn't be any overcharging and that did work well. All those people got fed for days. There were no food queues and no complaints about the food." - *Ray Foulk interviewed by the authors.*

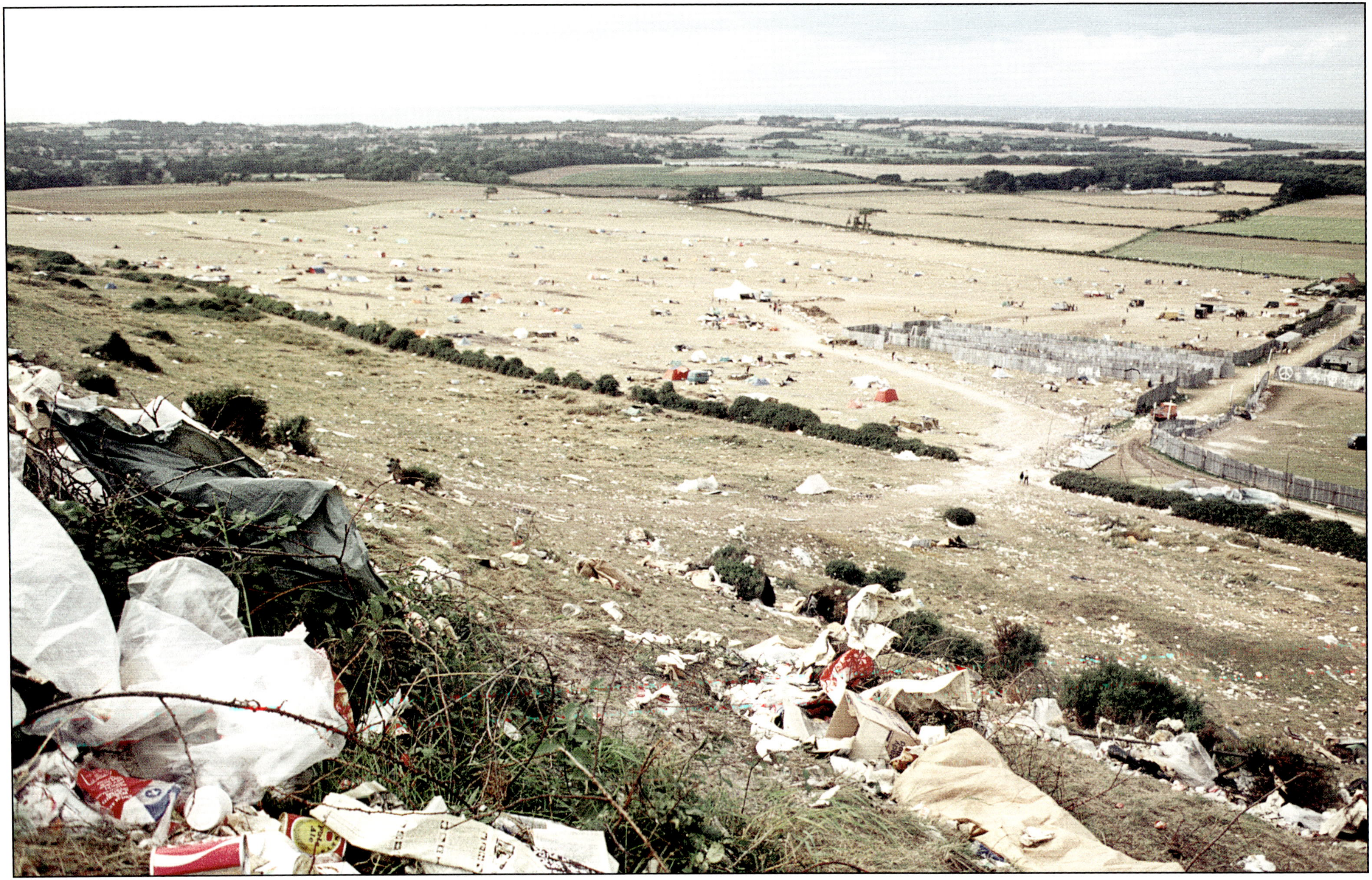

Ken Box

"The five young men, calling themselves the Fiery Creations who organised the festival, were unable either to drive the free-loaders off the hill or to make them buy tickets. So the festival has lost a lot of money. In other ways it went quite well. There was remarkably little trouble among the 250,000 teenagers, including every sort of hippie and drop-out who were crowded together in that small part of the Isle of Wight." - *Daily Sketch editorial, August 31, 1970.*

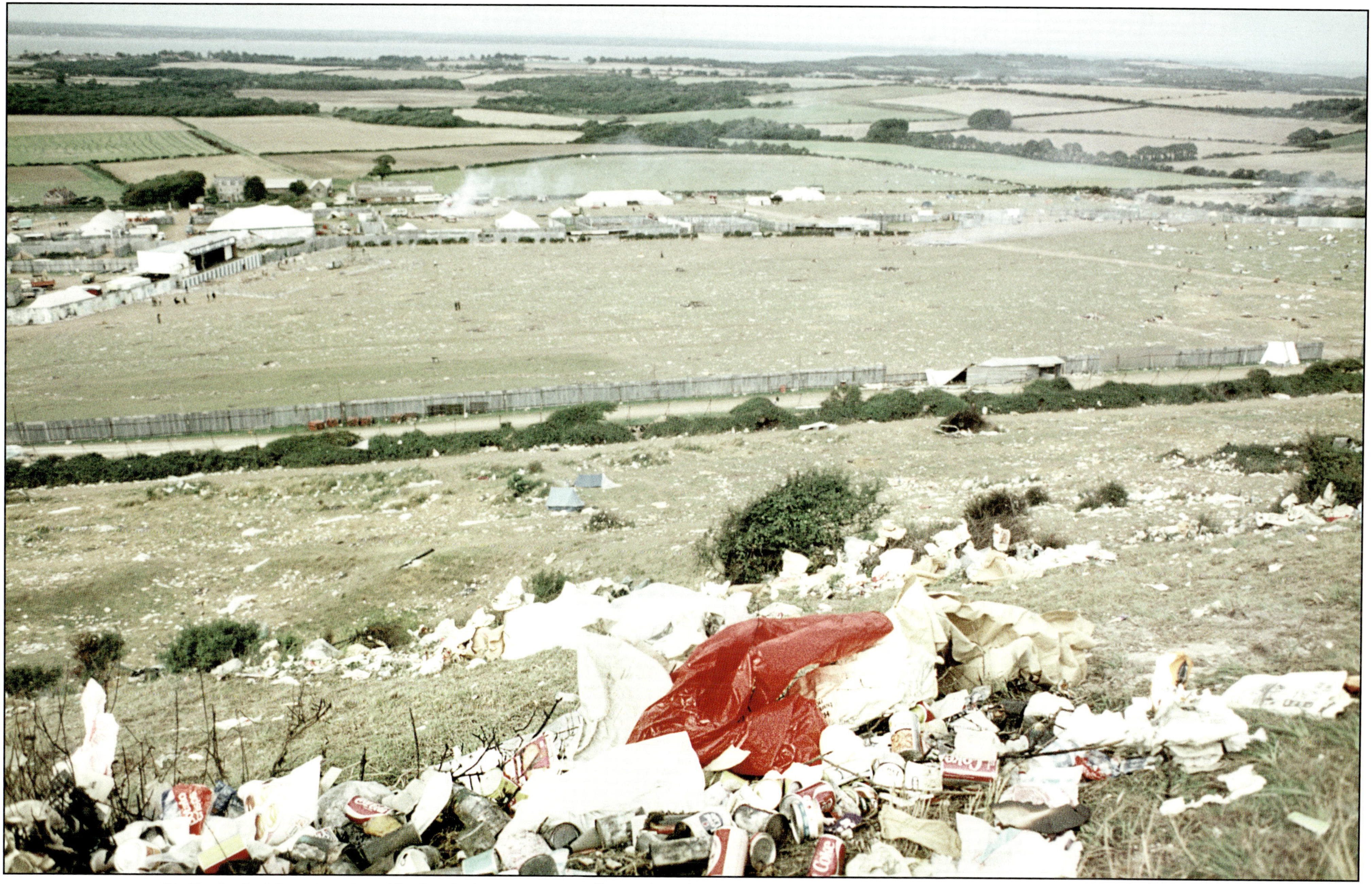

"To The Festival Organisers From The People On Devastation Hill : For three days we have listened to free music. We would like to show our appreciation of this by helping to clear up the litter on the hill. If plastic bags are provided we will do this on Monday For Free. PS: Some of us had tickets as well. We also dissociate ourselves from any wall-breaking activities. Kit, Hubback, V. Johnson and 10 others."
Announcement in 'Freek Press', on-site news sheet, August 30, 1970.

Ken Box

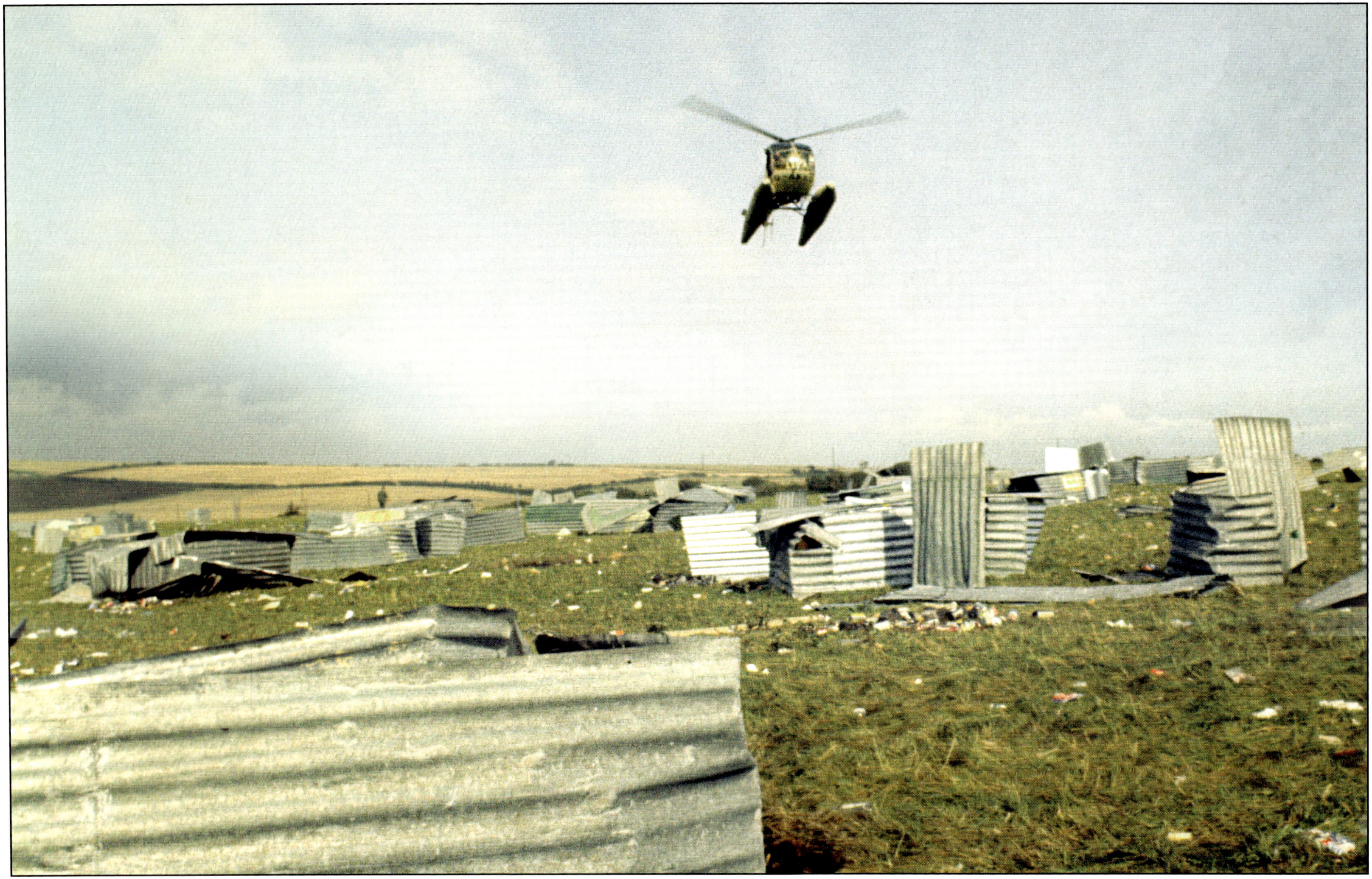

"The performers weren't exactly appearing for love. If someone had not paid the money out there would have been no festival. But the free-loaders on the hill were unwilling to contribute. "Pop should be free," they said. As one of the organisers admitted ruefully, an event which deliberately sets out to defy the conventions of adult society is liable to run into this sort of snag." - *Daily Sketch editorial, August 31, 1970.*

Ken Box

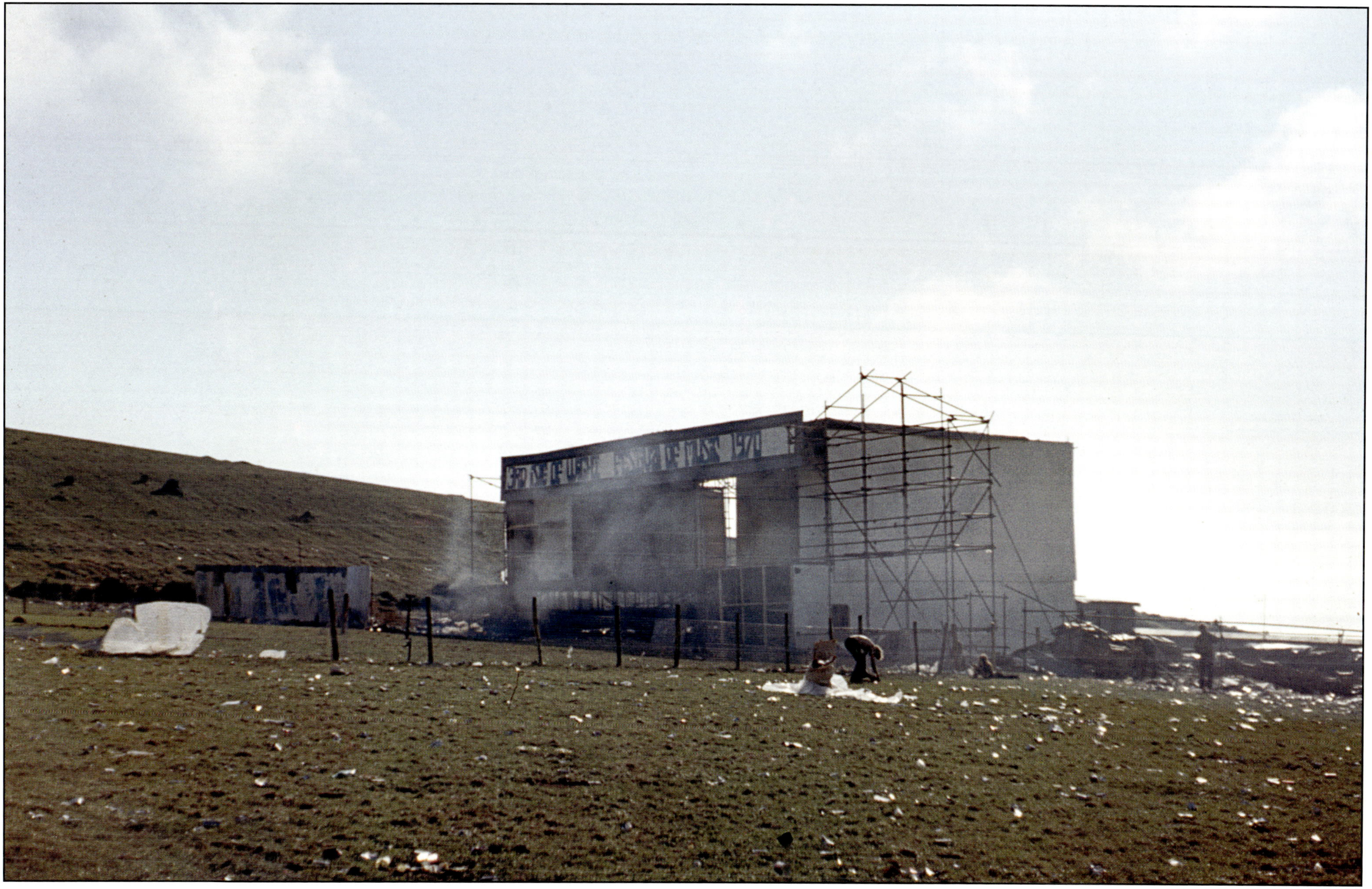

"If Fiery Creations are not entirely happy with the way things have worked out, most of the people who came are, and the police have been slightly surprised by the general good behaviour. They say probably about 250,000 attended. Mr Douglas Osmond, Chief Constable of Hampshire, said he had gone in casual clothes to sit on the down among the people and listen to the music. 'I found it very pleasant. There has been less violence from the great majority than you get at an English football weekend,' he said." - *David Wilsworth, The Times, August 31, 1970.*

Harry Matthews

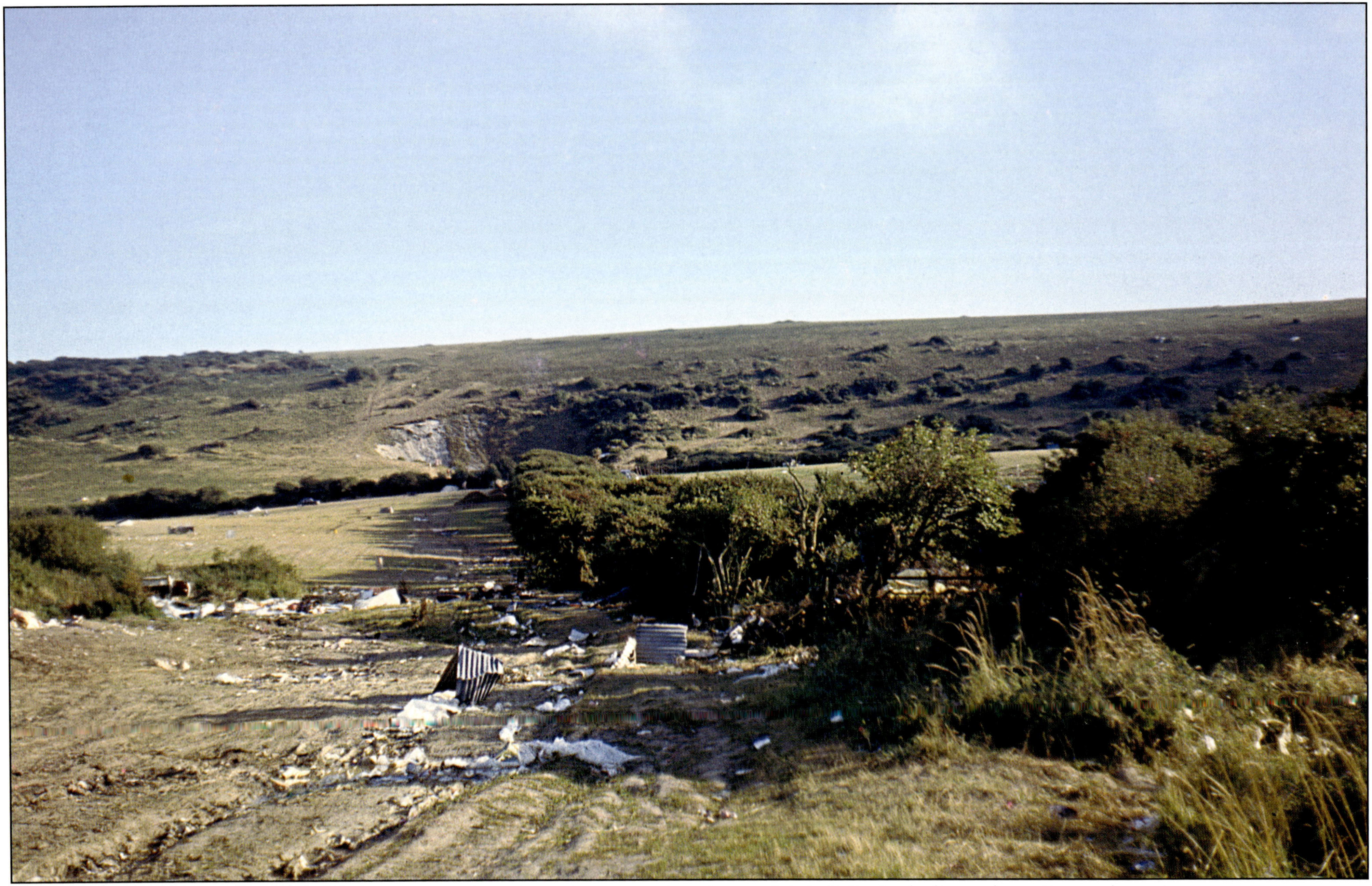

"On 'Devastation Hill' where the renegades against paying encamped, the air was polluted with the stench of joss sticks, marijuana and sweat."
I.W. County Press, September 5, 1970.

Harry Matthews

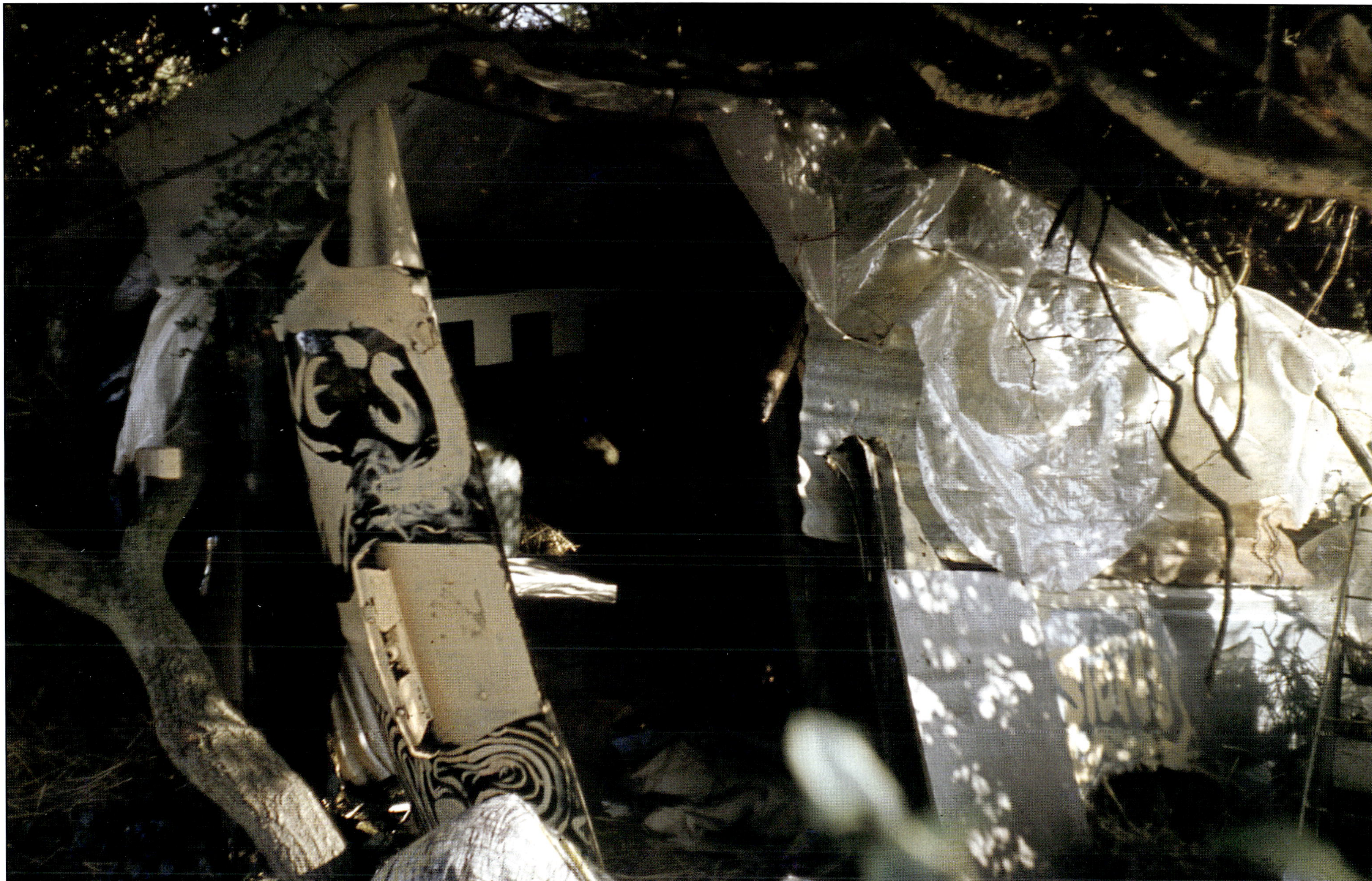

"Police were expected to stay on the site for a few days during the mopping-up operations and to supervise several hundred remaining campers. Inspector G. Cutliffe said that any hippies who planned to stay for the rest of the summer would be 'elbowed out'."
I.W. County Press, September 5, 1970.

Harry Matthews

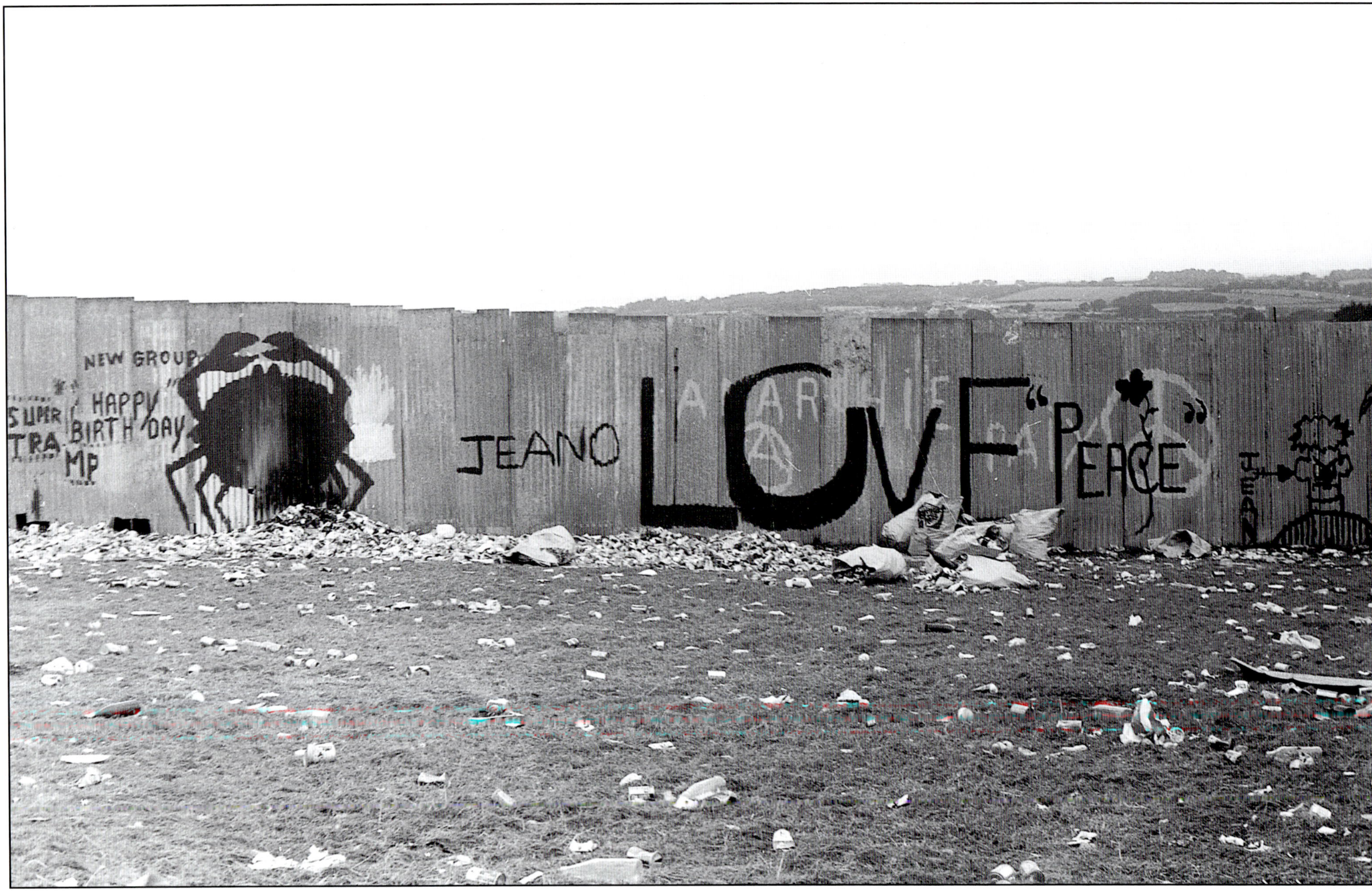

Alan Stroud

"Fiery Creations said this would be the last festival they will promote on the Island. The event has become too big and they have serious doubts as to whether they will make a profit this year. Experts on pop culture have long been saying that the large pop festival was a dying phenomenon and that this year's Isle of Wight Festival would be the last great event. Fiery Creations' assertion that the festival is almost unmanageable bears this out." - *David Wilsworth, The Times, August 26, 1970.*

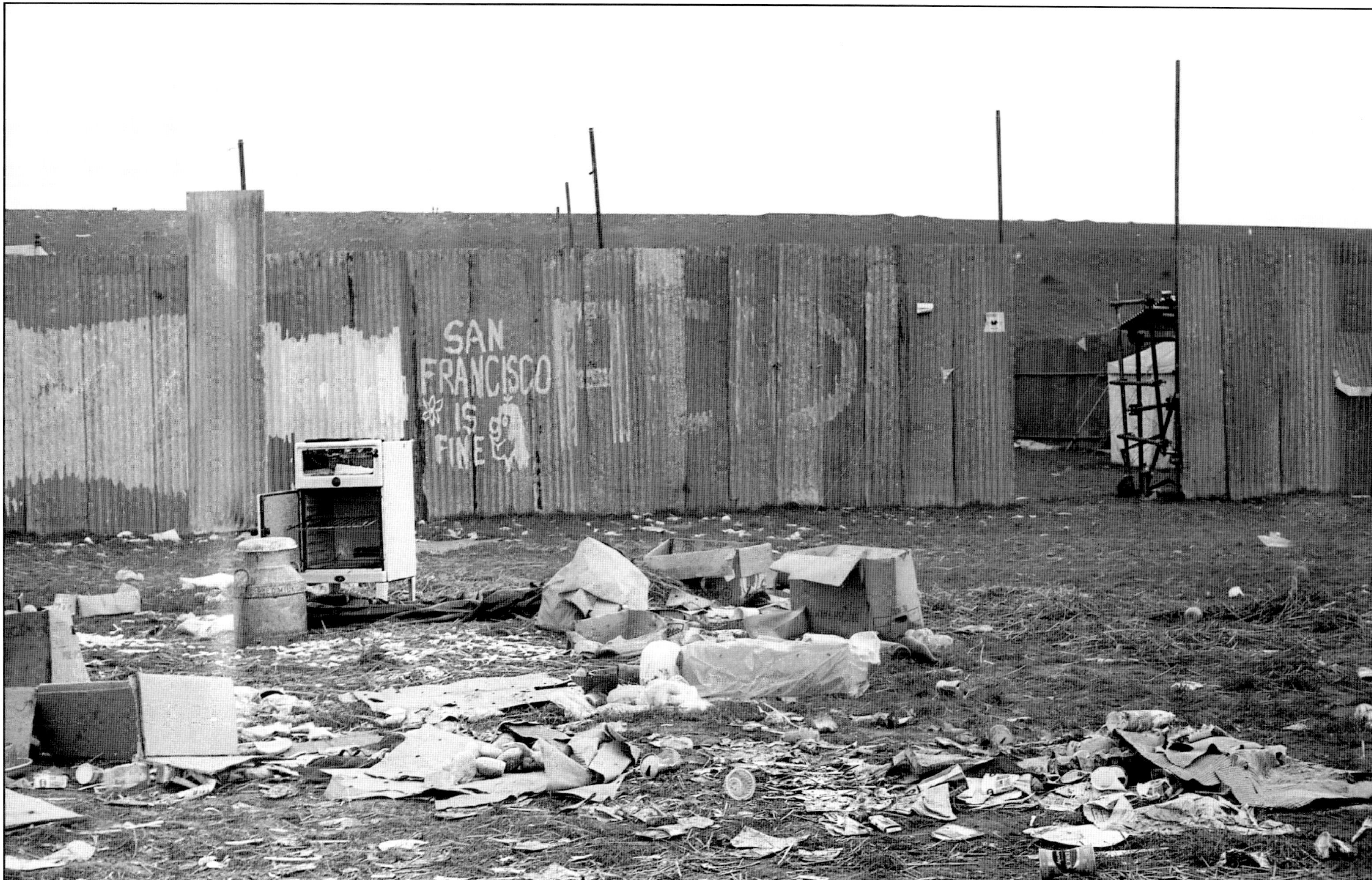

Alan Stroud

"Pop Goes The Profit. The organisers of the recent Island pop festival expect the loss on the event to be between £20,000 and £30,000, which would be more than covered by recording rights and a film, according to the *Daily Telegraph*. They add that creditors may have to wait for their money and that they would not be promoting another festival on the same scale." - *I.W. County Press, September 12, 1970.*

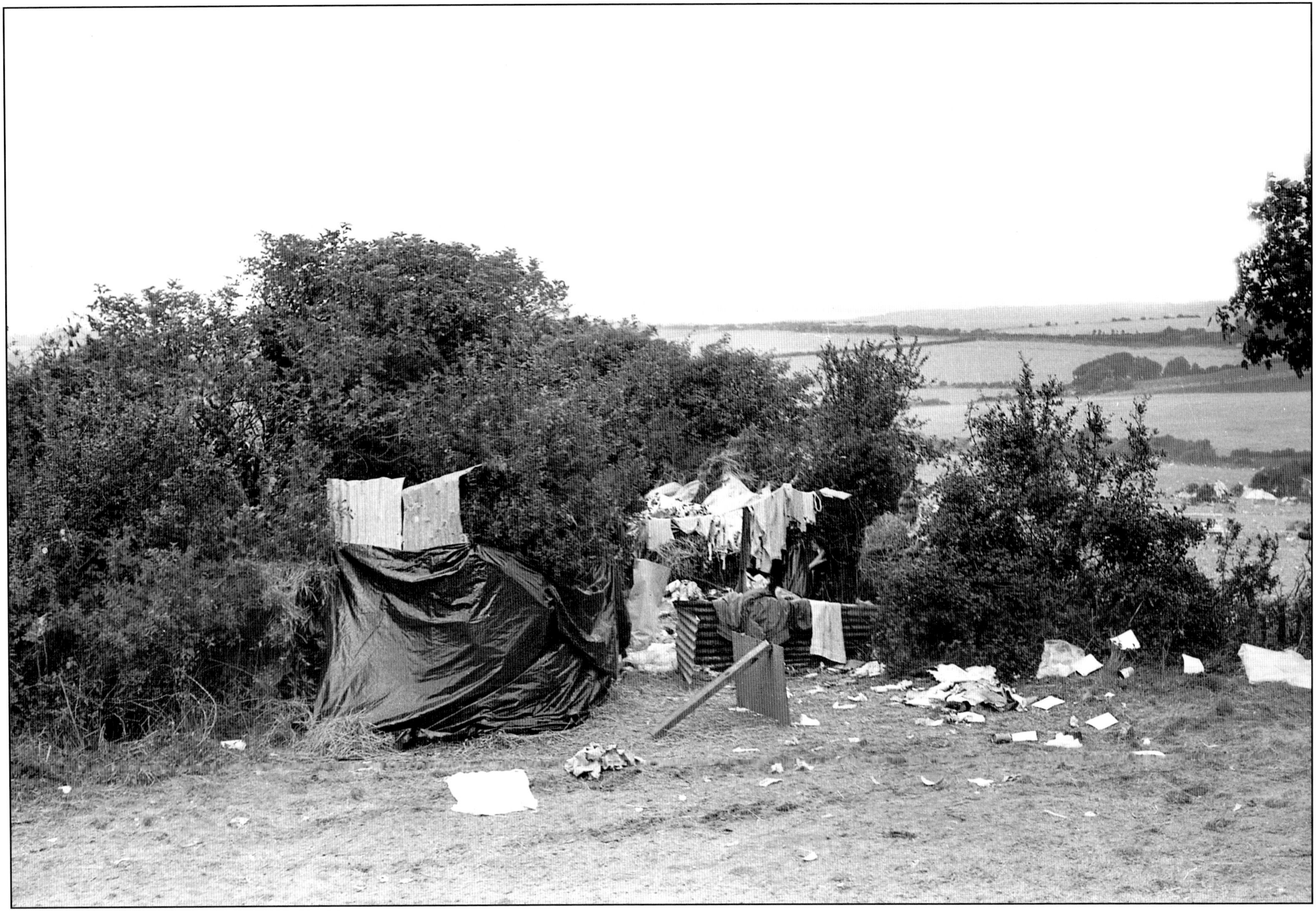

Alan Stroud

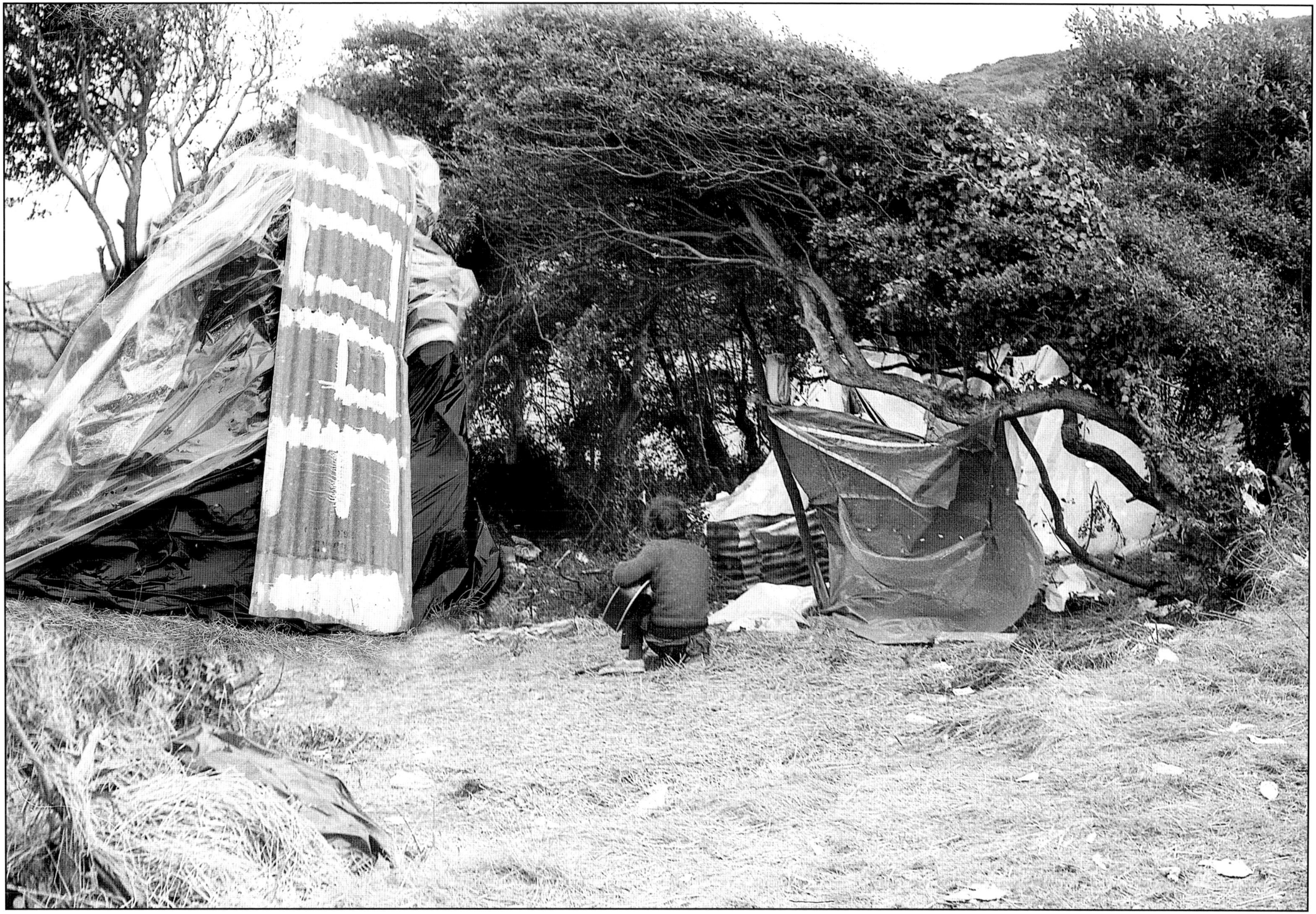

Alan Stroud

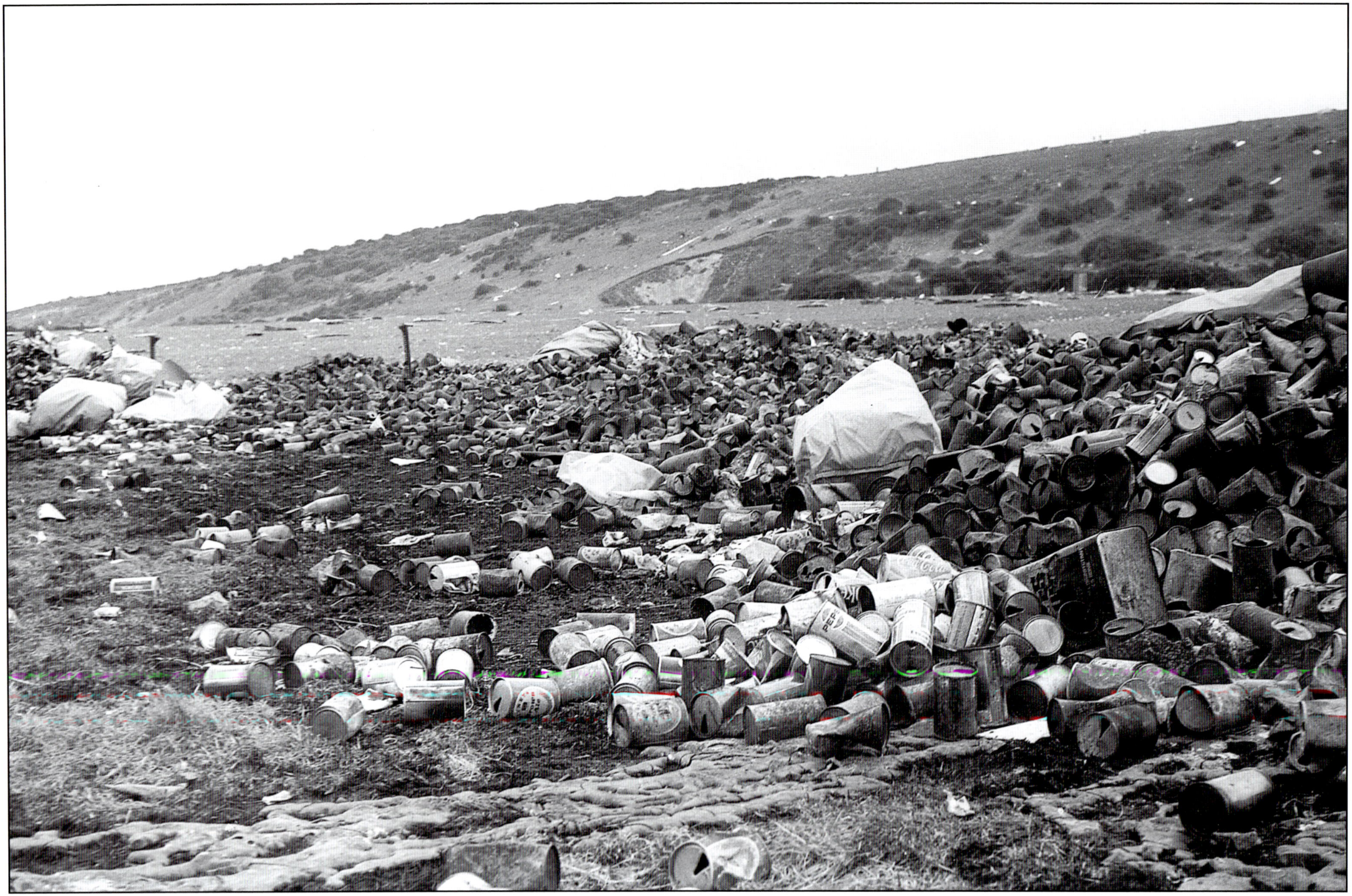

Alan Stroud

"Although litter left on the part of Afton Down adjoining the site was enormous, only about one tenth of the area of the National Trust land on the Freshwater Estate has been affected. On all the rest of the estate there is very little damage — no worse than on an ordinary Bank Holiday weekend." - *Secretary of the Island National Trust - I.W. County Press, September 5, 1970.*